BASS FISHING IN CALIFORNIA

Third Edition

Secrets of the Western Pros

by Ron Kovach

featuring these expert Western bass anglers...

- John Bedwell
- Fred Borders
- Chuck Boydston
- Bill Craig
- Jim Emmett
- Chuck English
- Mike Folkstad
- Bobby Garland
- Don Garland

- Larry Hopper
- Don Iovino
- Al Kalin
- Dave Mitchell
- Dave Nollar
- Don Payne
- Gary Robson
- Don Seifert
- Bob Suekawa

MARKETSCOPE
BOOKS

119 Richard
Aptos, CA 95003
(408) 688-7535

*"The leading publisher of
fishing books for California Anglers"*

About This Expanded and Updated Edition

The first edition of this book was a big surprise. We had no idea that so many thousands of Californians would buy a book about bass angling. Outdoor writers praised it and anglers obviously found it useful. It's still selling at a fast pace, but now we've decided to make it even bigger and better. More strategies. More tactics. More tips and tricks. More bass waters. More maps and illustrations. Quite simply, this new edition has more of everything for the California bass angler. We hope you like it.

The Editor

ISBN 0-934061-12-2

Cover Design: Electric Art Studios
                Mountain View, CA

Printed by: Delta Lithograph
                Valencia, CA

Illustrations: Linda Kovach

This book is dedicated to two people who have always supported me in my efforts to catch these little green fish. Thanks, Dad, for introducing me to the sport and for allowing me to always take that "one last cast." Thank you Linda, my lovely wife, for standing by me and encouraging me to pursue my dreams as a fisherman, guide and writer.

Ron Kovach

This expanded and revised edition of **Bass Fishing in California** would not have been possible without the help of the expert Western Bass Fishermen who were unselfish enough to share their secrets with the rest of us. These are the guys who pound the waters every weekend and have "paid their dues" in this wonderful sport. In alphabetical order, thanks especially to: John Bedwell, Fred Borders, Chuck Boydston, Bill Craig, Jim Emmett, Chuck English, Mike Folkestad, Bobby Garland, Don Garland, Larry Hopper, Don Iovino, Al Kalin, Dave Mitchell, Dave Nollar, Don Payne, Gary Robson, Don Seifert and Bob Suekawa.

Great Books

Fishing in Northern California,

Marketscope Books publishes the bestselling **Fishing in Northern California** (8 1/2 x 11 inches, 240 pages). It includes "How To Catch" sections on all freshwater fish as well as salmon, steelhead, sturgeon, shad, kokanee, lingcod, clams, sharks, rock crab, crawdads, stripers, etc. Plus, there are sections on all major NorCal fishing waters (over 50 lakes, the Delta, Coastal Rivers, Valley Rivers, Mountain Trout and the Pacific Ocean). All these waters are mapped in detail!

Fishing in Southern California,

Marketscope Books also publishes the bestselling **Fishing in Southern California** (8 1/2 x 11 inches, 256 pages). It includes "How To Catch" sections on all freshwater fish as well as barracuda, bonito, calico bass, grunion, halibut, marlin, sea bass and yellowtail. Plus, there are sections on major SoCal fishing waters (45 lakes, the Salton Sea, Colorado River, Mountain Trout and the Pacific Ocean). All these waters are mapped in detail!

Bass Fishing in California,

At last, a bass fishing book just for Californians -- both beginners and veterans. This book explains in detail how to catch more and larger bass in California's unique waters. But, most valuable, it includes a comprehensive guide, with maps, to 40 of California's best bass lakes, up and down the state. 8 1/2 x 11, 240 pages.

Trout Fishing in California

Trout fishing is special in California and now there is a special book for the California trout anglers. It covers, in detail, how to catch trout in lakes or streams, with line, bait or flies, by trolling, casting or still fishing, from boat or shore. And even better for California anglers, this is a guide to the best trout waters all over the state. Detailed info and precise maps are featured. 8 1/2 x 11, 224 pages.

Saltwater Fishing in California

California is blessed with over 800 miles of Pacific Ocean coastline. This is a marvelous resource for all Golden State anglers. And now there is a book that covers it all. Surf fishing. Kelp fishing. Harbor and Bay fishing. Poke poling. And more. Don't go saltwater fishing without it. Both veteran anglers and beginners are finding this book a necessity. It explains, in detail, how to catch albacore, barracuda, bass, bonito, halibut, rockfish, sharks, salmon, stripers, yellowtail and striped marlin. And there is a large "How-To and Where-To" Guide for hot spots all along the coast. And don't be without the Saltwater Sportfish I.D. Section. This book has become a standard because it explains in simple, straightforward language how to catch fish in the Pacific, off California. 8 1/2 x 11, 256 pages.

Pier Fishing in California

There are many marvelous ocean and bay fishing opportunities on California's piers. And now there is a book that covers each and every one of them--from San Diego to San Francisco Bay to Crescent City. Learn how to fish each pier, the species, best baits, proper timing, the underwater environment, fishing tips, and more. Plus, find out about the best techniques, baits, lures, and necessary equipment from an expert who has fished all these piers all his life. There is also an extensive pier fish identification section and cleaning and cooking info. 8 1/2 x 11, 256 pages.

Order your Copies Today!

	Price	Sales Tax	Total Price	Qty	Total Amount
___ **Fishing in Northern California**	$14.95	$ .95	$15.90	___	_____
___ **Fishing in Southern California**	$14.95	$ .95	$15.90	___	_____
___ **Bass Fishing in California**	$14.95	$ .95	$15.90	___	_____
___ **Trout Fishing in California**	$14.95	$ .95	$15.90	___	_____
___ **Saltwater Fishing in California**	$14.95	$ .95	$15.90	___	_____
___ **Pier Fishing in California**	$16.95	$1.40	$18.35	___	_____

Postage & Handling (1st book $1.75; no charge on 2 or more books) . . . . _____ *

Check Enclosed . . . . _____

*Special Offer (order 2 books, any combination, and we'll pay **all** postage & handling)

Name _____ Address _____

Send Your Order To: **Marketscope Books, Box 171, Aptos, CA 95001**
(Permission is granted to xerox this page.)

Contents

Contents (continued)

The California Bassin' Scene

California has long been a virtual mecca for a variety of saltwater fishing ranging from big game marlin and swordfish to tackle-busting king salmon and albacore tuna. What a lot of fishermen do not realize is that the country's #1 state in population is also home to a large population of the country's #1 gamefish - the freshwater bass. California lakes are habitat for largemouth, smallmouth, Florida-strain, and even Alabama spotted bass. California also has a wealth of organized bass fishing clubs and serious bass fishermen that according to the Bass Angler's Sportsmen Society (B.A.S.S.) is surpassed only by Texas.

This is a rather staggering statistic considering all the other recreational opportunities that exist in the Golden State. The scenic beaches, mountains and deserts, the variety of amateur and professional sports to choose from, combined with the arts and other cultural activities all compete for the weekend warrior's recreational dollar. Yet, it is estimated that over three million people fish for freshwater species in California and one out of every three fish specifically for bass.

However, fishing for California bass can be a very tough and frustrating proposition for the average recreational angler. In contrast to the rest of the United States, many of our lakes are subject to tremendous pressure. In addition to the hordes of fishermen that frequent the lakes, large numbers of water skiers and pleasure boaters also vie for their share of the water. Furthermore, for the most part, this heavy usage of our lakes is a year-round activity due to the state's relatively mild climate and lack of severe winter weather. Consequently, the bass population gets little rest from angling and recreational traffic.

California's bass population is exceptionally wary and typically very tough to fool. The daily limit in the state is five bass per angler and on a given lake, limits are usually few and far between. With the challenge there, the bass fisherman who is able to catch his five fish limit should feel very accomplished. But, it is also estimated that only 10 percent of the bass fishermen catch 90 percent of the fish. Why is this so?

When the first specialized bass boats were introduced on the market, some of the fishing public proclaimed that this elite group of fishermen would rape the bass populations in our lakes, especially with the unfair advantage of sophisticated electronic fish-finding gear. Many fishermen still believe that these are the guys catching all the bass in California.

Speaking as a professional guide and a veteran tournament bass fisherman, believe me when I tell you this isn't the case. The so-called bass "pro" with his arsenal of rods, reels, lures, and electronic instruments also struggles with the California bass. The electronics may tell you where the bass are holding, but not what they are eating or how to fish for them. There have been many times when I have seen the fisherman in his aluminum rental boat or the one walking the bank thoroughly wax the guy in the high-tech bass rig who's running from spot to spot frantically viewing his fish finder screen.

There is also the old adage that the more you do something the better you become. Some people simply think that the more you fish for bass, the better you become at it and it is these diehards that catch the most bass. To some extent, this might hold true. But if a basser persists in fishing the same way week after week without results, it really won't matter how much time is spent on the water, as the mistakes repeat themselves.

The key to successful bass fishing in California lies in technique. Without question, there are certain, very unique methods used in lure selection and bait presentation that have been designed especially for tough-to-catch California bass. Although many of these little "tricks" have been developed by the Western bass pros, it is just recently that they are being used by fellow pros to catch bass in other parts of the country (where the lakes are also facing increased pressure). Up until now, it was almost impossible for the weekend, recreational bass fisherman to learn about these special techniques.

In these next chapters let's look at the secret tactics devised by the Western pros. Whether you're the occassional bassin' man who fishes from the bank or pleasure boat, or the aspiring bass club member hoping to fare better in tournaments, **Bass Fishing in California** should provide you with many new and exciting insights, leading to more productive days on our lakes.

Serious Bassin': Getting Started

The very fact that you are reading this book suggests that you may want to get more involved in bass fishing. But you may be wondering, "How do I get started? I can only afford to spend so much, so what tackle should I purchase?" I'll answer all these questions in this chapter. We'll start with selecting the proper tackle, including the basics in rod, reels, lines, and some solid guidelines on what lures to purchase.

Most bass pros have a tendecy to go somewhat overboard anyway in assembling their tackle "war chests". You will see some of them carrying a dozen outfits and six or more tackle boxes in their boats. But, invariably they end up using just a few of those rigs and a handful of lures that are historically productive on California bass. So I'll keep this "shopping list" plain and simple and put together a tackle selection that is both economically practical and effective.

The Right Rods

You should have two if not three rods to effectively present a wide range of lures on California lakes. First, I recommend a 5 1/2 foot medium light to medium action graphite baitcasting rod. You'll need this stick for fishing plastic worms with a Texas rig using 8 to 10 pound line. Remember, unlike the South and the Midwest, you have to scale down to this lighter mono with smaller 3 to 6 inch worms for California style bassin! The rods should be graphite (or, if you can afford it, the more expensive Kevlar or Boron composites). In contrast to less expensive fiberglass models, these materials allow the rod to be very sensitive which is critical to working a worm on the bottom. The graphite blank is both light and very strong, providing a lot of power on the hook set.

This style rod will also have a lot of utility for other techniques. You can use it for crankin', spinnerbait fishing, and pitching 1/4 to 1/2 ounce jigs. In a pinch, it will work allright with medium-sized chuggers, poppers and stickbaits along with most buzzbaits. I've also used a graphite rod with this action for spooning with 10 pound test line down to 60 foot depths.

If I had to own only two bassin' rods for the West Coast, my other stick would be a 6 foot medium-action, single piece graphite spinning rod. I realize that this may be tantamount to "heresy" for the traditional basser raised on baitcasting rigs, but for light line fishing with 6 to 8 pound mono, a spinning outfit excels for both pro and novice alike.

More and more bass are being caught in the Golden State with methods that utilize diminutive subtle baits. Split-shottin' grubs, tube baits, darters, and P-heads are all techniques that match well with spinning tackle. Similarly, the small lightweight balsa and plastic minnow baits such as Rapalas and Rebels, twitch, rip, and jerk best with spinning gear. Many bass pros now realize that to be competitive here in California they must be versatile enough to fish both casting and spinning outfits.

Now, if you can afford a third rod, there are two ways to go. You might consider adding a 6 to 7 foot graphite baitcasting model in medium to medium-heavy action. The lengthier rod makes for longer casts and better control with big baits such as 5/8 ounce jigs or Zara Spooks. This rod should be able to handle 12 to 20 pound test line.

An alternate choice would be a 7 1/2 foot graphite flippin' stick. Along with the subtle baits, this very specialized technique has caught on like wildfire in the pro ranks and is exceptionally productive on certain Western lakes. The flippin' rod will handle up to 30 pound mono and heavy lures up to one ounce. I have seen pros use this "meat stick" for other things besides flippin'. You can "kneel'n reel" an ultradeep-diving crankbait such as a Bagley DB-III with this rod. It will also serve very nicely for throwing that #6 to #8 magnum willowleaf spinnerbait I talked about. Sometimes, you can also use a flippin' stick for wormin' in stained or muddy water. Match it with heavier 14 to 17 pound line and an 8 to 12 inch plastic worm and hunt for quality "kicker" fish.

Selecting a Reel

Try to buy the best baitcasting reel you can afford for you basic outfit. A good, high quality reel will last for many years. You can chose from either graphite or metal alloy frame models. The graphite frames are the lightest; the anodized aluminum the heaviest but strongest. Put the reel on the rod you select and see how it feels. Try comparable models to come up with the one that feels best in your hand.

You may want to spend a little more for a baitcaster with ball bearings rather than bushings. The bearings provide for a smoother retrieve and the manufacturers estimate they will enhance casting distance by 15 percent. To be honest, most bushing reels will cast very adequately. Most pros would be hard-pressed to see the difference between quality bearing and bushing baitcasters as far as casting distance is concerned.

Better baitcasting reels will also have some type of magnetic-braking system that keeps the spool from backlashing. To my knowledge none of these systems is totally fool-proof, but they really help. For years I resisted using baitcasters with the brake feature figuring I would cut down casting distance dramatically. But, after I used one of these reels with a large lure throwing directly into the wind, I quickly became a "convert" to the new technology!

Once you learn how to set the brake on these reels, you will probably never want to use one without this feature. The lower the setting, the less braking you will have, and the longer the cast. But, with the lighter brake tension the possibility for backlash increases. The higher the brake setting, the greater the spool resistance. Casting distance decreases but so does the potential for a "professional overrun" (i.e. backlash!!!). You have to experiment and determine how "educated" your thumb is at helping to control the spool. Also, if you wish, you can practically eliminate this feature entirely by setting the magnetic brake to "0".

There are two other things to look for in a quality baitcasting reel. The better reels have a line pawl that will disengage when casting. The pawl is the wire guard that goes back and forth and serves to wind the line level onto the spool. With cheaper reels, the pawl will continue to move from side to side as the spool rotates, paying off the line on the cast. With better reels, the pawl disengages from the level wind mechanism and remains stationary as the line strips off the spool. Baitcasting reels designed with this feature will thus throw with minimal line resistance, yielding smoother and longer casts.

The other thing to check for is a fairly high speed retrieve. For crankin' you have to have a reel with close to a 5:1 gear ratio. This means that for every complete turn of the handle, the spool will make approximately five revolutions. Although it is not always best to retrieve a crankbait super fast, at least with this type of reel, when you have to reel quickly you will be able to with minimal effort. Tournament fishing usually is done in a "run'n gun" style. The angler is continually pitchin' or chuckin' a worm, blade, jig, or crankbait to shoreline cover. A highspeed, quality baitcasting reel is an absolutely essential piece of equipment for this type of fishing.

For flippin', you can get by with a cheaper baitcaster. Most pros actually tighten the star drags down as far as they can, allowing for minimal line slippage when that dramatic hook set is made. The "cast", is really more of an underarm pitch of the line as it is manually held and then released. The fight at such close range is often over in a matter of seconds, with many bass being "bounced" like tuna into the boat. Thus, the reel for flippin' is more for storing line than actually casting or playing out the fish with drag. An inexpensive or older-style baitcaster will suffice nicely for this technique.

As for spinning reels, again you can pick from graphite or aluminum frame models. I like the graphite spinners best because they are so light. I also prefer the ball bearing models to bushing because they seem overwhelmingly smoother with this style of reel. All the better quality reels have fairly hi-speed gear ratios and can be simply converted to either left or right hand retrieves. One additional feature to look for is extra spools. This is important for California-style bassin' with spinning tackle. Fill one spool with 10 lb. test line for rippin', twitchin' jerkin' or crankin'. Have the other spool ready with 6 pound mono for split-shottin', working grubs, Gitzits, or fishing P-heads and darters.

Try to stay with name-brand manufacturers in selecting appropriate bassin' rods and reels. For the most part, off-brand cheapie discount house models will not withstand the heavy beating this tackle gets riding in a boat or yanking fish out of heavy cover. Stay with one-piece rods instead of two-piece models. The one-piece blank is stronger, although not as convenient to carry as the two-piece version. This inconvenience is worth it when you have to lean into a big fish nestled in deep structure.

Start out with these 2 or 3 basic outfits, and then you can add to them as you become more adept at specialized techniques and more seriously committed to the sport.

Why Premium Lines?

It is essential not to skimp on line. This is the all-important link between you and the fish. Don't get suckered into buying a bulk spool of low-grade monofilament at bargain prices. This type of line might be good enough for bluegill and catfish, but not for serious bassin'!

Premium monofilament will sell for as much as 3 to 4 times more than the line sold in the cheapie bulk spools. But it will have some very important differences that will be worth the investment. Top quality mono is fairly uniform in diameter and breaking test strength throughout the spool you purchase. In contrast, the less expensive bulk spools of cheaper line will often have a wide range of variance in diameter and line test throughout the spool. Basically, what you are buying is an average breaking test. Premium monofilament also has excellent abrasion resistance and good knot strength. The economy line will have a tendency to chip or crack from exposure to the elements and will break more easily at the knot.

As for color, I think this feature is really overrated, as far as being that critical. I like to "line watch" a lot, and I prefer colored lines in clear, stained and muddy waters. Some pros feel that either green or smoke works best in clear lakes while others prefer a brown or chameleon line for stained water. Experiment yourself and decide on your favorite. But do spend a little more money to get the best monofilament you can afford.

Perhaps the most revolutionary innovation to hit the premium line market in recent years is Berkley's tri-polymer Tri Max monofilment. For a long time, fishermen found that although certain lines had great strength and limited stretch when dry, these qualities diminished when the monofilament became wet. Most lines typically lose about 20% of these optimal characteristics as the water is absorbed into the nylon core. Berkley's chemists have minimized this absorption problem, with Tri Max demonstrating only 6% reduction in qualities shifting from a dry-to-wet state. They did this while also extruding a monofilament of ultra fine diameter compared to lines of similar breaking test. Although monofilament of this class is distinctively higher priced, serious bass fishermen will appreciate its tremendous sensitivity and hook-setting properties.

The Tackle Box

A good tackle box is an essential piece of equipment for the bass angler. A well designed box can save the pro bass fisherman a lot of time under tournament conditions. The last thing the pro wants to do is to search frantically through his boat to find the "hot" bait. If you listen to what the accomplished bassers say about their tournament success, invariably, they will mention how critical organization of tackle and lures is when they are on the lake. Time is money, and they must know precisely where all their equipment is located to keep that lure in the water.

Veteran pros will usually organize their boats with a variety of tackle boxes, each storing a selection of specialized baits. For example, one box will have jig heads, trailers, and pork; another, plastic worms, bullet weights and worm hooks. You don't have to be this specialized to get started. A single tackle box, well thought out and organized will suffice.

I recommend one of the briefcase or satchel style boxes with two usable sides. These are very compact yet have a lot of lure compartments. The better models have double latches on each side to guard against accidental spillage and are actually designed for bass fishermen. Use one side for soft plastic baits, assorted lead heads, worm hooks and bullet weights. Flip the box over and store your crankbaits, top-water plugs, spinnerbaits, and jars of pork rind. After a few trips, you will begin to memorize exactly where all your lures are located so you can make changes quickly as needed.

Avoid buying tackle boxes with the single or double cantilever trays, at least for getting started. These take up more space in a boat and often the compartments have been designed more for trout lures than the larger bass plugs. If you decide to fish bass tournaments as a "non-boater", the satchel style box will be the most convenient and accessible while taking up little space in the other guy's boat. Manufacturers such as Adventurer, Fenwick, Plano, and Rebel all make a variety of this type of box to chose from. Now, let's work on filling the box.

A Basic Lure Selection

Start with buying an assortment of plastic worms. Refer to Chapter 5 and use Western pro Don Iovino's guidelines for popular California worm colors. You should have two or three crawdad patterns in soft, hand-poured, 4 inch straight or paddle-tail worms for doodlin'. Next, add a few shad tones in a 4 inch spaghetti-thin, curl-tail worm for split shottin'. Buy a few of the injection-molded baits in curl-tail 4 and 6 inch models to use as trailers or when the bass want a bigger, thicker worm fished Texas-style. Mix in a few brown/black Superfloat worms to flip with or to use as jig trailers along with some 1/8 ounce P-heads or darters, #3 to #5 split shot, 1/8 to 3/16 ounce bullet weights, and #2 and #1/0 worm hooks. This will give you a solid array of soft plastic baits.

You can also keep your selection of crankbaits tight and simple. You should have #5 deep-running Rapala Fat Raps in a silver foil finish. For crawdad-colored alphabet-style plugs, pick from the Storm Wiggle Wart, Rebel Deep Wee-R, Bill Norman Baby N, Bomber Model A, or again, the #5 Rapala Fat Rap. All of the above (except the Rapala) are also made in a Tenessee shad finish which is the third most important pattern to own for California bassin'. If the bass seem to prefer a thin profile, shad-like bait, keep a few #7 Rapala Shad Raps in silver foil and natural shad finish handy.

Finally, if you need a super deep-diving crankbait, throw in a Bagley DBII or DBIII in either silver foil or Tennessee shad patterns. This assortment of top-notch lures should cover you for much of the crankin' you'll have to do in California waters.

If you want to give spoonin' a try, you need just three models to keep you competitive. In a larger spoon, buy the Hopkins #075 in the chrome finish. This heavy 3/4 ounce lure will handle almost all the spoonin' needs of the serious basser. Also, carry a Kastmaster spoon in 1/2 ounce silver finish if a bait is needed with a slower, more fluttering fall. To round out your spoon choices, add the 3/8 ounce Haddock Structure Spoon in one of the more exotic color schemes to give deepwater bass something different to see. Purchase this spoon in either smoke, shad, blue, or baby bass finish.

You can also keep your top-water selection uncomplicated and down to a minimum of good, productive lures. Start with a #11-S floating Rapala minnow for twitchin' and jerkin'. Add a smoke phantom-colored Storm Chug Bug, a chrome twin prop Devil's Horse, and a Heddon Zara Spook in 3/4 ounce silver flake shad finish to your top-water collection. Round out the selection with a 1/2 ounce single chrome blade buzzbait in white and chartreuse patterns and you are ready for most surface activity you will encounter.

Your jig selection has to be divided simply into pork and plastic combinations. Pick out some 3/8 and 1/2 ounce live rubber skirted jigs in black, brown, and maybe brown/orange colors. Match these with the Uncle Josh #11 Pork Frog, stocked in brown, purple, and black. For plastic jigs, either the Garland Spider or Haddock Kreepy Krawler in smoke/sparkle finish will day in and day out be your best bets when the fish want a shad-patterned jig fished deep. Match these with some 3/8 ounce spade-shaped jig heads.

Spinnerbaits are the simplest of all to select. Stay with the two basics: a tandem 3/8 ounce white with nickle blades, and the companion model with a chartreuse skirt and gold blades. You can't miss with these two.

For the subtle baits, keep a good stock of the Twin-T's single tail grub in the salt'n pepper combination matched with a 1/8 ounce P-head or darter jig. Along with the grub, add some Fat Gitzits in smoke/sparkle and smoke/red flake color to complete your subtle bait selection.

All of the lures listed in this chapter can be deadly on any given day in California. There are no "stiffs" in this collection -- all of these have been time-tested by the Western pros and are truly productive bassin' baits. Believe it or not, you can fit this array of lures into one of those compact double-sided satchel boxes. This little assortment of baits will make you very competitive on your favorite lakes if you master the special techniques used to fish them!

Conclusion

Try to invest in good tackle whenever you buy a rod, reel, and especially line. If you take care of it, quality equipment will provide you with many years of dependable service. Don't go crazy buying every new gizmo that comes out on the market. Out of each year's crop, there are only a small number of truly productive new lures.

Many of the newest offerings are gimmicks or variations of older, established ideas. Don't misunderstand this. You have to be somewhat cagey and creative to master the finicky California bass. Just try to be selective in your tackle purchases. A lot of items that allegedly work down South or in the Midwest will not be that effective in our clear, deep, and often heavily-pressured California waters. A lot of finesse and forethought is required for any of the tackle you purchase for this unique fishery.

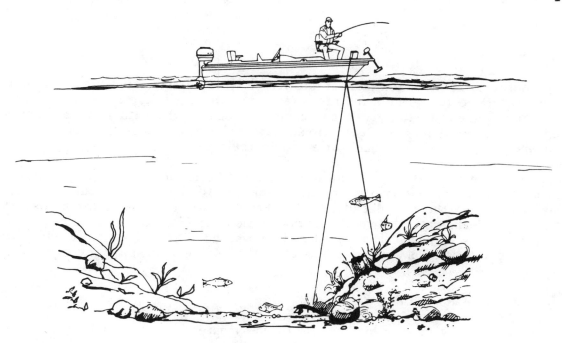

Bassin' Electronics: Gadgets, Gizmos and Serious Tools

It is certainly true that quality bass can be caught fishing from the shore as well as from the family pleasure boats. However, a majority of big fish in California are taken from boats equipped with sophisticated electronic instruments. The angler committed to serious bass fishing in the Golden State must learn to move off the bank and fish what is known as "structure". To do this, he has to have some basic knowledge of how to utilize his boat's electronics. Before we talk about this equipment, let's examine this notion of "structure".

Structure Fishing - A Must for California Bassin'

Don Iovino is the only pro in the history of U.S. Bass to win the prestigious Northern and Southern divisions in the same year. Many of these tournaments occurred on lakes scattered throughout California. He attributes much of his success to being able to catch fish from deep structure.

Iovino defines lake "structure" to be anything on the bottom that is not within the norm of the flat, muddy surface found in most California lakes. This could be rocks, boulders, brush, old car bodies, truck tires, broken concrete pipe -- simply anything that deviates from the typical mud bottom. Largemouth bass need ambush points to survive. These kinds of underwater structure serve as holding areas that the fish can use to prey upon the forage bait.

The secret to Iovino's tournament prowess is to find this structure. But most importantly, he looks for structure away from the bank, typically in water 35 to 60 feet. Better sanctuary can be found at these depths with minimal boat and angling pressure evident. Recreational bass fishermen across the country have a tendency to be simply too bank-oriented in their routines.

Biologists concur that for the most part, larger bass prefer the deep water haunts. If you follow Iovino's amazing track record, it would appear to support this position. In the last decade, he has caught 110 bass over 8 lbs in water 35 to 45 feet deep, capped by a 14:11 pound monster from Lake Castaic. This Western pro is emphatic that if such data was accurately kept, it would prove that more big bass in California are caught at 45 feet than at any other depth.

The Graph Recorder

Iovino specifically credits his success to the mastery of the graph recorder. With this piece of equipment, the basser will get a paper print out of the underwater terrain in great detail. He can then keep these readings filed away for future reference and analysis when he returns to the lake. Iovino uses his graph to decipher what is going on in the underwater environment. To quote this veteran pro, "The graph recorder is the heart of bass fishing." He uses his graph to locate at least three key things in a given lake: (1) structure, (2) baitfish, and (3) the thermocline.

For Iovino, structure not only includes the obvious brush piles and rocks, but also the deep ledges and "breaks" where schools of threadfin shad are found. The graph will also actually show the schools of shad and individual bass. On California lakes, it is imperative to find these schools of bait. With the grayline function of the graph turned on, the shad schools will appear as dark "clouds". Where you find these concentrations of bait, you will invariably see bass activity. Bass not lying on the bottom will appear as arches either mixed in, to the side, above or below the clouds of bait.

How completely symetrical the arch appears depends upon where the bass is located in relation to the transducer. This is the device mounted under the boat which picks up the sonar signal bounced off the fish. The arch may appear to be more incomplete if the bass is on the outer perimeter of the transducer's range. This perimeter can be imagined to look like an inverted ice cream cone. A perfectly symetrical arch represents a fish directly under the transducer in the center of the cone.

The graph can tell you even more about the fish. For instance, an arch that seems longer than normal is typically an indication that the fish is swimming in the direction of the boat. A shorter than normal arch means the fish is moving away from you. The thicker the arch appears, the bigger the fish. Furthermore, if there are a lot of different size arches surrounding the clusters of baitfish, this is a good sign that the bass are actively moving and feeding on the shad. In contrast, arches that appear to be nearly identical usually mean that the bass are inactive and suspended.

In pro tournament circles, there is an ongoing debate as to whether or not it is possible to distinguish bass nestled right on the bottom with the graph recorder. Don Seifert is a long-standing member of the Western pro ranks. He is also a field representative for one of the largest marine electronic companies. Seifert fishes California lakes extensively and has seen just about everything possible on graph paper.

In Seifert's professional opinion, a lot depends upon whether or not the boat has top-of-the-line equipment properly rigged. With good electronics, you can see fish 4 inches off the bottom with a flasher. With quality graphs, it only takes a 5/8 inch separation from the bottom to read the fish. Seifert also notes that the further the fish is from the center of the cone, the further off the bottom it has to be to get recorded.

The third feature discernable with the graph is thermocline. This is a stratified layer of water with a distinct temperature variance of usually one half a degree per foot of depth. This appears as a straight band of dots across the paper. Iovino will use these two variables, location of shad schools and thermocline to bracket where the bass should be. For example, if the thermocline reading occurs at 12 to 15 feet and the shad schools are located from 5 to 15 feet, you should look for structure and hence, bass between 0 and 15 feet. Iovino emphasizes that there is no more than a 10 foot difference between the thermocline and the location of the bait fish. Proper interpretation of the picture on the graph recorder will thus help you to eliminate up to 75 percent of the areas **not** to fish.

Flashers and LCR's

Many bass fishermen think of the flashing sonar units that heralded the electronic age for this sport when electronics are mentioned. These "fish finders" as they are sometimes termed, are still an intregral part of a bass boat's electronic system.

Most pros mount these units to their electric trolling motor shafts so that they can monitor the bottom as they silently cruise the lake. The flasher will not give as detailed a report of the bottom as the graph recorder. However, it will still allow you to determine if the bottom is hard or soft. You can also see clusters of bait fish and individual bass. (All of the manufacturers provide excellent instructions and illustrations with these units to facilitate proper usage.)

Too often however, the neophyte basser spends excessive time running his graph or fish-finder frantically searching for active fish when the bass are hugging right on the bottom. At times like these you may simply be better off casting to seemingly good water and worrying less about viewing the fish on you instruments. I have repreatedly returned to deep lakes like Castaic and fished favorite breaks, spoonin' fish right off the bottom, when I could see no visible life on the graph or flasher. I had confidence based on past experience in the area, that there would be fish there. So I continued to fish, watching my front bow flasher. I monitored the flasher not so much for bass or shad, but rather to be certain that I stayed along a certain ridge or drop off.

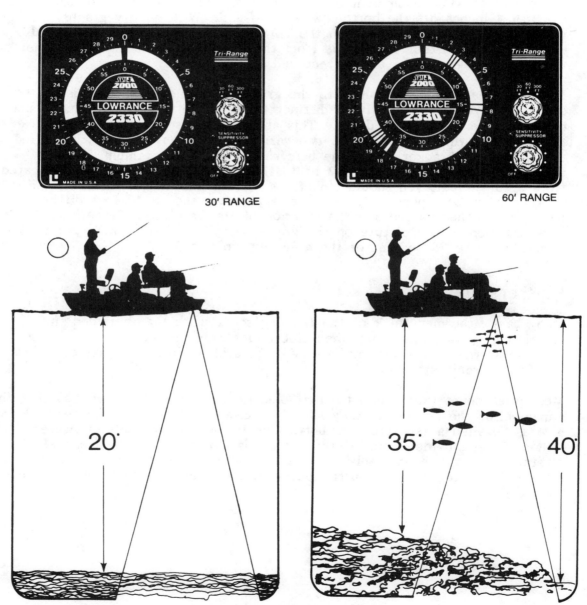

Typical Flasher Readings

Many pros speculate that the new liquid crystal recorder units (LCR's) will replace traditional flashers. The LCR's are more compact than flashers and in the long run may prove to be the more accurate of the two types of fish finders. For the recreational weekend basser, the LCR may be the simplest way to go. They are the easiest of all to read and operate and you never have to worry about running out of graph paper.

There are now LCR's on the market that take a lot of the guesswork out of making the proper settings. The most current units have an automatic feature that will dial in their own range and sensitivity settings. With some of the more sophisticated LCR's, you can actually enlarge the view to get a better look at the bottom 10 to 20 feet of water. In this way, the extraneous water all the way to the surface is eliminated and you can concentrate on this lower strata where the fish may be holding.

A final point to be made in favor of liquid crystal units is their ability to report in really deep water. The top models can work quite well in 60 to 90 foot depths, which is definitely a viable range on many California lakes. Iovino has put on demonstrations for nonbelievers in which he shows them that bass can be caught down to 100 feet as they follow the schools of shad. Flashers simply will not provide the quality of picture at these depths that is possible with the best LCR's.

A natural progression for the future of bassin' electronics will be video recorders. Working in a manner similar to a television set with a cathode ray tube, these units are already being used in saltwater fishing. Many commercial and sportfishing boats have these video, CRT recorders. The most sophisticated color CRT's can report the underwater environment so thoroughly that you can distinguish the different densities of the fish appearing on the screen. This unique feature allows you to separate bait from larger gamefish when they school tightly together. You will actually get different colored readings depending upon the size and density of the fish.

At present, most of these CRT's are somewhat expensive and cumbersome in size and weight for bass boat adaptation. They may also be less able to withstand the rigors and pounding that electronics take with high-speed boats. Also, a video recorder is very difficult to read in daylight conditions. Another possible drawback is that the CRT's require a greater amount of power than most other electronic instruments. Smaller, thinner profile units will be available soon. These will mount nicely on a bass boat console. The CRT's will do just about everything that graph recorders and LCR's are capable of doing. Some of the newer LCR's and CRT's also provide a constant surface temperature readout on the screen.

Temperature Gauges

The pros here in the West do not seem to overwhelmingly rely upon these instruments. Temperature gauges are used primarily in the Spring. When the largemouths are looking for shallow water in which to spawn, a one or two degree difference in water temperature can be critical. Western bassers will use their surface temp gauges to especially find coves that have warmer water than others on a particular lake. These are the areas where you will find active fish in preparation for the spawning ritual.

Sometimes during the heat of the Summer, the temperature gauge can also serve to help you find slightly cooler water and more active fish. It is important to keep in mind however that these gauges primarily measure water temperature down just a few feet below the surface. If you want to more accurately measure the temperature down deeper, I recommend that you purchase an inexpensive pool thermometer that can be lowered to the bottom. This will also work well for the rental boat fisherman who might want to take temperature readings in the Spring.

The pH Meter

There is some evidence that the acidity or pH level of the water can influence the overall ecology of the bass fishery. Studies have shown that fluctuations in water pH can effect the basic metabolic functions of the various bass species. This includes their ability to spawn, combat infection, manage stress and utilize oxygen. Such variables as runoff water flowing into the lake and quality of the surrounding watershed in a given locality can effect the pH levels at a specific lake.

The proliferation of large scale vegetation and the influence of sunlight and ensuing photosynthesis from the lake plant life can also create daily fluctuations in the pH levels. The pH meter can help the seious basser to measure which coves, for example, on their favorite lake have optimal pH levels. Such areas are commonly best for spawning and consequently tend to hold populations of bass throughout the year. So why do so few Western pros utilize this piece of electronic wizardry to find such choice pH levels?

One key explanation put forth by some of these pros themselves is that the bass lakes in California are typically deep, often clear, face minimal runoff, and overall provide a fairly stable environment pH-wise for the bass fishery. California lakes are not affected as much by irrigation flows from nearby fields as are lakes elsewhere in the country. There aren't that many lakes in the Golden State that evidence a major alkalinity problem from the local watershed either.

Furthermore, in contrast to the South, for example, California lakes are fairly barren of heavy aquatic vegetation that can affect pH levels. Largescale plant growth such as hydrilla, hyacinth, other waterlilies, and massive moss beds are noticeably absent on most California lakes. Thus, most of the Western pros with whom I have spoken, simply feel that the pH meter is unnecessary for the deepwater lakes they fish.

Still, for popular bassin' areas such as the Sacramento River Delta or the lower Colorado River, the pH meter might be a prudent investment. These waterways are characterized by numerous backwater lakes, small hidden pockets known as "pretty water", and sloughs that branch off from the main river. There are also a variety of smaller water channels that flow into these areas. It is a good bet that the pH levels will change more dramatically in these shallow fisheries or on any lakes that receive runoff water.

The Color-C-Lector

Recently, the invention of the Color-C-Lector has added an exciting new dimension to bass fishing, especially for the plastic worm and crankbait enthusiast. The Color-C-Lector will actually key in on one of a series of distinct colors that the fish can most readily see. Serving as a unique light meter, the hand-held unit can definitely enhance wormin' and crankin'. Here are a few helpful hints to keep in mind when using the meter.

First in viewing the meter and the band of colors, also look at the adjacent color on each side of the dominant color selected by the needle. Then try to choose, for example, a plastic worm that combines two or three of the colors to maximize the chances that the bait will be seen by the fish. To illustrate, if the Color-C-Lector needle points to dark purple as the dominant color, look for a dark purple worm that might also have blue and light purple bloodlines. These are the colors on each side of the dark purple band. A similar effect can be achieved by using a dark purple bodied worm with a contrasting blue tail section. More and more plastic worms with corresponding Color-C-Lector schemes are being manufactured in both injection molded and hand-poured models.

As mentioned, many pros make crankbait selections depending upon the forage bait available (i.e. foil and Tennessee shad finish for threadfin shad populations, "baby bass" for fingerling schools, and crawdad, for crayfish). However, the advent of the Color-C-Lector meter has removed a lot of guess work and added a critical tool to use in the selection of crankbait colors.

Study after study has shown the Color-C-Lector to be right on in recommending which color will be most visible to the fish at a given depth and under different water and light conditions. One key to remember in using the meter is that you must reference the color reading to the depth that the crankbait runs. For example, if you are positioned in, say 40 feet of water, and throwing up to the bank working out, the plug obviously isn't going to bounce the bottom all the way back to the boat. It would be futile to lower the meter's light probe directly below the boat to the bottom for a color reading.

Instead, the angler must have some prior knowledge of the diving depth of each crankbait that he uses. This information is provided by most manufacturers. If the lure runs, say 8 to 12 feet deep on the standard retrieve, the probe should be lowered to that depth for an appropriate color reading.

Almost all of the major crankbait manufacturers have now marketed their baits in special Color-C-Lector colors. Some, like Bill Norman, have brought out a popular model in all 26 colors represented on the meter. Others, like Bomber for instance, feel that an individual crankbait's depth will vary on the retrieve so they bring out plugs in tri-color combinations that will cover more range.

Still other lure makers such as Cordell, Heddon, and Rebel have interesting do-it-yourself kits you can purchase to customize your lures to match the Color-C-Lector colors. They provide the bass fisherman with a bone white plug and quick drying paints to color the lures under field conditions. Special Color-C-Lector coded, felt-tip pens and other lure paint kits are also now available to color your old lures quickly to adjust to different readings from the meter during a day on the water.

I have spoken to many bass fishermen who will relate how one unique experience with the Color-C-Lector meter made them believers in the units. My personal "revelation" came one day at Lake Hodges when the fishing had been shut down all day. I had tried the usual menu of crankbaits that had produced time after time for me on this lake, but without a single strike on this day. By late in the afternoon, I decided to try the Color-C-Lector since, as bad as conditions seemed, I had nothing to lose.

I lowered the probe to the depth I figured the crankbait should run and got a reading of color "C", light red (closer to pink). I happened to have a plug that was especially designed in this particular Color-C-Lector color, tied it on, and threw it. I caught six fish in the span of about 15 minutes on a bank I had tried numerous times earlier in the day with no success. There is absolutely no question in my mind that the distinct "pink" color did the trick. I also have no doubt that there was certainly no way I would have thrown such an unusually colored bait if the meter hadn't recommended it.

One final tip: lower the probe into the water at fairly regular intervals during the day to test for changes in dominant color preferences. Fluctuations in weather conditions, water clarity, temperature, underwater structure, and even changes in turbulance from wind action or water skiers can affect the choice of color selection made by the meter. Conduct a new test as you move to a different spot on the lake or if weather and cloud cover change dramatically.

Be prepared to switch colors quite a few times if you have faith in this electronic instrument. For many serious bassers in California, the Color-C-Lector has become an intregral part of their boat's electronic system. It can be a very valuable tool on these heavily pressured lakes.

Conclusion

Most Western pros agree with Don Iovino that the graph recorder, along with a bow-mounted LCR or flasher are the most important pieces of equipment on their bass boats. Because California's lakes are usually so deep, it is imperative to learn to locate schools of shad and structure if you want to catch bass all year long. There will always be a certain amount of fish to be caught in shallow water throughout the year. But, the veteran basser out West knows that he will have to eventually move out to deep structure if he is to be competitive in tournament circles.

Don Seifert notes that there are two common mistakes the neophyte basser makes using electronics. Both of these entail making very simple corrections to get the maximum reporting from these instruments.

First, Seifert feels that most anglers have a tendency not to turn the sensitivity setting up high enough on their electronics. He points out that the soft mud bottom found on most of these California waters is a difficult surface from which to receive a good electronic echo. This bottom has a tendecy to absorb the signal and not shoot it back to the boat. Increase the sensitivity on the unit and you will get a better picture of the structure on the lake bottom.

Secondly, don't be overly concerned with conserving graph paper. To get the best possible reading, the tracking speed for the paper must be turned up to a fairly fast pace. If the paper speed is too slow, you will not get what Seifert terms the complete "parade of action", displaying what is going on in the underwater environment. By turning up the paper speed, you receive better relative feel of the action occuring under your boat.

A quality graph recorder will get from 7 to 10 hours of play from one roll of paper. The average pro will get 3 to 4 days worth of recordings from this roll under most tournament conditions. A graph recorder is like a good underwater camera. Just as you wouldn't cut corners on film, don't be too conservative with graph paper. The results you receive could be catching that trophy bass from deep structure.

Some Tips and Tricks from the Western Pros

There are a number of little special tricks and tactics devised by the Western pros that do not involve lure selection or use, yet add to their tournament success. Here is a brief rundown of some of the less obvious tips that can lead to more productive days on the water.

The Question of Scent

Long before commercial bass scents were on the market, California pros were dipping their plastic worms into a variety of concoctions in an effort to enhance their catch ratios. In those days, the "secret" mixture was oil of anise, the licorice scented liquid sold in drug stores. To keep the injection-molded worms from drying out and becoming too hard, the pros would put them in a plastic bag with some mineral oil and a few drops of anise. The mineral-anise oil combination would give the bait both a glossy sheen and an appealing smell.

Today's commercial bass scents are basically divided into two types: attractors or stimulators. Some manufacturers claim their scent attracts the bass with a tantalizing aroma. Others believe their scent stimulates the attack-feeding response in the fish. Regardless of the school of thought to which you subscribe, one thing is certain-- bass do feed not only by sight but also by smell. As with other fish species, their olfactory senses are relatively keen.

Furthermore, there is good scientific documentation that bass give off a "danger" odor when caught and then released back into the water. This is known as the "Schreckstoff Response" and research clearly indicates it is very powerful among members of the bass family. Bass will actually emit an odor that will warn their companions of impending danger. The only exception appears to be fish that are hooked outside the lip.

I have personally experimented with a wide variety of these commercial scents and in my opinion, they definitely work. I have used fish oil base products in standard, crawdad or shad flavors, as well as other scents that are prepared from a natural biochemical strike-stimulant. I have also used scents in liquid, paste and roll-on form. They all seem to work.

I do a lot of plastic worm fishing and throw a lot of the subtle baits such as grubs and P-heads. I always add some type of scent to these lures. Usually I'll put a few drops on about every third cast or so. Many of the manufacturers package their scent in large pump spray bottles. The problem with these is that 80% of the liquid ends up in your boat or out in the water and not on the bait. Purchase a small squeeze bottle similar to that used for backpacking or for medicines and transfer the scent into it. You only need a few drops of this concentrated mixture to work with the lure.

Veteran Western pros like Don Iovino are emphatic about applying scent to all the plastic baits for these touchy California bass. Iovino puts a few drops of scent in a little plastic sandwich bag, then rolls his 4 inch "Doodle King" worm around in it before he makes the vertical drop. I also believe that if you add scent to the lure after each fish you catch, you will eliminate the possibility of its brethren spooking away because of the Schreckstoff Response.

A final note on scents. Many of these compounds will stain clothing or affect the gel coat on expensive fiberglass boats. Keep a wet towel handy to wipe up any spillage and try to work away from the boat. Take that extra effort to add scent to your lures. The results may be well worth it!

Important Eyewear

There are a wealth of accessory items that the serious basser can purchase at his local tackle shop. Some of these appear to be pure gimmicks; but, others are worthwhile investments that may lead to better catches.

For the plastic worm affecionado, polaroid sunglasses are an absolute must. So much of this type of fishing is done by sight or by "line watching". The polaroid lenses cut down on the glare and really highlight the line as it enters the water. Polaroid sunglasses are also important because they can actually let you penetrate through the water and often see your quarry. On clear lakes in particular, this can be critical because you may have to stay way back from the bass so they won't spook. Quite often, with a good polarized lense, you can see the bass lazily cruising or playing hide'n seek in the brush many yards away before you cast.

There are a number of manufacturers that make polaroid sunglasses in plastic or glass lenses. My favorite was pioneered by Western trout guides and are made with heavy duty glass lenses. The frames also have polaroid side panels that keep harsh light from entering from this angle. This style of sunglass is distinctively heavy riding on the nose so to speak, but it does give optimal protection and handles a lot of abuse from dropping, scratching, etc. I also recommend you purchase an eyeglass strap with these glasses. Too many times, the angler leans over to unhook a fish and the sunglasses slide off and fall into the drink.

Line Strippers

The Berkley Company has devised a unique little gadget termed a line stripper that can literally save you many hours of tedious work over the course of a year. Many bassers have a tendency not to change line often enough. They buy line and expect it to last all season. The pros realize that the line -- not the rod, reel, or hook -- is the most important link between themselves and the fish. They purchase top premium grade monofilament and keep their reels filled at all times. Exposure to the sun, heat, rocks, brush, and structure will even wear down the best of lines. Thus, the pros will often change lines every time out.

This can become a major project if you have 6 to 12 reels that you use in a tournament situation. Here is where the line stripper pays for itself. Powered by two "C" batteries, an efficient miniature roller forces the line off the reel and through the stripper. To remove 150 to 200 yards of monofilament takes just a matter of seconds with this inexpensive little device.

Also built into the stripper is a rotating whet stone that serves as an excellent hook sharpener. Throughout this book I have harped on how important it is to sharpen the hooks used on all artifical bass baits. The same holds true for live bait hooks. You can sharpen hundreds of hooks with this little miniature grind stone, quickly and efficiently.

Other Handy Tools

Often the novice bass fisherman decides to customize his pork rind frogs and he has nothing in the boat to cut through the tough bait. Similarly, he may need to trim back a vinyl or rubber skirt if the lure appears to be too bulky. A pair of scissors designed especially for fishing can be a very helpful tool here. Most of these instruments also have a cutting, knife-like edge on the outside of the two scissor blades. You can use the scissor function to cut the pork or trim the skirting material, then use the sharp outside edge to make cross cuts in the pork rind without going all the way through the bait.

Izoreline markets an absolutely indispensible little gadget called the "Dr. Fisherman". These are basically a surgical hemostat that makes the dandiest hook remover you'll ever use. This inexpensive tool also has a cutting edge adding to its versatility. I won't leave home without one stashed in my boat.

Finally, if you are going to split-shot plastic worms or fish live bait with the older style, crimp-on shot, then be sure to carry a pair of pliers with you. Many manufacturers such a G-96 and Sampo market small compact pliers designed especially for fishermen. Don't try to use your teeth with this style shot. The potential damage isn't worth it. Invest in a pair of good pliers.

Keeping Fish Alive

If you own a bass boat, then it is important to make an effort to keep your fish alive in tournament conditions. Most tournament organizers will actually penalize you for weighing in dead fish by deducting a prescribed amount of weight from your total catch for each dead bass brought to the scales. Outside of making sure that your live well pumps work, there are a couple of other things you can do to insure the safety of your catch.

First, keep a jar of "Catch'n Release", a special crystaline chemical, added to the live well water. Follow the instructions as to how much to add based on well size. This chemical does two things to maintain healthy bass in the live well. It will tranquilize the fish to keep them from thrashing around in the well. But, interestingly, it will also help to regenerate the protective slime layer on the outside skin of the bass.

Secondly, learn to "lip" your fish as much as possible. Grasp the bass by the lower lip and try not to handle them any further if you can help it. If you have to touch the bass, wet your hands to keep that protective slime coat from coming off. This layer of slime serves as an anti-fungal barrier that wards off infection and keeps the fish healthy. Avoid letting the bass make contact with the boat's rough carpeted surfaces as this too will strip off this layer.

Here's another tip worth noting. Make it a habit to examine the contents of your boat's live well during the course of the day. Check the bass themselves. If their teeth seem intact, many pros feel that this is an indication that they are feeding on soft, threadfin shad. If the teeth appear somewhat mashed down, they most likely have been crunching hard shell crawdads. Also look at the bottom of the live well. Sometimes bass will regurgitate pieces of forage bait after they have been caught and placed in the well. This can be a real windfall. For example, you may have lucked into catching a bass on a shad-style lure when the contents in the live well indicate they are actually feeding on 'dads. By then switching to a crawdad pattern bait, you may start catching even more fish.

In extremely warm weather, keep your live well water constantly circulating. You can also add a little ice to the wells from your ice chest to cool the water down. If you want to get an accurate reading of the water temperature where your fish are being kept, add an inexpensive pool thermometer to the live well.

Should you decide to fish tournaments, you will need a measuring device to determine if your bass is a "keeper" fish based on either a 12 or 13 inch size limit for most California events. The most commonly sanctioned device is Jimmy Houston's "Will-E-Go" board. This is basically a ruled, plastic board with a cupped trough at one end. The bass have to be placed, mouth closed, against the cupped end. Then you measure from nose-to-tail to see if it will "keep". Just as with weighing in a dead fish, bringing a "short" bass to the scales can also be costly with similar weight deduction penalties resulting. (Keep in mind that many bass contests are decided by mere ounces!)

Two tips that the pros use to maximize their catch involve this measurement process. Before you measure your fish, wet the Will-E-Go board with water. On hot days especially, the fish may actually "shrink up" from the shock of being layed out on the hot plastic surface. Wetting the board minimizes this in addition to protecting that important slime layer.

Next, if the bass seems just "short" (e.g. 11 7/8 inches), the pros will often put them into the live well anyway, add Catch'n Release, and remeasure the fish later in the day. Bass are often traumatized in the fight and will sometimes have a tendency to shrink up as they are boated. The chemicals will calm the fish down and give it a chance to relax its muscles. Often a "short" becomes a bonafide "keeper" if handled carefully in this manner.

One final point: if you are just fishing recreationally and want to practice catch'n release, then turn your bass back immediately after you catch them. Unless they are being caught in water over 35 feet deep (whereby the fish may be killed from the bends anyway), there is nothing better than to release bass right after you catch them. A live well is not an alternative to putting the fish back into its natural habitat. If you are fishing for fun, try to "lip" your bass, and get them back into the lake as quickly as possible. Also, treat them with T.L.C. Don't toss them back, ease them into the water gently. The bass you preserve today may be your tournament-winning fish tomorrow!

Conclusion

In this chapter, I have tried to pass along a smorgasboard of tips from the Western pros that have nothing to do with lure selection or presentation per se. Make no doubt about it however, with big money on the line, the professional basser will take advantage of every legitimate angle possible to bring legal size fish to the scales.

Plastic Worm Fishin': California Style

It has been said that throughout the country more bass are caught on plastic worms than all the other artificial lures and live bait combined. This is definitely true for California bass fishing, and particularly for the Florida-strain bass, which are very selective feeders. Day in and day out, all year 'round, the plastic worm is the most versatile lure in the bassin' man's or woman's arsenal. However, in contrast to other parts of the country, "wormin'" for California bass requires more finesse and considerably more forethought in lure selection with regard to style, size and color.

Article after article has been written about fishing the plastic worm in the South or the Mid-west for example. Invariably, the featured pro will comment that any worm will produce on these lakes "as long as it's blue" or "if it's a 6 inch black grape firetail", etc. Such broad generalizations simply won't work for California lakes. Again, due to the tremendous angler pressure, California bass become "educated" very quickly, often "turning off" completely on Sunday to a plastic worm pattern that was dynamite on Saturday. To be a successful worm fisherman in these lakes, you must broaden your selection of baits and be ready to change patterns a number of times during the day.

Worm Size

Again, making a general comparison to the South and Mid-west, the plastic worms that produce in California are typically much smaller in length. In other parts of the country, a 7 inch plastic worm is acceptable table faire for seldom-pressured bass. Larger models up to 9 or 12 inches also produce with some regularity.

In California, a 6 inch plastic worm is large, with more and more anglers now opting for 2, 3, 4 and 5 inch patterns to use on congested waters. Perhaps this smaller length matches better with a natural nightcrawler or a small western newt. The larger, 7 to 12 inch worms most closely resemble a small aquatic snake which for the most part are very rare on California waters, but are not so uncommon in the South. Similarly, these smaller 2 to 4 inch worms also come closer to the size silhouette of two other natural forage foods for California bass, the crayfish and threadfin shad.

Bass fishermen tend to subscribe to the theory that big fish want a big bait. This clearly isn't so with plastic worm fishing in California. Many bruiser-class bass, 10 pounds and over, are caught annually here with these miniscule 4 inch worms. It is important to note that there are still quite a number of fish caught on the 6 inch patterns mass produced by the lure manufacturers and sold all over the state, particularly when the bass indeed prefer a large bait. Interestingly, I have found that the larger worm will sometimes work even better in a "customized" color and/or using more unconventional presentations which I will discuss shortly.

Invariably, when the fish are feeding on shad or conditions are particularly tough, more and more of the good plastic worm fishermen will switch to a very small 2 to 3 inch pattern. It seems that these wary fish will more readily strike diminutive baits when they are not aggressively feeding, sometimes more so than larger, live, natural baits. Many of the better worm fishermen will thus start with a 4 inch worm and then either switch up to a 5 to 6 inch pattern, or scale-down to a 2 to 3 inch worm, depending on the size of bait the fish prefer that day.

Injection Molded vs. Hand-Poured Worms

Plastic worms are made from two basic manufacturing processes. The mass produced worms manufactured by such popular tackle companies as Mr. Twister, Creme, Culprit, Action and Manns make their plastic baits from an injection-molded process. Here a great number of baits are made from molten plastic which is automatically injected into a large series of molds. Injection-molded baits tend to be fairly hard, and are available in a modest number of color selections and patterns. But they are inexpensive. Injection-molded worms will average less than 10 cents per bait.

On the other hand, a selection of plastic worms that are fairly unique to California (although the word is spreading east) are termed hand-poured baits. Many serious bass fishermen feel that they must continually stay one step ahead of the fish, constantly seeking out new and innovative lures to which the bass have yet to get accustomed. Custom hand-poured worms definitely offer something in this regard. These baits are derived from a more deliberate process in which each worm is made from a layer or layers of molten plastic poured by hand into a custom mold. The manufacturer can come up with an endless variety of colors and hues by pouring one layer of plastic on top of the other. For example, he could start with a clear belly, then add a dark blue, thin center (a "bloodline") followed by a purple upper portion. Additionally, a special tail section of clear plastic with sparkle glitter for example, could also be added, producing a very customized worm.

Hand-poured baits are more expensive, averaging about 25 cents per worm, although sometimes discounts are available for purchases of 100 of a particular color and style. This type of plastic worm is also usually softer, and sometimes will tear apart after catching just one fish.

Local California manufacturers such as Teazer, Worm King, C-O, P.R.O. and A.A., offer the California basser a tremendous selection of colors and shapes from which to chose. These plastic baits are most often sold only at tackle shops and pro shops that specialize in bass fishing equipment. Thus, serious bass fishermen eagerly purchase these more unique, customized worms hoping that the less knowledgeable anglers simply won't stumble on their "hot" bait.

Now the question arises, are hand-poured worms that much more productive, and are they worth that much more money than the commercially available injection-molded baits? The answer, very often, is yes.

There have been many times in my guiding and tournament experiences where I have seen the bass in a virtual frenzy over some new, unusual, hand-poured color. The angler having the "hot" worm will often dramatically outfish the other bassers, who are using standard, injection-molded worms. This is often the case when angler pressure is very intense on weekends and during large tounaments.

A custom hand-poured worm can simply offer the hook-shy bass something new to grab. Also, since most of these worms are poured by knowledgeable local manufacturers -- many of whom are accomplished pros themselves -- the fisherman can be fairly certain that the shapes, lengths and colors are very up-to-date on what the fish are currently biting.

Worm Color

When the first plastic worms appeared on the fishing scene over 30 years ago, the fisherman had his choice of primarily three colors: black, purple and red. Although these three basic colors are still effective today, the California bassin' angler can now select plastic worms from a virtual rainbow of colors.

The most common worms sold by name brand manufacturers are injection-molded baits found in solid colors. In addition to the three basic colors, manufacturers now include brown, amber, blue, violet, green, white, motor oil, silver, and smoke in their selections. These solid colors are sold in either opaque or clear, see-through shades. Some suppliers have also added metal flake to these solid colors or have molded two colors together (known as a laminate pattern) to produce an even more attractive bait. The addition of a "bloodline" -- a solid color stripe down the center of a light or clear-bodied worm -- can also be very productive when all other combinations fail to get bit.

Custom hand-poured worms are also made in solid colors, with or without metal flake or the bloodline effect added. However, the custom worm maker can produce batch after batch of unique shades that are variations on the basic solid colors. Again, these are to be found primarily in selected pro shops. For example, the basic brown worm sold in the injection-molded styles can be found in hand-poured colors in such subtle shades as "smoke brown", "crawdad belly" "rootbeer" and "cinnamon brown". There are definitely times when the basic solid brown color will not produce while one of the custom variations will.

The current rage in hand-poured coloration is a variation of the bloodline in the form of a "neon" stripe. The neon color produces a very brilliant, almost electrifying stripe down the center of the bait that really sets the worm off in both clear and stained water. The most common neon colors being used are blue, green and purple.

Another color variation to consider in selecting plastic worms is the addition of a contrasting tail section. Quite often this feature added to the bait will also offset the tail from the main color of the worm and results in a more aggressive strike. At Lake Havasu on the Colorado River for example, a black worm with a fluorescent pink or a brown worm with an orange "firetail" can be excellent at times. Similarly, a smoke/sparkle worm with a fluorescent green tail can be a sensational producer at such lakes as Casitas and El Capitan Reservoir.

On this note, it is important to add that the angler visiting a new lake should check with the local tackle stores to determine which colors in plastic worms are currently producing. Quite often, one special worm pattern will become known as the legendary "hot bait" for a particular lake. For instance, at Lake Hodges in San Diego County, a 4 inch curl tail hand-poured worm in cinnamon brown with light blue bloodline has been a great bait year after year on this trophy water. At Lake Perris, home of world record Alabama spotted bass, the hawg hunter would be wise to carry a stock of 4 inch "mean green" Super Float worms. Similarly, there are times at Lake Lopez where the bass seem to bushwhack only a solid chartreuse worm, a regional secret at this lake.

Colors that may be mentioned in books and magazine articles as effective in other parts of the country may prove to be "stiffs" here in California. In contrast, some worm patterns that are hot in the West are rarely found elsewhere. For instance, brown is consistently one of the best colors for worm fishing in California. In my travels, this seems to be more of a Western phenomenon with limited usage elsewhere. The dominance of crayfish as a forage food for the California bass population may contribute to some of the effectiveness of this color.

Likewise, plastic worms in shades of clear or smoke with colored metal flakes are equally popular in the West. This is probably due to the abundance of threadfin shad that seem to match closely to these color patterns. Another similar innovation made popular in the West are the new worms in "salt'n pepper" colors. These are basically clear, smoke-colored worms with large flakes of black glitter added throughout the worm body. This unique coloration has proven to be a year-round winner, a truly universal bait throughout the California lakes.

Don Iovino is a Western pro with national prominence as an expert worm fisherman. He is one of the all-time top finishers on the prestigious U.S. Bass circuit. He also guides over 100 clients per year on local California lakes. He feels that bass fishermen have a tendency to make their lure selections overly complicated. Iovino passes along the following tips that should help the California basser more easily choose the color of plastic worm to use.

Firstly, he recommends carrying 9 basic colors in your worm arsenal: red, blue, cinnamon, orange, pearl, chartreuse, purple, smoke, and black. On a given day, one or more of these colors should work. He emphasizes that the worm should be changed frequently if one color isn't producing. You can also mix and match the colors to increase your chances of getting bit. For example, try a purple worm with a chartreuse tail.

Secondly, he succinctly categorizes what colors will work best under certain water clarity conditions:

Clear Water	Stained Water	Muddy Water
smoke	chartreuse	chartreuse
blue	black	black
pearl	orange	orange
red	cinnamon	
purple		

Finally, there are some additional color rules you should follow for California worm fishing. Darker patterns seem to be better in the early morning or at dusk with the worm silhouetted nicely against the dimly lit sky. The more transparent worms with metal flake seem to be particularly effective on bright days with little overcast. Plastic worms with the fluorescent firetails are very productive in muddy or stained water. Keep in mind that these are very general recommendations. Successful plastic worm fishing in California requires the basser to constantly be willing to experiment with color selection.

Worm Styles - All Kinds To Choose From

Like color choices, plastic worms are available in a smorgasbord of styles. The most common patterns purchased are either straight-tail or curl-tail designs. The straight-tail worm is styled after a live night crawler in both size and shape. Popular sizes are 4, 5 and 6 inch models. Mr. Twister, Creme, Manns, and Reds all make a variety of these worms available in sporting goods stores through-out the state. Custom hand-poured versions are sold in the pro shops by local manufacturers including Teazer, Worm King, P.R.O., C-O, and A.A. (See diagram on next page.)

Straight-tail worms work particularly well when an ultra-slow retrieve is in order. During the winter and early spring, these baits, especially the 4 inch patterns, can be very productive when the fish are somewhat inactive and will not move very far to attack a bait. A small straight-tail worm will also work very effectively in the Summer when the bass retreat to deeper water during mid-day heat, or when greater pressure on the lake requires a slowed down presentation.

Curl-tail worms are characterized by some form of a crescent-shaped or ribbon-like tail that provides the worms with a distinctive swimming action. The faster this type of worm is retrieved, the more rapid the swimming effect will be. Curl-tail worms are also available from all the aforementioned manufacturers in 4 through 7 inch lengths. Some other manufacturers who primarily specialize in curl-tail baits are worth mentioning for California bassin'. The Twin T's and Culprit series of 4 and 6 inch worms have become very popular for their sensational, snake-like tail actions. Similarly, the Ditto GatorTail worms in 5 and 7 inch models with their dramatic large sickle tail, enjoy a large following among fishermen "flippin'" the shallows.

Finally, the small 4 inch spaghetti-thin worms manufactured by Fluttercraft have become a staple for the bass fisherman who relies upon a very subtle bait. On heavily pressured lakes, these baits "split-shotted" or "shake'n baked" can be deadly. (I'll explain these specialized worm fishing techniques in greater detail shortly.)

Curl-tail worms work particularly well when the bass are more aggressively feeding and especially when there are schools of shad nearby. The swimming tail action resembles the natural movements of the bait fish. This type of worm is an excellent choice for fish actively cruising the banks. The larger curl-tail patterns will often induce large, quality "kicker" fish to strike when smaller worms are producing the smaller bass. The larger curl-tail will displace a significant amount of water, generating more vibration which will often induce a strike. Curl-tail worms in general, can be worked at a much faster pace than straight-tail baits, since only a modest retrieve rate is necessary to produce the proper waving tail action.

Popular Plastic Worm Styles
for California Bassin'

Paddle-Tail

Spaghetti-Curl Tail

Doodle Worm

Straight Tail

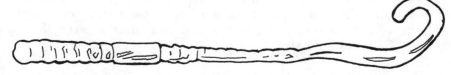

Curl-Tail

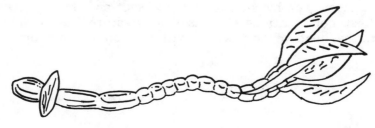

Multi-Tail

For the tournament bass fisherman, this last feature can be an important criteria in selecting a worm style. This is especially true on big lakes where a lot of territory must be covered in a short amount of time. The curl-tail worm allows the tournament angler to work the bank faster, similar to a "run'n gun" presentation used in crankbait fishing. In contrast, the straight-tail worms are usually most effective at a much slower retrieve and cannot be worked as fast as the curl-tail patterns.

The paddle-tail worm is sold primarily in 4 and 6 inch hand-poured models. This type of worm can be fished slowly like a straight-tail bail or it can be retrieved faster like a curl-tail worm, with the paddle-tail generating a slightly different and tighter type of swimming action. The paddle-tail worm in 4 inch lengths is also very popular for vertical "doodlin'", when the bass have moved off into deeper structure and along outside ledges or "breaks" in the underwater terrain.

Don Iovino, the veteran California touring pro who pioneered the "doodlin'" technique has perfected the usage of these paddle-tail baits producing outstanding catches day after day when other anglers are stymied by the bite. Iovino has designed his own custom hand-poured Teaser "Doodle King" worms in color shades that precisely match the indigenous crayfish population in both colors and in the paddle-tail action. This type of worm can also be used with such other techniques as "split-shottin'", "shake'n bake", "line feelin'", and "p-headin'".

Split-tail worms are manufactured commercially by Haddock Lures in 3 and 5 inch styles. This unique plastic worm consists of a tail section that has been divided or split into four separate tails, each with its own little spade-like paddle on the end. This split-tail construction yields a very sensual effect in the water as the four tail sections sway while the bait is at rest.

A variation of this split-tail bait can be created by the angler himself by customizing either a 4 or 6 inch Super Float worm. These straight-tail worms have been around for a long time but are not an overwhelmingly popular seller. They feature a tremendous number of little air pockets molded into the plastic, which provides the worm with outstanding buoyancy. By taking a razor blade and slicing the worm from the sex collar down to the end of the tail section, a split tail results. With the skill of a surgeon, the angler can then cut each of the two newly formed tail sections down the middle with the final product resulting in a four-tailed bait.

This is a little known trick of the Western pros. The Super Float worm straight off the shelf is thick, hard and very unappealing in its simple color combinations. However by slicing the tail section, the pro basser creates one of the deadliest combinations ever used in Western bass fishing. Rigged with a worm sinker, the head of this worm will rest on the bottom with either the double or quadruple tail sections sticking up waving back and forth like tentacles in the water. Many pros feel that this effect resembles a crawdad being backed up when attacked as it raises its claws in its first line of defense.

The customized Super Float worm can also be effective using a split-shot rig, again when a very slow presentation seems best. In some lakes where night fishing is allowed, the ultra-flotation of this bait produces a very slow-moving tantalizing silhouette against the evening sky, often resulting in strikes from larger fish. Finally, as we'll discuss soon, the customized Super Float worm is a "must" bait for the basser doing some serious "flippin'".

Customizing the Super Float worm

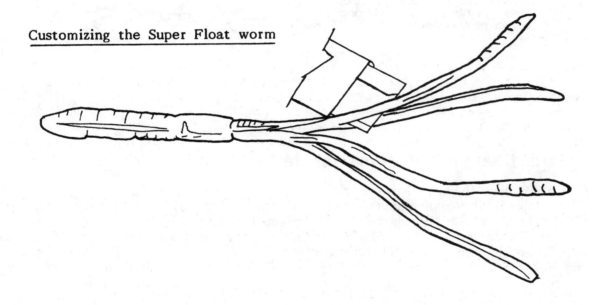

The Texas Rig

The most common way to rig a plastic worm for California style bass fishing is the standard Texas rig. With this rig, the hook is inserted into the worm through the head, then pushed through the plastic about 1/4 inch from the tip end. The hook is then rotated 180 degrees and re-embedded into the underbelly of the worm creating a full weedless bait. The worm weight is a bullet-shaped sinker that is designed to slide freely up the line above the worm.

THE WEED-LESS TEXAS STYLE

FIG. 1 Insert barb of hook into head of worm. Push hook through worm just below collar.

FIG. 2 Pull hook through until eye of hook is buried in worm's head. Turn hook 180° degrees and insert hook point back into worm body.

FIG. 3 Be sure worm is straight on hook so as not to twist line. If worm is not straight pull barb from body and replace point slightly higher.

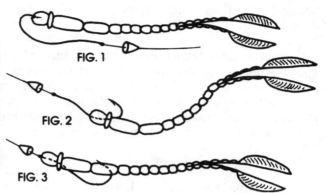

Hook and Weight Selection for Texas Rig

California bass fishermen use a wide variety of worm hooks for this rigging. Some popular styles include the dark blue Mustad #33637, the Tru-Turn hook and the Eagle Claw .45 Automatic. Hook choice basically comes down to a matter of personal preference. Regardless of what style worm hook you decide to use, be certain to sharpen each hook before using it with the worm. Although this requires extra work, the hooks straight from the box are simply not sharp enough for proper penetration. Almost every successful pro I have ever talked to has noted that each hook he uses is hand-sharpened, whether it is a worm hook, a spinner bait hook or a treble hook on a crankbait.

It is important to remember that the plastic worms used here in California are smaller than those used, for example, in the South. Hence, hook size should be scaled down somewhat. For the larger 6 inch worms, a #1/0 to #3/0 hook is very adequate. The popular 4 inch baits require a smaller hook, ranging from size #2 to #1/0. The minuscule 2 inch worms match well with a #2 or #1 straight shank worm hook.

Mustad also makes an ultra-sharp wire hook, #3777 (size 28 or 30), that also works well with the 2 inch baits and the spaghetti thin 4 inch worms. This hook requires no additional sharpening and yields fast penetration on the hook set. The trick is that it works best when it is hooked just barely through the plastic layer off to the side of the bait. This particular hook also allows for maximum buoyancy and works especially well with the 4 inch Super Float worm when the angler desires the bait to float well off the bottom. Because this uniquely designed hook is wire thin, it must be fished with 6 to 8 pound test line. A light drag setting is also necessary to minimize the chances of the hook bending out from too much pressure.

Also, in contrast to other parts of the country, it is recommended that lighter, bullet-shaped worm weights are used for the Texas-rigged bait here in California. The most common size worm weights used in our local lakes range from 1/8 up to 1/4 ounce. Heavier weights, up to 1/2 ounce are occasionally used with larger baits, in windy conditions, and sometimes for deep water wormin'. However, since lighter lines ranging from 6 to 10 lb. test are so often used here, a 3/16 to 1/4 ounce worm weight will get the bait down quickly with minimal line resistance.

Crawlin', Line Feelin', Shakin'n Bakin' and Doodlin'

The Texas-rigged worm can be retrieved and presented in a variety of ways to entice the hook-shy California bass. The most common technique is to simply cast, let the worm sink, and slowly retrieve "crawlin'" the worm back to the boat or the shore. Strikes will often occur on the "fall" as the bait is dropping. Thus, it is imperative to watch your line for the tell-tale little "tick" as the line jumps when the fish inhales the bait as it is dropping.

A variation of this "crawlin'" technique is affectionately known as "line feelin'" or "stitchin'". This constitutes the ultimate slow down in bass fishing outside of still fishing live bait. "Line feelin'" originated on the San Diego city lakes where the first Florida-strain largemouths were stocked in California many years ago. The San Diego bass fishermen on impoundments such as San Vicente Reservoir, Lower Otay Lake and Lake Miramar, found these Florida bass to be very spooky in the clear water and very tough to fool. These "Floridas" are very tricky feeders. The San Diego locals started to fish these bass with large, 9 to 12 inch plastic worms, very s-l-o-w-l-y creeping them along the bottom. Rather than retrieving the line strictly with the reel, the "line feelers" hold the rod in one hand and very slowly pull the line up with the other free hand. Then the slack line is reeled in. By "line feelin'", the angler forces himself to retrieve the bait in the slowest, most deliberate fashion. He is able to do this while also maintaining an excellent feel for even the slightest pick up.

"Line feelin'" continues to bring big bass to the scales, as this wormin' technique has now spread to other lakes outside of San Diego. This method works well from a boat at anchor in strong winds retrieving the worm up-hill along outside points where bass are known to congregate. Smaller 4 and 6 inch worms also adapt very well with this technique. However, I might add that not enough good worm fishermen try the larger 9 and 12 inch baits today. "Line feelin'" with these jumbo baits is still worth trying, particularly on lakes where trophy-size Florida bass are found.

A Texas-rigged worm also works perfectly for "doodlin'" in 20 to 60 foot depths. The 4 inch, hand-poured worms in straight-tail or paddle-tail styles, matched with #2 to #1/0 worm hooks, and up to a 1/4 ounce worm weight are the typical set ups. Lighter lines, preferable 6 to 8 lb. test, are standard choices for this type of vertical fishing, again with the worm weights sinking fairly rapidly.

"Doodlin'" requires both patience and a steady hand. The angler must impart a shaking action to the worm by jiggling the rod in constant, quick little side-to-side or up-and-down motions. The strike, particularly in deeper water along ledges and breaks may appear only as a form of mushy pressure. The fisherman should use a gradual sweeping motion to make the hook set in this deeper water while using the light monofilament to minimize shock and potential line breakage. Doodled fish have a tendency to rapidly plane to the surface, so it is important that excessive slack line is reeled in quickly, maintaining constant pressure on the fish.

A similar technique that is used with the Texas-rigged worm combines some of the elements of "crawlin'" with those of "doodlin'", known by locals as "shake'n bake". With this presentation, the angler casts the worm out and retrieves it back to the bank or the boat while gently shaking it, making it "dance", so to speak, and occasionally pausing. Sometimes the strike occurs while the bait is being shook erratically, and at other times it occurs during the pause period. On many occasions I have witnessed two fishermen using the identical worm rigs side-by-side, one crawlin' the bait occasionally getting bit, while the other used the "shake'n bake" action to generate many more strikes.

Sometimes, the worm fisherman who really masters the "shake'n bake" technique, casts a comical pose from a distance. It's as if he is afflicted with some strange fisherman's palsy as his rod, reel, hands and arms shake incessantly after every cast. But, believe me, on these wary California bass, this technique is continually productive under the toughest conditions.

Flippin'

A final technique should be mentioned. "Flippin'" utilizes the Texas-rigged worm. More and more fish are being caught using this method that has been refined by western pro Dee Thomas. Flippin' involves using fairly heavy lines ranging from 12 to 30 lb. test, with a stout, 7 to 8 foot flippin' rod. The lure must be gently and quietly lobbed underhand into shoreline cover. Many pros feel that flippin', above all other methods of bass fishing, allows the angler to keep his lure in the strike zone 90 percent of the time. This is because the casts are quickly made in short distances to potentially good fish-holding cover. The heavier test lines are necessary to literally yank the bass from the dense cover. For those who have ever seen commercial fishermen "jackpole" tuna on the open seas, the similarity to flippin' is immediately apparent.

Pork rind baits (which I will discuss in a separate chapter) are used quite often with this technique. However, during the summer months when the bass are more active, a plastic worm flipped into shoreline brush can be a very "hot" method. The 6 inch worm is used quite frequently for this summertime "flippin'". Both curl-tail and straight-tail patterns are popular.

In the straight-tail variety, the 6 inch Super Float worm in brown/black, black with chartreuse tail and solid purple are excellent producers. This worm sinks very slowly. If the tail is sliced into the four sections as I mentioned with the 4 inch model, the bass holding to tight cover can't resist this tantalizing morsel.

Other commercially made straight-tail baits are equally effective in both 4 and 6 inch patterns. Occasionally, for example at Lake Hodges in San Diego, the banks are lined with endless tules if the lake water level is full. Anglers, literally from all over the world, visit this lake in search of a 10 lb. plus trophy. Hodges' bass population retreats deep inside the tule banks when heavy boat traffic occurs on the lake. Veteran tournament anglers who fish this lake will sometimes opt for a small, 4 inch, straight-tail worm, flipped very delicately through the small pot holes and cracks that are found in the matted down tules. Often, this small 4 inch worm will dramatically out-produce larger worms flipped in the same spots.

At other times, the bass holding to shallow cover can be best enticed with a larger worm that displaces a lot of water. The 5 and 7 inch Gator Tail worms with the large sickle tails are good choices. Also, a 9 or 10 inch worm flipped in this same water might be worth a try. These worms probably resemble a small garter snake that has fallen into the water and larger, quality fish will often annihilate this little-known bait. Don't be too overwhelmed by the size of this large, snake-like bait. Strikes usually occur right at the head of the worm, making a quick hook set possible.

Worm hooks up to size #5/0 can be used for flippin'. As a general rule, a fairly large, extra-sharp hook is recommended. Quite often when flippin' the worm, the strike is an aggressive reaction as the bass attacks the intruder falling into its sanctuary of cover. Thus, thicker diameter lines and larger hooks will often not affect the presentation. However, I found many times on a very crowded lake where many boats are lined up flippin' a particular bank, that working behind another boat with much lighter line will often out-produce the boat in front.

For example, most flip fishermen working a bank will be using 17 to 30 lb. monofilament. If the bite is spotty at best, scale down to 12 or 14 lb. line and a small worm. Time after time, the results have been remarkable. Granted, some fish might be lost in the heavy cover with the lighter lines; but still, I'd rather get bit and lose some fish than not get bit at all.

Other times, the worm bite is more subtle when this type of bait is flipped.   A gentle "tick" or slight pressure can be felt.   The first inclination is to set immediately as flip fishermen do with pork rind baits, but patience may be a virtue here.   Allow the fish to take a few inches of line, i.e. eat the bait a little longer, then swing hard.   This little trick works very well sometimes when the fish are just not aggressively feeding in this heavy cover.

Rigging the Worm for Flippin'

Sinker selection for using the Texas-rig under flippin' conditions can require some forethought.   If the plastic bait is being fished through dense, heavy cover, such as broken brush and deadfall, a heavy 1/2 ounce weight is needed to penetrate through the cover.   But other times, the bass seem to want a bait that falls very slowly and thus a light 1/16 to 3/16 ounce worm sinker would be in order.   Regardless of the size of the weight used, it must be affixed to the line in a way that eliminates the sliding effect.   If the worm weight is allowed to slide under flippin' conditions, it will have a tendency to get entangled in the brush.   This is because there is some slack or belly to the line as the cast is initially made.   Here the angler does not have complete control over where the sliding weight goes as with tight-line casting.   The worm weight can be immobilized in one of two ways.

First and most common is to place the end of a wooden toothpick into the hole at the top of the sinker which the line passes through as the weight rests against the bait.   Firmly push the point of the toothpick down into the sinker against both the line and the lead.   Then break off the toothpick flush with the hole.   This leaves a small pointed piece of wood wedged between the sinker and the line, which resists the worm weight and keeps it from sliding any further.   Pros term this "peggin" the bait".

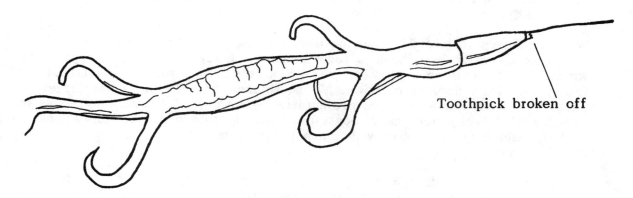

Toothpick broken off

Another less complicated way to secure the worm weight is to push the sinker next to the head of the worm and simply crimp together the very tip of the sinker.   This flattens out the hole, making it nearly impossible for the line to pass through the weight. If this is done carefully, the crimping will not nick or hurt the monofilament in any way. By either pegging or crimping the worm weight, the flip fisherman will be able to maintain a very sleek-looking bait that is weedless and won't get fouled in the brush.

Plastic Lizards and Crawdads

Two other plastic baits often grouped together with wormin' techniques should be mentioned. Although California worm fishermen do not rely upon these baits as much as they should, the plastic lizard and crawdad imitations can be tremendously productive offerings for the flip fisherman. Often, the lizard will work under these conditions when the plastic worm won't. It has been theorized that a finicky bass may pass up the worm placed in front of its nose, so to speak, but not the lizard due to the shape of this bait.

Some researchers speculate that the bass will attack the lizard with its four little legs swimming about in preference to the worm, because it senses that this creature will be able to scurry away too quickly if not eaten. The worm simply doesn't appear overly mobile to the bass, and there is less urgency to make the kill.

Plastic worms that are half worm and half crawdad in shape and full-scale crawdad imitations also sometimes work very well during a flippin' situation. These baits can be used with a standard Texas-rig or laced onto an accompanying jig head. Both plastic lizards and crawdad imitations seem to produce best in the spring when bass are actively working the shallows in preparation for the spawning period.

Carolina Rigs

If the California bass fisherman isn't wormin' with the Texas-rig, he's probably employing some variation of the Carolina rig extensively used throughout the United States. There is nothing real complicated about this basic rig and many bait fishermen have been using a modified form of it for years. The basic setup includes a sliding weight (either a bullet style worm sinker or a sliding egg sinker) with a swivel attached to keep the weight from sliding into the leader. A lighter leader line of 12 to 30 inches is tied to the other end of the swivel with the plastic worm tied to the other end of the leader line.

In deep water lakes such as Lake Mojave, bass fishermen have used up to a 3/4 ounce weight to get this rig down to 40 to 60 foot depths and to hold in the river current flowing through the lake. For most of our lakes a lighter 3/16 to 1/4 ounce weight will usually suffice. The fisherman can use this rig with heavier line than normally would be used for California worm fishing, as long as a lighter leader line is attached.

CAROLINA RIG

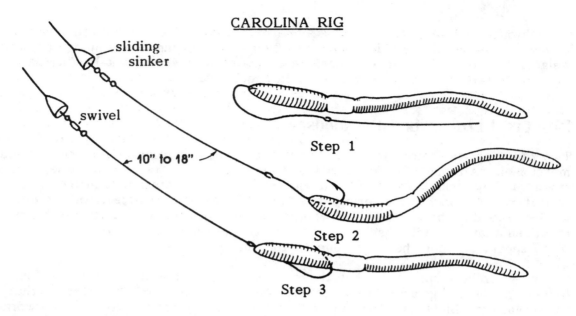

A popular combination would be about 12 to 17 lb. test fluorescent line with a 6 lb. clear monofilament leader. The heavy fluorescent line allows the angler to very easily visually monitor for the strike, while the lighter, clear monofilament is appropriate for clear water, highly pressured lakes. All the popular worm sizes from 2 to 6 inch models, in straight, curl and paddle-tail models will work with this presentation. The worm is retrieved fairly slowly with the rod raised dragging in a small amount of line and then lowered as the slack is retrieved. This retrieve produces a tantalizing rise'n fall action in the worm that simulates the movements of shad and crayfish.

National pro Jack Chancellor refined this basic Carolina method somewhat with his famous "Do-Nothin" rig that is now popular throughout the United States. Chancellor uses the same basic set up, but adds a fluorescent bead between the sliding weight and the swivel. The bead does two things for this variation of the Carolina rig: (1) it acts as an attractor to the fish; and (2) as the worm sinker knocks up against the bead, the clacking sound may also bring bass to investigate the noise.

JACK CHANCELLOR'S DO-NOTHIN' RIG

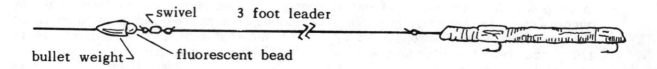

Chancellor has designed and marketed a plastic worm that is now starting to be of more interest to California bass fishermen, his short, stubby, "Do-Nothin'" worm. He rigs this worm with two small hooks threaded into the bait, one in the head section, the other in the tail. These hooks are exposed and are technically non-weedless. However, because they are rather small, they are very unlikely to get hung up in the weeds. The worm is tied to the lighter leader line, cast out with the sinker and bead combination, then retrieved slowly, often pausing. As with "doodlin'", the strike is often very "mushy" at best and sometimes is detected as nothing more than subtle pressure. The small hooks really do hold the bass quite well. The hook set, however, should be done in a steady, sweeping motion of the rod to avoid breaking the lighter leader line. This Do-Nothin' rig should be tried more often on the deeper clear water of California lakes. It is very easy to fish and it can be remarkably productive.

Split-Shottin': A California Secret

A final variation of the Carolina rig has been truly a well kept secret among California tournament bassers for sometime. "Split-shottin'" as it is termed, is another specialized slow-down technique popularized in California tournament circles. Boy oh boy, does this technique work on these California lakes! There are many bass fishermen who fish popular trophy fisheries such as Lakes Casitas, Vail, Hodges and Isabella who wouldn't think of leaving the dock without a split-shot rig tied on. Anglers fishing in Central California at lakes like Nacimiento and San Antonio have also discovered the tremendous power of this wormin' method to produce strikes year 'round. What makes this specialized technique so effective here in California?

To begin with, we have to remember what has been said about pressure on the lakes. During the weekends when pro tournaments are scheduled, boat and skier traffic is heaviest. Bass will often move from shoreline haunts to find quiet sanctuary in deeper water and outside structure. "Split-shottin'" with light line and delicate baits permit the angler to reach these cautious deep water bass.

Plastic worms fished behind a split-shot setup will also often entice suspended fish to strike when less subtle presentations fail. The slow falling of the lure as it sinks behind the lead shot on the cast, and the gentle rising and falling motion of the retrieve often tantalize fish suspended off the bottom. A split-shotted bait will thus stay in this strike zone longer than, say, a worm crawling along the bottom rigged Texas-style. Plastic worms that are split-shotted also imitate the two most dominant natural baits found in our local waters, shad and crayfish. The split-shot method produces particular actions in these plastic baits that most closely resemble the darting and pausing action of school shad and the crawling and swimming movements of crayfish.

The typical split-shot setup starts with 6 lb. test line. Occasionally 8 lb. test is used in heavy cover, or 4 lb. in gin clear water. It doesn't seem to matter whether the line is clear, colored, or fluorescent. The lead shot used should be the old-fashioned, round split shot, not the removable type that can be crimped on with hand pressure. Removable shot seem to get hung up on brush and rocks more than the rounded shot which must be crimped on with pliers. The weight of the shot depends upon depth fished, brush concentration and wind conditions. I have found a #4 or #5 spit shot to work best overall for both shallow and deep-water split-shotting. The shot should be crimped firmly to the monofilament, 18 to 30 inches above the bait.

Popular Split Shot Rigs

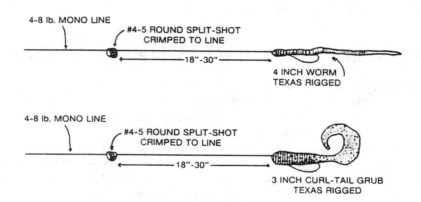

4-8 lb. MONO LINE

#4-5 ROUND SPLIT-SHOT
CRIMPED TO LINE

18"-30"

4 INCH WORM
TEXAS RIGGED

4-8 lb. MONO LINE

#4-5 ROUND SPLIT-SHOT
CRIMPED TO LINE

18"-30"

3 INCH CURL-TAIL GRUB
TEXAS RIGGED

Some split-shot fishermen vary this rig somewhat because they are concerned that crimping the shot to the monofilament line weakens it at that spot. Some have replaced the split-shot with a bullet-worm weight, pegged with a toothpick ahead of the lure to keep it from sliding down the line. Others use a heavier weight (up to an ounce) combined with a swivel and a 2 to 4 foot, 6 lb. leader to fish these small baits. This is similar to the Carolina or Jack Chancellor's "Do-Nothin'" rig previously discussed. For the most part, line breakage at the spot where the shot is crimped is rare, particularly with today's premium monofilament lines.

Most split-shotters opt for spinning reels over conventional baitcasters, although either will work. For many California fishermen, the spinning reel has become an excellent weapon in their tackle arsenal, especially when light-line fishing. However, many of the new, lightweight casting reels will now very nicely cast 4 to 8 lb. test lines. No matter which style of reel is used, it is important to match it with the proper rod.

Because of the 18 to 30 inch length of leader line from the bait to the shot, a 6 to 7 foot rod is recommended. This setup can be very cumbersome to cast with the shorter 5 to 5 1/2 foot worm and jig rods. Distance, accuracy, and ease of casting are enhanced with these longer rods when split-shotting. Rods with slightly softer tips are also popular for this method of fishing. They will allow you to detect the often very subtle, "mushy" bite that is so common with split-shotting.

The serious split-shot fisherman can select from a virtual smorgasbord of lures. Plastic worms in three and four inch patterns are particularly effective. I have found thin, curl-tailed worms to work the best with this method when the fish are feeding on shad or are suspended. Fluttercraft, Teazer and Twin T's all make small, curl-tail worms that fish well split-shotting. Popular colors include smoke/sparkle, smoke/red flake, smoke/blue flake, cinnamon brown, and electric grape.

Paddle-tail and straight-tail patterns in 4 inch lengths seem to produce best when the bass are on crawdads, working around brush and rocks. Teazer, Ambusher, and P.R.O., to name a few, all manufacture these baits in unique, hand-poured earth-tone colors that work sensationally with this method. Favorite combinations include cinnamon/blue neon, brown/green neon, brown/black, brown/orange, and brown/shad. The Haddock 3 inch split-tail and the Super Float 4 inch worms should also be used "split shottin'".

Standard worm hooks work fine with most of the plastic baits used in split-shottin'. Again, the main thing to keep in mind is to scale down in size. A #1 or #2 worm hook is best with these smaller plastic baits and will allow the baits to sink slowly. The Mustad "3377 wire hook (size 28 to 30) also matches well with these lures. This hook allows the worm to sink even more slowly, with many strikes occurring on the fall. A #6 to #8 standard baitholder hook rigged open-style can also be used with these small worms. This hook style works especially well in brush-free open water and also allows for that slow sinking action.

Split-shottin' can be effective utilizing a variety of presentations all year long. In the winter, throwing out from the bank into deeper water and working slowly uphill often produces outstanding catches when other baits and methods fail. Similarly, working this rig off of ledges and breaks in deeper 30 to 60 foot depths can work well during the tough winter months.

In early spring, a split-shot worm worked through brushy coves, rocky banks, and shoreline stick-ups can be deadly on fish feeding up in the shallows or on the flats. Crawdad-pattern worms in particular are popular for Spring split-shotting.

Summer and fall fishing can also be excellent times to use the split-shot rig. Working shad-colored pattern worms slowly through schools of bait and near points and deep-water rock piles can produce results during heavy-use months on our lakes. Split-shotting also can entice bass to strike that are laying in the thick summer mass beds and are difficult to fish using standard worm rigs.

Whatever the time of year, the best split-shotting technique is to retrieve the bait **very slowly**, occasionally pausing. Sometimes, the fish will respond best to a slight shaking action added to the retrieve, especially with the curl-tail baits. Other times, strikes will occur only if the bait is crawled ever so slowly with no action imparted at all on the retrieve. Occasionally, the fish will only strike a "dead bait". If the fish are striking short and not hooking on to the bait, allow the worm to rest on the bottom following a short strike. Let it rest for up to a minute or so. It is during this long pause that a more pronounced pickup often occurs.

Split-shotting can also be very effective on super windy lakes where conventional worming techniques would be difficult to use. Dragging a split-shotted bait behind the boat as it is slowly drifting has produced many catches under these tough conditions. This technique is a favorite among the local fishermen at Lake Isabella where the winds can hamper most methods of bass fishing.

The final point to keep in mind when using the split-shottin' technique is to stay alert. The strike with this method is often a very gentle "tick" or just a straight pressure on the end of the line. Many strikes will also occur on the fall after the cast so it is important to watch your line. I have found the best rule to follow when split-shotting is if anything feels different in the way of pressure on the line -- swing and set!

Summary

At the beginning of this chapter, I noted that more bass are caught on plastic worms than on any other single type of lure. Hopefully, the reader will now have some better ideas about how to go out and use this versatile bait to catch the elusive California bass. I feel that if any one single tip can be passed along more than any other with the wormin' techniques, it would be to slow down. Too often I have observed novice bass fishermen working the plastic worm too quickly. Their retrieves are too fast with no action at all imparted to the bait. With strikes coming far and few between with this fast retrieve, the fisherman gets frustrated and quickly changes to another type of lure.

I often draw upon some advice I read over thirty years ago as a young boy just starting to learn about this exciting new bass bait: **when you think you are working the worm too slowly, it's time to slow down your retrieve even more.** Be patient when wormin', change baits and experiment often with the different techniques. Day in and day out, wormin' will be your most consistent means to catch California bass!

Crankbait Fishin': Chuckin' and Windin'

Many veteran bass pros started out in this sport by first throwing a crank plug from the shore. "Crankin'" is an absolutely essential part of the serious basser's repertoire. California bass will strike a crank plug all year long. These versatile lures can be fished in all types of weather and are an excellent choice under difficult, windy conditions. They are not overly complex to master and "crankin'" allows the tournament angler to make many casts during the day, covering the greatest amount of territory.

But, like wormin', successful crankbait fishing involves certain tricks in lure selection and the refinement of some specific techniques. For example, how do we know what style of crankbait to buy? Should it run shallow or deep, cranked slow or fast? Should it wiggle a lot or not so much? What color should we pick? Should we buy one made out of plastic or wood? All these questions are definitely worth considering in selecting a crankbait for a particular California lake.

Choosing the Right Crankbait

Crankbaits are made from different materials, each with its own unique pluses and minuses. The most popular baits are made from plastic. These lures are generally the easiest and cheapest to manufacture. They are thus the most inexpensive on the market. The next advantage to plastic crankbaits is that they are very durable. They will take incredible abuse as they are bounced off of shoreline boulders, shook from overhanging tree limbs, and clobbered time after time by big bass.

Plastic crankbaits must have air cavities built in the body of the lure to maintain proper buoyancy. This is because the plastic material has a density that is heavier than water. Plastic crankbaits will generally vibrate much less than those made from other materials. They can be fished more slowly and deeply than a comparable size balsa plug, and are a good choice for less aggressive fish.

In contrast, lures made from natural balsa wood offer the best flotation, since the wood's density is lighter than water. The wood is soft and extremely workable which allows the manufacturers to create some very distinctive natural bait reproductions and actions. When the bass want a fast-moving, vibrating lure, go to a balsa wood crankbait. However, balsa plugs are much more susceptible to chipping and cracking than plastic. Balsa wood crankbaits also usually cost more than their plastic counterparts.

There are other considerations in addition to material that affect the manner a particular lure performs. The shape or size of the plug, the vibration or tracking pattern, the color and its sound producing ability all should be considered. The size of the lure is probably the first characteristic to look at in selecting a crankbait.

Crankbait Sizes and Shapes

There is some evidence that during the late Spring and Summer months, bass prefer to eat a bigger bait because they have a higher metabolism. The fish simply need more food to sustain the increased activity level. Conversely, in winter when the metabolism slows, a smaller morsel will support the limited feeding activity. Keep this in mind when selecting a crankbait size.

However, I should be quick to point out that bass fishing is far from being a precise science and rules such as this one are not etched in granite. There have been times when the exact inverse (for crankbait size versus time of year) held true on a lake on a given day. Thus, when such generalizations are made in any book about bass fishing, it is important to understand that they are basically just guidelines. But they are at least a good starting point in choosing a particular bass lure or technique.

The two most dominant shapes of crankbaits used in California are the fat-belly and the shad silhouette baits. The fat-belly baits are best represented on California lakes by the Bomber Model A, Rapala Fat Rap, Bagley Balsa B, Storm Wiggle Wart, Bill Norman's "N" and Rebel's "R" series. Most of these lures are floating-diving baits that will float at rest and dive on the retrieve. They are made to imitate larger shad, crayfish, small bluegill, and fingerling bass.

These fatter crankbaits usually have more surface area for the wide diving lip to work against. This results in a deeper diving bait than a plug with a more slender profile. For most conditions, the smaller versions of these baits will dive from 2 to 12 feet and are available in shallow, medium, and deep diving models. Plugs such as the Rapala Fat Rap #5, Rebel Double-Deep Wee R, Bomber Model "A", and the Storm Wiggle Wart are popular choices in this medium sized crankbait. If the fish seem to be on a slightly larger bait, the Bill Norman Deep Little N or the Rapala Fat Rap #7 are popularly used models. If greater depth and slightly larger profiles are needed from a fat-belly plug, the Bagley DBII and DBIII, Bill Norman's Deep Big N and the Rebel Deep Maxi R will usually do the job on California waters.

The fat-belly styled crankbaits are usually a good choice to start with when beginning to crank a particular lake. But there are definitely times when the fish want a thinner profile lure which most closely resembles a threadfin shad. The Rapala Shad Rap in sizes #5 and #7, and the Rebel Fast Track Shad come to mind as bonafide winners when the bass want a classic shad look-alike. Recently, Rapala has added a large #9 to their collection that is producing well on larger fish. These thinner, shad-profile baits offer considerably more wind resistance than fat-belly plugs. For this reason, more and more serious bassers have opted for a medium action spinning outfit spool with 8 to 12 lb. line to get maximum casting distance from these lures.

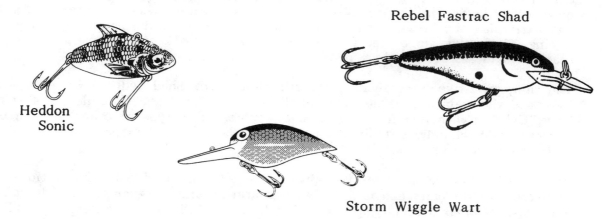

Rebel Fastrac Shad

Heddon Sonic

Storm Wiggle Wart

Oldies but Goodies

There are a few other styles in crankbaits that are occasionally used on California lakes with some level of success. Some of these lures enjoyed their greatest popularity before the invention of the alphabet-style, fat-belly baits. Still, many of these "oldies-but-goodies" will produce today and are worth taking out of mothballs once in a while just to give the fish something different to look at.

The original Bomber and Hellbender plugs in black and yellow, perch, black and white, and white with green glitter ribs (known as "Xmas tree") all occasionally still work. These two plugs are excellent bottom bouncers and due to the oversized diving lip, run fairly weedlessly. Similarly, the Heddon Sonic and the Cordell Spot are two slab-style baits that are worth trying. These lures work particularly well during the hot summer months when bass are feeding on schools of shad. These lures offer little wind resistance and can be worked with either spinning or casting outfits (diagram 9).

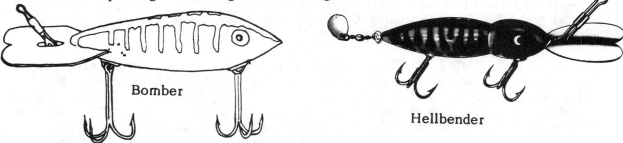

Bomber

Hellbender

Crankbait Actions, Colors and Retrieve

Crankbaits evidence a variety of vibration or tracking movements with the bass quite often keying in on one over all the others. Sometimes their preference for one particular action will even shift from one to another during a single day's fishing. It is thus important for the serious basser to keep a stock of basic crankbaits in assorted actions in his tackle arsenal.

The thin, shad-like lures such as Rebel's Fast Track Shad and the Rapala Shad Rap, and the slab-style plugs such as the Hedden Sonic and Cordell Spot track very "tightly" with minimal side-to-side wobble. This type of crankbait can be retrieved very quickly with little chance that the plug will plane to the surface due to overcranking.

Fat-belly plugs with medium-sized diving lips offer more side-to-side action than thin profile baits and usually have greater lateral movement. The Rapala Fat Raps, Bomber Model A's, Storm Wiggle Wart, Bill Norman's Deep"N" and the Rebel Deep "R" series again, are the best choices for California lakes.

Crankbaits with an extra wide lip such as Bagley's popular DBII and DBIII models track deeper with a lot of vibration than most smaller plugs. However, these big-lipped lures can also be overcranked if you're not careful. Let's talk about this overcranking effect for a moment.

As water passes over the crankplug diving lip, an inevitable amount of surface resistance is built up. The plug must dissipate this resistance in some manner. Typically, the lure is designed to channel this resistance from the side of the diving lip, first from one side than the other. The extent of the channeling effect varies from plug to plug and is precisely what gives a particular crankbait its own unique vibration. If this type of lure is cranked too fast, the resistance will also be discharged from the front portion of the body of the plug. The lure will then rise to the surface, planing in a manner similar to a water ski.

Novice crankbait fishermen tend to retrieve too fast, particularly with the ease of today's super high-speed retrieve casting reels. This contributes to the plug waterskiing on the surface. Slow it down a little, a moderate retrieve will work very well with most of these baits. During the winter months especially, an even slower retrieve is sometimes most effective on sluggish, less aggressive fish.

After the size and action of a crankbait have been narrowed down, color would definitely be the next factor to consider. For California bass fishing there are certain basic color schemes that seem to produce time after time. The silver foil and crawdad finishes would have to rank #1 and #2 in popularity. The Tennessee shad finish and "baby bass" are also quite productive, depending upon the type of forage on which the bass are feeding. Another crankbait coloration gaining in popularity has a portion of the plug opaquely colored and the other half in clear, see-through plastic. Storm calls this the "phantom" effect in their Wiggle Wart plugs. Bill Norman has a similar Reflect'N finish in their "N" series of baits.

The Question of Sound

Most Western pros agree that sound is an important feature to consider in crankbait selection. Most prefer to use a crankbait with some type of rattle in stained, dirty water. The sound chamber in a crankbait adds to the overall vibration pattern of the bait, and can definitely "call" fish into striking in water with low visability.

On California lakes that have particularly clear water with visability sometimes over 25 feet (e.g. Lakes Almanor or Casitas), the pros opt for a crankbait without the sound chamber. They feel that the presentation on these waters has to be so delicate and subtle to begin with, it is best to keep the lure simple as to not spook or overwhelm the fish. There are times on clear water where two anglers can be fishing near identical-looking crankbaits, but the only one getting bit is the guy with the "quiet" plug. In the clear water the fish were simply turned off to the rattle effect and hit only the quieter lure. It is thus best to carry a modest stock of both rattling and non-rattling crankbaits in comparative sizes and color patterns.

Crankin': The Pro's Pointers

Chuck Boydston is a well renowned crankbait specialist on the California tournament scene. Over the years, he has come up with a number of little "tricks" that have helped him put lots of crankbait bass in the live well. Boydston is very selective when it comes to choosing a crankbait. Above all, he wants a lure that runs straight. He relies upon manufacturers whose plugs historically require no tuning. That is, they can be used right out of the box.

With regard to color, Boydston is also very specific as to what to use for California bass. For most general conditions, he'll start with either a shad or crawdad-colored plug. However in stained, dirty water he relies upon crankbaits with a chartreuse belly and a sound chamber. But here's a little secret he passes along: take an orange marker pen and draw a stripe down the center of the chartreuse belly. Time after time, this trick has made this color plug doubly effective in stained water. For what reason, who knows? But the fish seem to key in on the added orange stripe.

A similar effect created by Boydston works with baits used in clear water. Here he takes a popular crankbait in a Tennessee shad finish and scrapes off a small white patch on the top of the black head of the plug. Again, the fish seem to really get excited in seeing the white spot. Perhaps this makes the lure appear as the weakest member of a shad school, a crippled or wounded bait, and something that appears easiest for the bass to catch. Whatever the reason, this little coloration trick really works.

A similar trick I ran across involves enlarging the "dot" near the gill area on silver foil Rapala Fat Raps. I have seen times when two guys were working these popular plugs side-by-side and the only one getting bit had customized his lure. This is done by taking a black marker pen and making the black gill dot twice as large. This trick, like all the coloring tricks, simply gives the bass something different to look at in contrast to all the stock factory lures they see. I'm sure some of you fishermen have your own ideas that you might now want to try in custom coloring crankbaits.

On many of California's lakes that are very clear, there are a few other useful crankin' tips worth passing along. Many of these lakes such as Shasta, Trinity, Almanor or Castaic also have a rainbow trout population. Always keep at least one crankbait in a rainbow trout finish in your tackle box when venturing out on this type of water. Solid chrome, blue and chrome, or blue and clear finish plugs are also very productive on clear water lakes. In addition, keep a bone-colored crankbait handy for clear water bassin'. Occasionally, this very boring color will work when all others have failed to produce.

Finally, most Western pros feel that it is important to change hooks on many factory stock crankbaits. They remove small bronze and all silver wire hooks and replace them with larger bronze treble hooks, hand honed to needle point sharpness. Some pros are very adamant that the silver wire hooks add a flash or an unnatural look to the crankbait resulting in the bass passing up the offering. Buy replacement bronze treble hooks and change over to these before using a new crankbait.

As for retrieving these lures, most recreational bass fishermen make the mistake of being too conservative or unimaginative. They cast the plug out and crank it in, often throwing it only to "safe" water where it can't get hung up. For a pro to fish a crankbait successfully, he knows he will have to throw it to where the bass live. You have to cast to weeds, brush, boulders, tules, and deadfall, and plan on losing some lures. It is inevitable that you will loose lures that get hung up on this structure but that is where many bass are to be found.

One very successful technique is to cast in and around stickups, start your retrieve, but when the lure strikes the brush, keep reeling. Novice crankbait fishermen have a tendency to immediately stop the retrieve when they feel the lure hit the trees or brush. Instead, reel hard to force the diving lip to plow through the cover. Invariably, a bass will strike the crankbait as it passes through and deflects off of the tree limbs, stickups and similar brushy structure.

Another retrieve commonly used throughout the U.S. is the "stop'n go". With this technique, the lure is allowed to rest for a brief second or two intermittently through the retrieve. Typically, the strike often occurs as the bait is stopped, suspended for a moment, simulating a wounded baitfish or erratically moving crawdad. Pay close attention when using this crankin' technique. The angler is often caught off guard when the bass decides to strike the lure as it is stopped.

Often the pro basser wants his crankbait to run as deep as possible. There are a couple of little tricks outside of selecting a deep-diving plug that will get the lure to dive deeper. First, there is the retrieving technique known as "kneel'n reel". Here the angler casts out and then kneels down in the boat with his rod actually extended down into the water. By "kneelin'n reelin'", he is able to keep the lure in a deeper strike zone, while minimizing the chance that the plug will plane to the surface. With other crankbaits, it is equally effective to cast the lure, crank very quickly for a few seconds, then back the retrieve speed off dramatically. This gets the lure down deep quickly, then it can be retrieved at a more moderate pace.

Many bass pros feel that heavier, 12 to 17 lb. test monofilament is imperative for tournament crankbait fishing as it allows for easier retrieval through thick cover. They reason that the heavy line prevents lost lures, which translates into saving time by not having to retie baits in a hectic tournament situation.

Chuck Boydston is a real maverick on this issue, but more and more pros are taking his advice to heart. Boydston has had tremendous success throwing medium-sized crankbaits. But he does this with light line and spinning tackle when others are being blanked "chuckin' and windin'" with 15 to 17 lb. test. By light, we're talking 6 lb. test! On lures such as the Rebel Double Deep Wee R, Rapala #5 Fat Rap and Shad Rap, Boydston relates that the lighter line gives him the best "feel" for the plug as it kicks off from brush and rocks. The strike is telegraphed better with the lighter line and the crankbait's action is significantly enhanced. The lighter line also allows the lure to swim deeper with minimal line resistance. Overall, not that many of these medium-sized crankbaits are lost with this technique.

"Crankin'" can also save the day in rough wind conditions or when your local lake is being subjected to heavy boat and water skiing traffic. Often the weekend bass fisherman in California gets frustrated and angry when the water skiing activity creates a lot of turbulence at his favorite lake. The water becomes choppy from the constant ski boat wakes, with a lot of wave action against the shore. It becomes tough to hold the boat steady and to use slower techniques like wormin' under such conditions.

A crankbait can be deadly under such pressure. The bass populations on these heavily used lakes become very acclimated to water skiers and pleasure boat congestion. As a matter of fact, at popular water skiing lakes such as Lake Castaic knowledgeable anglers will use the waterskiing zone of the lake to their advantage. Quite often the water skiers churn up the bait and the wave action pushes the bait into the bank. The bass will follow the bait into the shallower, cloudy water stirred up by the skiers. A crankbait fished along these shorelines and off the points can be super productive under these conditions. The bait is concentrated near the bank, and the bass feed more aggressively in the cloudy water. When other anglers move off from this kind of activity, tie on a crankbait and use this water to your advantage.

Summary

Although crankbaits are not the most complicated bass lures to master, as you can see, there is more involved than simply throwing out the plug and retrieving it. Successful California pros are very meticulous in selecting the precise crankbait to use, the right size, the proper color and the correct retrieve. Furthermore, they rely upon certain little "tricks" that allow them to customize these lures, making them more unique and fish-appealing than the common factory stock baits everyone else is throwing.

Crankbaits are perhaps your best way to locate bass on California lakes. You can find fish faster with a crankbait than any other lure. Spinnerbaits, as I'll discuss later, are also good for finding fish, but are best suited for lakes with brush. On many California lakes, there is little visual brush and a lot of rocks and submerged structure. You can get a crankbait to dive deep quickly and generate reaction strikes as it kicks off from the structure. Crankbaits can be kept in the strike zone with relative ease compared to other bass lures. But don't overcrank, keep your speed moderate, and try to be a little creative in the retrieve and in your selection of colors.

Top Water Tricks: Twitchin', Buzzin', Walkin' the Dog, etc.

Top-water fishing is, without question, the most spectacular bassin' the angler can experience in the Golden State. There is nothing more heart-throbbing then to see, and hear, a big bass coming up and crunching a top-water bait. The main difference between California top-water fishing and that found in the South and Mid-west is the noticeable lack of lily pads on our waters. Very few of our lakes have this type of aquatic vegetation. Many of our top-water presentations are made to rocky shorelines, tule banks, shallow flats, mossbeds and even deeper water.

In this chapter we'll examine some of the special top-water techniques used in California that have become particularly productive over the years. But first, let's talk to some of the local pros and find out when to use these baits and which ones to pick.

Top-Water Time and Baits to Choose

Dave Mitchell and Gary Robson are two veteran pros that have earned the respect of fellow tournament fishermen by being exceptionally proficient with top-water lures in Western bass competition. Both agree that the best time to fish top-water in California's tough lakes is after the bass have spawned in the Spring all the way into late Fall. They will fish top-water until the surface temperature drops into the low 60's. It is often written that top-water fishing is best early and late in the day. In contrast, Mitchell and Robson will throw these baits all day if the conditions are right.

Top-water lures can be categorized as floating minnows, chuggers and poppers, stick baits, prop baits, buzz baits and plastic frogs. As far as lure selection goes, these pros cite wind conditions as the single key variable. In calm water, a subtle top-water lure is recommended. This could be a light, floating minnow such as the Rapala, a little larger chugger-style bait such as the Storm Chug Bug, or a large stick bait like the Heddon Zara Spook. If it's big fish you're looking for, the Zara Spook is the best choice. On this note, the pros agree that top-water bass tend to be larger than those caught with plastic worms, cranks or spinnerbaits. Subscribing to the adage "big bait = big fish", they go for the Zara Spook when they are looking for larger fish.

Bill Norman Rip-N Minnow

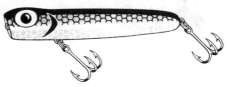

Storm Chug Bug

Heddon Tiny Torpedo

Heddon Zara Spook

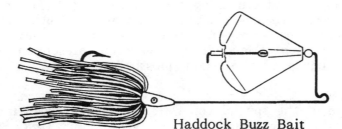

Haddock Buzz Bait   Arbogast Hula Popper

Prop baits can also be used in calm water. These lures are best fished in little pockets formed by shoreline brush, moss beds, and rock formations. The pro bassers use a prop bait to draw fish up and out of these quiet, little pockets.

When the weather gets very hot with a warm surface temperature or when the wind comes up, many pros choose a buzz bait. This top-water bait can be fished the fastest of all the surface lures and can cover a lot of water. It can be pulled through heavy cover, brush, and over summer moss beds without hanging up. Buzz baits work especially well when the bass are feeding aggressively and are sometimes thrown all day from early dawn to sunset.

Robson also notes that the location of the bass on a given lake is critical to selecting the correct top-water lure to use. During the summer months, the bass will often suspend over submerged tree tops. Here, Robson throws a slower moving, but noisy bait such as a popper, a large stick bait, or chugger. The noisier, gurgling lure will draw fish out of the submerged tree tops up to the surface to investigate the commotion. Surprisingly, he will also use this type of top-water bait in water 35 to 45 feet deep if he feels the fish are holding in deep rocks and brush.

When the fish are near the bank with schools of bass fry nearby, Western pros prefer a very quiet, subtle bait such as a floating Rapala. This type of lure is also a favorite for fishing shallow 10 to 15 foot flats where small underwater rockpiles and brush are known to be.

What Color Top-Water Lure?

As for color in top-water lure selection, both Mitchell and Robson are quick to suggest that the lure should be matched with the forage bait. For example, when there are schools of shad in the area, silver foil, glitter shad, smoke and clear top-water lures would be a sound bet. If the bass are feeding on small frogs or bluegill, a frog pattern plug with a yellow belly will work. If the fish have spawned and bass fry are plentiful, a good choice would be a top-water plug in "baby bass" finish. Both pros recommend solid chrome top-water lures for hot summer days on California lakes.

These pros also volunteer some rather exotic coloring tips that have often given them a unique edge under tournament conditions. Sometimes Robson will scrape off all the color on a particular surface lure until it is pure bone. Like the crankbait tip we talked about in Chapter 3, for some strange reason the bass will often go crazy for this bland bait when all others fail. On the other hand, another trick is to take a clear Zara Spook and match it to a dominant Color-C-Lector color. The pros will take fluorescent paint and put a solid stripe down the center top of the lure. They do this instead of using a solid colored fluorescent Spook that is sold commercially. The single stripe against the clear background makes for an unusual subtle bait. A locally favorite combination is clear with a fluorescent blue stripe.

Buzz Baits

Buzz baits present another issue as far as color and style are concerned. "Buzzers" as they are also termed, do not float and must be retrieved a little faster and steadier to be kept on the surface. The bass therefore do not have time to carefully "study" the bait as they do with a more traditional floating surface plug. The strikes tend to be vicious reactions to the noise and splash produced by these lures.

The most popular buzz bait colors used in California are white or chartreuse. Many pros prefer white in clearer water or on bright days, chartreuse in dirty water or with overcast skies. Bob Suekawa has been making lures for the Western market for many years and is considered a resident authority on buzz bait fishing. Although he sells a tremendous variety of colors in his Haddock lure line, he feels that buzz bait color is more a matter of what the angler feels most confident with. As he says, "the bass don't hit the buzz bait color, they strike at the commotion it creates."

Suekawa passes along some key pointers that should help both novice and pro in selecting these unique top-water baits for California bassin'! First, he recommends a fairly large buzzbait (3/8 to 1/2 ounce) for most conditions. Buzzers, by their very design, are bulky and have a lot of wind resistance. The larger lure will cast more easily but it will also have more torque. This means more commotion, which is what this reaction bait is supposed to create. He likes to throw a buzz bait around very heavy cover where other floating surface plugs would be difficult to fish. The bigger "buzzer" plows through the thick brush and stickups more easily than the lighter buzz baits.

Smaller buzzers (say 1/8 to 1/4 ounce) are a good choice for using in the backs of quiet coves where a more subtle presentation is required. Keep in mind however, that these smaller buzzers have a tendency to pop out of the water with faster retrieves due to the minimal torque they generate. Still, if the fisherman is a light line enthusiast, or prefers to use spinning tackle, these smaller buzz baits will be an appropriate choice.

As far as blade type goes, Suekawa recommends a simple large, single-blade, buzz bait. This blade produces a lot of splash, fouls very infrequently, and can be found in chrome, bronze, clear or painted surfaces. In contrast, the double-bladed buzzer has two separate smaller blades spinning in counter directions to each other. This is a more subtle bait and can be used when less commotion is desired. Another option would be a large tri-bladed buzzer made by Bill Norman, called the Triple Wing. This surface lure produces perhaps the most gurgle and splash of all. The Triple Wing looks like a small outboard going across the water (Roostertail and all) and can really call in the bass when a lot of noise is needed.

A lot of Western pros prefer to use a buzz bait without a trailer, feeling that the bass have a tendency to strike "short" often hitting just the trailer portion and missing the hook. Others feel a pork rind or plastic worm trailer is a must. They theorize that it adds just another element of attraction to the lure. Again, like buzz bait color, this is probably a matter of personal preference. I have seen buzzers with and without trailers work equally well on a given day fished side by side.

Twitchin', Jerkin' and Rippin''

Let's focus now on some of the specific top-water techniques used by the Western pros on California waters.

"Twitchin'" has become one of the most universal top-water techniques used in the West. The basic gear for serious "twitchin'" involves a medium action, 6 foot spinning rod, spinning reel with 6 to 12 lb. line, and some type of floating minnow-shaped bait. The most popularly used lure is the Rapala floating minnow in sizes #11 and #13. The silver foil finish black back is the favorite color, although gold with black back, and silver with blue back also will work at times. Other popular choices would include the Bagley Bang-O-Lure and the Rebel floating minnow.

"Twitchin'" works particularly well in the early morning in still water. These light weight lures can be cast fairly long distances with a spinning outfit, and then gently "parachuted" down, making a very soft landing in the calm water. This part of the "twitchin'" technique is very important in order to keep the bass from spooking off. Veteran twitch fishermen kind of "feather" the line in their free hand to make certain the lure hits the water with minimal disturbance. The minnow bait is then allowed to rest for a few seconds until the ripples clear. This is often when a surprise strike occurs catching the angler off guard. Be ready as soon as that bait lands on the water!

The actual "twitchin'" involves making the minnow bait "dance" from side-to-side while staying on the surface. By either rhythmically or erratically twitching the rod tip, the bait is made to dance, resembling a shad dying on the surface. Sometimes the bass prefer some splash with a constant twitching action. Other times they prefer an intermittent "twitch-pause-twitch" retrieve, often attacking the lure as it is floating at rest between twitches. With "twitchin'", the plug stays on the surface with varying amounts of splash and noise added.

Pro Gary Robson especially likes this "twitchin'" technique when there are schools of young bass fry tight to the bank. After the bass have spawned in an area Robson will look for these schools of fry. He'll then throw a floating Rapala near the fry, let it rest, then the key is to give it a single twitch. The adult bass do not want any creature to intrude near the fry, and the single twitch often aggravates them into an explosive strike.

"Jerkin'" is not exactly a top-water presentation in the strict sense. I've placed it in this section because it is often modified to include certain elements of top-water techniques I'll mention in a moment. California pros use a floating-diving lure dragged below the surface in quick, short jerks with this method. Both spinning and bait-casting outfits will work with "jerkin'".

The Bomber Long "A's" are especially popular with this technique, in 3 1/2 and 4 1/2 inch lengths. The Bomber is stroked back often with a brief pause to allow the bait to float up a little. This is similar to the stop-n-go retrieve used with a crankbait. As with "twitchin'", be prepared for a strike to occur after the bait is stopped and the "jerkin'" retrieve is resumed.

Some of the local pros fishing known big-fish lakes such as Vail, Isabella, and Silverwood go "hawg hunting" in the Spring using this "jerkin'" method. The secret here is to use a BIG bait. The popular choice is a Bomber #16 Long "A". This is a large, 6 inch, shallow-running, minnow-like bait designed primarily for salt water. The local pros use this plug with 15 to 20 lb. test line, a medium-action 7 1/2 foot saltwater spinning rod, and an intermediate size saltwater spinning reel. You need to use this heavy rig to jerk this lure properly. The larger, saltwater spinning reel with the greater spool diameter, picks up line faster than freshwater baitcasters. This type of "jerkin'" is a lot of tiring work, but the results can be astonishing when trophy-size largemouths are around.

"Rippin'" is basically an exaggerated version of "jerkin'". Here, it is important to use long sweeping "rips" or jerks with the rod tip often dragging the bait down three of four feet below the surface. The Bill Norman Rip-N-Minnow plug is an excellent bait for this method along with the larger #13 Rapalas, and Bomber Long "A"s. I cannot emphasize enough how important it is to be prepared for the strike as the "rips" are stopped. As the minnow-like plug is allowed to slowly start to float up for a brief second or two, the bass who have been following the lure practically bump into it during this pause period.

Another method that I have found to be very successful was pioneered down south on those San Diego lakes where the touchy Florida-strain bass prowl. This technique is actually a "twitch-jerk" combination. The lure to use is either a #11-S or #13-S Rapala floating minnow. Following the cast, the bait is twitched with short, little strokes and is kept submerged most of the time. You should stop twitching intermittently, but the trick here is to never let the lure totally resurface. As the twitching action is paused, watch for when the lure floats up to about 1 to 2 inches below the surface. Then quickly start another series of twitches, dragging the lure down again.

Many times the bass can actually be seen as it rolls or "flashes" on the minnow-like lure. It is so tempting to quickly rear back and set at that moment. Invariably, I have found that you will lose the fish if you do. The key to this technique -- and I might add all top-water fishing -- is to wait until you feel the pressure of the fish to set the hook. This requires some patience, but a lot of times, the bass will make a pass at the surface bait without ever hitting it. To set the hook, simply on the visual assumption that the bass is "on", often results in pulling the bait away from the fish. Thus, set by "feel" rather than sight -- the fish might come back for a second look and a solid strike.

Prop Baits

Propeller-equipped surface plugs are one of the easiest baits to fish, but some patience is required. This is particularly true immediately following the cast. Too often I've seen the fisherman throw his prop bait out and then immediately start his retrieve. I'm a "traditionalist" with these old-time top-water lures. I prefer to let the lure sit still until the concentric ripples clear from where it landed. Then I'll give the bait a short little "pop", just enough to get the propellers moving. I let the bait rest for a moment, followed by a slightly longer and louder pop. I'll repeat this retrieve until I feel the plug has moved out of the strike zone, then I reel it straight in.

Dave Mitchell fishes this bait in a similar fashion, but perhaps a little faster under tournament conditions. Mitchell throws out, lets the prop bait sit for a moment, gives it three or four good pulls, then reels it straight back to the boat. Occasionally, a vicious strike will occur as the bait is speedily retrieved. It is as if the bass senses that the baitfish floundering on the surface has got its second wind and is now high-tailing it out to deep water. Not wanting to miss an easy meal, the bass gets excited and moves quickly to make the kill before the bait gets away.

Mitchell will fish the prop baits even faster in windy weather, when the fish seem more active. On calm days, he recommends a single propeller. He feels a double prop works better in the wind when the fish will have a tendency to move further and more aggressively toward the noisy lure.

A lot of bass caught on prop baits are actually foul-hooked. Many of these plugs have double and triple treble hook configurations. With the plug tumbling from side-to-side, combined with the bass often rolling on the plug, foul-hooked fish are inevitable. To maximize your chances of landing these fish, make sure that treble hooks are sharpened before you start casting these baits.

Popular prop baits used on California lakes include the Smithwick Devil's Horse, the Ozark Mountain Woodchopper, Creek Chub Injured Minnow, and the Boy Howdie. The best colors are in shad, chrome, and perch finishes. Occasionally, when the bass want a slightly smaller top-water plug, the Heddon Tiny Torpedo is a local favorite.

Poppin', Chuggin' and Walkin' The Dog

Poppers and chuggers are some of the most exciting lures to use. Most poppers are characterized by a large, scooped out nose that cups the water. This type of lure makes a distinct "pop" when it is given a quick jerk. Some pros cast a popper, let it sit and then give it one single jerk. The old standby, the Fred Arbogast Hula Popper, still produces with this technique and is a local favorite at lakes like Pardee, Berryessa and Folsom. Other pros prefer to cast the popper and then quickly give it a series of short, quick twitches -- a "pop-pop-

pop-pop" effect -- letting it rest every third or fourth "pop". A long-time little-known favorite of the Western pros has been the Rebel Pop-R plug for this technique. This top-water lure was out of production for some time. Occasionally an old pro would find one gathering dust in some out-of-the-way little tackle shop. Rebel is now making the Pop-R again due to its secret popularity in Western pro circles. Other poppers that work for California bass are the Creek Chub Plunker, Burke's Pop Top, and the Heddon Lucky 13.

Chuggers do not have as prominent a scoop nose as poppers. Lures such as the Storm Chug Bug, Bagley's Chug-O-Lure, the Heddon Chugger Spook and the Heddon Baby Lucky 13 are popular choices. A chugger can be worked similar to a popper without as much noise. The chugger can also be made to swim from side-to-side like a stick bait, a technique termed "walkin' the dog". We'll go over this shortly. First, let me mention that not enough serious bassers in California fish the chugger-style baits. Because they combine the elements of both a noisy popper and the swimming action of a large stickbait, they often produce when neither of the other two plugs are working. Chuggers are exceptionally versatile top-water baits and are a good bet when a modestly noisy, subtle swimming bait is needed. Now let's talk about how to "walk the dog".

This technique is used primarily with the grandaddy of all top-water baits, the cigar-like Zara Spook. Floating stickbaits like this have no propeller and no scooped nose to generate noise. It is up to the angler to orchestrate the movements of this popular bait to create the tantalizing retrieve known as "walkin' the dog". After the cast is made with this large 3/4 to 1 oz. plug, it is allowed to rest for a second or two. The rod tip should then be kept low to the water, and with quick wrist action, give the bait a series of short, little twitches. The Spook will then rhythmically weave a path, moving from side-to-side in a zigzag pattern. This effect resembles a small baitfish floundering on the surface. Sometimes, short sharp jerks are used to produce more sound and splash. I've watched California pros like Mitchell and Robson work the Spook, "walkin' the dog", and it is really exciting to see a bass come up for this enticing presentation.

Both of these pros offer some very key pointers to fishing this large tricky bait. First, try to keep the line on top of the water. This creates less line drag than if the line is underwater and it allows for the bait to swim better where the knot is tied. On this note, the pros emphatically recommend adding a split ring to the lure. Tying the line to the split ring allows the Spook to dance more freely from side-to-side. Also, by keeping the line near the surface, greater tension is maintained for a quick hook set.

Quite often the California basser will have a fish blow up on a Zara Spook without eating the bait. Frustration sets in when you see a good bass miss this big bait. But the California pros have a few tricks that might salvage the strike. Robson uses this bait often in professional tournaments to find quality bigger fish. When a fish hits and misses his Spook, he will immediately stop the retrieve, let the plug rest for a second, then twitch it just once.

Often a dramatic strike will occur following that brief pause-twitch. This requires nerve racking patience, since the first inclination following a missed strike is to quickly reel up and fire off another cast.

If this little trick doesn't work, try one other. A lot of Western pros always keep a backup rod rigged with a plastic worm or a Fat Gitzit jig when fishing the Spook. If the bass misses the Spook, they will cast the soft baits right back to where the fish boiled. Quite often the fish will aggressively strike these quiet, more subtle baits after making an initial pass at the Spook. A few local pros are now actually attaching a trailer leader behind the Zara Spook with a Fat Gitzit tied on. This rig is cumbersome to cast, but will sometimes work.

Buzzin'

As I mentioned, buzzbaits are a very different kind of surface lure in that they do not float. It is entirely up to the angler to provide a fast enough retrieve to keep this lure churning on top. There are a couple of things that the serious bass fisherman can do to maximize his success with this unique lure.

To start with, the key to keeping the buzzer on the surface is to begin your retrieve immediately once the lure hits the surface. A lot of times bass feeding on top-water baits will instantly attack the lure as it lands on the water. If you wait a second or two after the buzzbait lands, a lot of those aggressive reaction strikes will be missed. Once these baits sink, it takes some time before they can be retrieved on top again. By the time they are pulled up, the lure is often out of the strike zone.

Next, be aggressive when "buzzin'"! Although these lures look very awkward and are not the most aerodynamic baits around, they are remarkably weedless. I have watched veteran California pros fish these baits in super thick stick-ups. They will cast into the heaviest concentration and then steadily retrieve the buzzbait allowing it to deflect from stickup to stickup. The wire frame of the bait serves as an excellent weed guard and the buzzer can work just like a "bumper car" as it moves in and about the cover. Many strikes occur in the thickest cover as the lure deflects from branch to branch.

Look for moss beds when using a buzzbait on California lakes. This lure is absolutely a killer when cast over the thick moss. At Lake San Antonio in Central California for example, the summer mossbeds are thick and very slimy. It is virtually impossible to fish these with any other surface lure. But the bass hide under the moss for shade and greater oxygen levels. A buzzer passed over this slimy vegetation will not get hung up. This lure will really bring the fish crashing through small pockets in the moss beds to attack the noisy intruder.

Two other little tricks are worth mentioning to help improve your buzzbait fishing. Dave Mitchell is an absolute maestro with this bait and depends on it for fishing the summer moss beds on desert lakes such as Havasu. If he misses a strike with the buzzbait, he immediately throws a Zara Spook to the same opening in the moss. This requires pin-point accuracy. But again, the fish are often aggrevated when first a buzzbait, and then a big ole' cigar plug invades their mossy sanctuary.

An interesting situation that I stumbled across occurred while fishing buzzbaits at Lake Skinner a few years ago. We had been scratching an occasional bass on the buzzers along tule banks throughout the late afternoon, but we had also missed a lot of strikes. We switched from trailers to no-trailers, we followed by throwing a plastic worm, but still no dramatic improvement. There is a good shad population in this lake and I happened to have a small #7-S floating Rapala tied on another rod. The shad were particularly small that summer and I was hoping to do a little "twitchin'" that evening with the scaled down Rapala. Following my umpteenth missed buzzbait strike, I cast the small Rapala to the same location. I got bit instantly and a keeper fish headed for the "Live Well Motel".

The rest of the afternoon was history as fish after fish succumbed to the presentation. It was as if the buzzbait drew them out of the tules just enough to get them interested. The follow-up cast with the Rapala was just too much for the bass to refuse. I might add that in the late afternoon I experimented with the Rapala by itself but with no results. I have used this "buzzin'-twitchin'" combination on other lakes, often with remarkable success.

Suekawa passes along one final tip: don't bother tuning a buzzbait trying to make it run straight. It's too difficult with all the torque. Often a buzzbait will have a tendency to run to one side or the other. Suekawa will keep this in mind when he must retrieve one of these surface lures to the right or left of some type of structure. He then uses the unbalanced lure to his advantage to cast to some hard-to-get spots.

Plastic Frogs

There is one final, rather esoteric bait that is worth talking about for top-water fishing in California. The Bill Plummer Super Frog is about as close as you can come to throwing the real thing. This is a soft plastic bait, molded and colored to look like a small frog. They are sold in a variety of colors and are a real secret bait for small California farm pond fishing. The Super Frog has a single weedless hook that allows the fisherman to put this lure in the thickest cover. I have used it on some small ponds with super thick moss beds. It can be cast with spinning tackle and thrown in the small pocket formed by moss, brush and other shoreline weeds.

Like the Hula Popper with its sensuous, slow-moving, rubber skirt, the Super Frog has two long legs that just dangle below the surface. So often the strike occurs with the Frog just sitting at rest with those legs dangling underneath. Fish this surface bait slowly, giving it an occasional jerk to extend the legs and create a little "pop". Let it rest, and be prepared for the strike when you least expect it.

The Super Frog has been producing catches at alpine elevation bass lakes such as Lake Hemet in Riverside County where there is a large frog population. For a change of pace, try this unique top-water lure on your favorite lake during the warm summer months when the bullfrogs let their presence be known.

Summary

If you want to improve your recreational bass fishing results, or compete in serious-level bass fishing in California, it is essential that you become an accomplished top-water fisherman. Time after time, the Western pro relies upon these techniques to catch the one or two larger fish -- the "kickers" -- to round out his five fish limit during the warmer months. Top-water fishing consistently produces quality fish.

Keep your eye on prevailing wind conditions and select a top-water lure to match. Minnow-like baits are excellent in calmer water, buzzbaits are similarly good in the wind. Poppers, chuggers, stickbaits, and propbaits can work in all conditions, but try to be selective in matching the lure to the forage fish in the lake. Above all, don't fall into the trap of using a top-water lure strictly in the early morning and twilight hours. During the warm summer months, these lures can often work throughout the day.

The most common error of all when working a top-water bait is to set too quickly. Avoid over-reacting to the visual strike, go more by feel. This requires discipline and patience, but the results are worth the effort. Another mistake is using too light a line. Many big fish are broken off by bassers using 6 to 10 lb. test line with their larger surface lures. Remember, many of the top-water bass you'll be catching will be bigger fish, 2 to 3 lbs. and up and will be in heavy cover. A heavier 12 to 17 lb. test line will allow you to move the fish from the cover and you'll get a better hook set with less line stretch. Surface fishing for bass involves a lot of aggressive reaction strikes so that heavy lines will not usually spook the fish.

Finally, watch your bait and use a fairly stiff rod. So often big bass will strike a top-water lure more by "sucking" it under the surface than by crashing on it. Watch for the flash and then the feel of the fish and get a good solid hook set with a strong, quality rod.

Spoonin': The Pro's Deep Water Tactics

"Spoonin'" is perhaps the singlemost underrated, seldom used technique in the California bassin' scene. A lot has been written on spoon fishing but most of it has been relegated to an explanation of Winter deepwater techniques. More and more serious California bass fishermen are using spoons to catch sluggish winter fish. But by the time March rolls around, the spoons are put back in the tackle boxes and usually stay there until the following November.

Dave Nollar is a well-known pro in California tournament circles. As a fishing tackle sales representative, a professional guide and accomplished taxidermist, he comes into contact with many local bass fishermen and has charted which lures have been working on the California lakes for many years. Nollar is considered to be a virtuoso spoon fisherman of sorts. When asked what the most common error novice bassers make when spoonin', he replied: "Not doing it enough. Too many guys simply lack the confidence in this method." California bassers tend to be no different from those across the United States when it comes to spoon fishing. They are simply too oriented to shallow water. They often believe that once winter rolls around, the fish that have moved off the bank have now become dormant in deepwater retreats. This is not the case.

Actually, as the baitfish move out to the greater depths, the bass follow. The shad will begin to have some die-off in the Winter with the bass waiting for the crippled bait to flutter down. The fish will continue to feed during this time of the year, perhaps at a slower pace.

There is a real simplicity to Wintertime spoon fishing that, when mastered, can be employed throughout the year. But, to become proficient with this method, a boat equipped with proper electronic gear is a must.

Where to Find Spoon Fish

Spoon fishing is easiest in the Winter, so let's start here in determining how to find these California bass. Using an LCR (liquid crystal recorder) or a chart recorder (graph), finding underwater structure and schools of shad are the key. Turn up the sensitivity control somewhat and begin by monitoring for sharper ledges. In the Winter the shad will often be layered in 25 to 60 foot depths on California lakes. They will often cluster where a ledge begins to drop off or "break". The bass will have a tendency to move up or down along these breaks to feed on the schools of bait.

Once the shad are found, it is then best to work off the bow of the boat with either an electronic flasher unit or an LCR. With these electronics, you can actually see more active bass pass in and out of the screen, usually feeding under the bait. Nollar notes that most often fish seen on top of the shad schools are trout that are commonly stocked in many of these popular bass lakes. He will usually waste little time when he only receives this type of reading, perhaps dropping his spoon one or two times and then moving on.

Nollar also comments that, particularly in the Winter, the bass in these lakes will be either mixed in with the schools of shad or right on the bottom. In either case, it is sometimes very difficult to distinguish bass on the graph, flasher or LCR. But when schools of bait are found in the winter clustered around good structure, the Western pros will still spoon the area because there is a good chance that bass are down below.

Types of Spoons

When the beginning angler first hears about spoonin' for bass, he often confuses these specialized lures with those used for trout or other gamefish. In contrast to trout spoons, the bassin' variety typically do not have the wide, concave surface that gives the wobble to such traditional trout favorites as the Daredevil, Wobble Rite and Hot Shot lures. Bass spoons as a rule are much narrower in width, much heavier in weight, and much less spectacular in action. The wobble effect is not that critical in the design of a bassin' spoon since few of these lures are retrieved near the surface as is done with the trout lures. Most spoonin' for bass is done with some variation of a vertical jigging retrieve -- although there are a few exceptions, that I will mention. Thus, it is imperative that the lure sinks fairly quickly and makes good, solid contact with the bottom. Hence, the need for the heavier spoon is obvious for this kind of bass fishing.

Nollar recommends trying to match the spoon with the size of the shad in the baitfish schools. As a general rule, he selects a 1/8 to 3/8 ounce spoon for smaller shad and a 1/2 to 1-1/8 ounce model when the larger baitfish are present. He also prefers to use as large a spoon as possible without overwhelmingly dwarfing the baitfish. The larger the spoon, the better control and feel for the bottom you will have when working for these deepwater bass. Quite often, small 12 inch "keeper" fish will strike the larger spoons without any problem. Other times, larger fish will only hit the smaller 1/8 ounce spoons. This is particularly true in shallower water, at the 20 to 30 foot depth.

The most popular spoon used for California bassin' is without a doubt the Hopkins #075. This spoon features a hammered solid chrome finish and weighs 3/4 ounce. For smaller spoons, the Hopkins 1/8 and 1/4 ounce, and the Cordell "C.C." are good choices in a hammered finish. All of these spoons also come in a hammered gold finish. The chrome is most popular but there are many times when I have seen the gold produce outstanding results even when the chrome wasn't working.

If you want to use a spoon that has more of a fluttering effect on the fall, the smooth, flat-sided Kastmaster would be a good choice in either gold or silver. The Kastmaster spoon is available in 1/8 through 3/4 ounce sizes. If you want a little more flash and color, Nollar suggests adding reflective prism tape to these spoons. Better yet, the Haddock Jig'N Spoon and Structure Spoon are available in a wide selection of prism tape finishes. The 3/8 ounce Jig'N Spoon has a thin tapered design and is good for vertical spoonin' with minimal flutter.

In contrast, the 5/8 ounce Structure Spoon is a fat, wider bodied lure made to flutter down slowly with long sweeping rod pulls. These spoons are available in smoke, shad, baby bass and a variety of other finishes. A "hot" secret for lakes that have Florida bass has been to use either a blue or chartreuse pattern in this spoon. For ultra-deep spoonin', the thin Jig'N Spoon is also made in a 1-1/8 ounce model. At Lake Castaic for example, this heavier spoon works very well when the shad are found all the way down to 75 feet.

Ways to Spoon

The most popular way to fish a spoon on these waters is with a vertical jigging approach. After you have pinpointed the baitfish, watch your electronics and get right on top of the school. Drop the spoon straight down. Once the spoon hits the bottom, raise the rod in a short pop. Then, lower the rod tip just fast enough to maintain contact with the lure. You want to minimize the slack line effect on the fall since this is where most of the strikes occur. Excessive slack makes a strong hook set difficult. Work the rod at about nine o'clock which allows you to make small "pops" on the lift, while maintaining good contact with the spoon as it falls.

Hopkins NO-EQL

Hopkins #075 Shorty

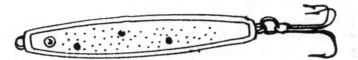

Haddock Jig 'N Spoon

Johnson Silver Minnow

Schurmy Shad

Haddock Structure Spoon

Kastmaster

Sometimes, the bass are fairly active and prefer to hit the spoon on an extra long fall. This requires a long lifting effect of the rod which allows a greater amount of line to drop. Nollar is especially effective with this long sweeping technique on these aggressively feeding fish. But he points out the the trick is to use a longer than average rod. He prefers a 6 1/2 to 7 1/2 foot stiff action baitcasting rod. This allows him to pick up slack line quicker, with the backbone providing a strong hook set. This is especially necessary with bass that are snagged which happens frequently with vertical spoonin'.

Nollar also emphasizes that whenever he fishes deep on these California lakes, he wants to minimize the "spongy" feeling that often occurs with deepwater strikes. This stiffer, longer rod also helps to transmit the strike better in the 30 to 60 foot depths.

Other Western pros modify this technique somewhat and use a unique flip-floppin' presentation. They firmly believe in maintaining contact with the bottom. For this reason, they will often stay with a 3/4 ounce Hopkins spoon when others opt for a smaller lure. They will let the spoon sink to the bottom then use short, little rhythmic pulls and falls to make the spoon sort of do a flip-flop dance on the bottom. This technique is particularly effective on slow-moving, lethargic bass that are nesting right on the bottom.

An alternative to the vertical jigging approach would be to fish the spoon similar to the way you swim a jig, hoppin' it down or across underwater points and ridges. Select a heavy spoon, cast it out along a point or ridge, and retrieve the spoon back, hoppin' it downhill. As with jig fishing, the strike will often occur on the fall. Be particularly observant and if you see the spoon suddenly stop falling after you cast before it hits the bottom, swing and set. Other times, you will feel the bass "on" the spoon as you lift or pull the rod, picking up the slack. Again, wind the line tight and set.

Bass invariably relate to these points and ridges almost all year long on most of the California lakes. Few serious bassers use this hoppin' technique except for Winter spoon fishing. This is a real oversight since this method can be effective throughout the year on this kind of structure.

Other Spoonin' Tricks

On many California lakes from late Spring through early Fall, large concentrations of bass will push schools of shad to the surface in a spectacular feeding frenzy. I have witnessed this phenomenon on lakes such as Sutherland and Hodges is San Diego County where the water surface looks like an eruption of tuna boils. For years, local fishermen have tried to figure out ways to get these surface feeding bass to strike an artificial lure. Rippin', jerkin', twitchin' and crankin' all work to some extent at times. But so often the bass stubbornly pass up these offerings, feeding only on the natural shad. This is one of the most frustrating sights you will ever see on these lakes, as the water is being churned all around with no biters.

In recent years, Western pros have relied more upon spoons to entice these surface-feeding bass. One very critical thing to keep in mind here is that if you are in a boat, stay as far away as possible from these feeding fish. Too often, the neophyte in his new bass boat runs on these boils and crashes into the school. This puts the fish "down" in a hurry. The trick is to make long casts on the outside perimeter of the schools of shad. Try to cast somewhat beyond any of the boils you see, and retrieve the spoon steadily across the surface.

The lighter metal spoons such as the Haddock Structure Spoon and the Kastmaster are very suitable for this technique, especially since they can be cast a long way with minimal wind resistance. These smaller spoons also obviously sink less than their heavier counterparts and can thus be kept nearer to the surface. A special, ultra-light aluminum spoon, the Schurmy Shad, is a California innovation designed especially for this unique condition. This spoon casts tremendously well with light line, and "shimmys" across the surface with limited sinking effect. The Schurmy Shad is made in a wide range of reflective colors and fishes best when retrieved directly across the water. On San Diego lakes in particular, this lure can often save the day when the Florida bass are constantly busting shad on the surface.

Gently pitchin' a spoon underhand into shallow brush or tules also works very well sometimes, but is a technique infrequently used by the California basser. Again, this is probably more a result of associating spoons with deepwater fishing than an intrinsic difficulty with the method. It is really very simple. Just pitch the spoon underhand like you would a jig and hop it back to the boat. Hopkins, Cordel C.C. and Kastmaster spoons all work with this method. The Johnson Silver Minnow, with its single weedless hook, can also be very productive with a white pork rind trailer pitched into heavy deadfall and tule banks.

You might also want to try pitchin' a spoon along steep rocky walls like those found on some of the Colorado River lakes. Let the spoon tumble down the steep walls and be prepared for a strike on the fall. Occasionally, the shad will find radiant warmth along the walls in Winter and cool shade in the Spring and Summer. The bass will lie up against the walls under the bait waiting eagerly for the dying shad.

Conclusion

Dave Nollar closes his seminars on spoonin' technique by mentioning two final tips. First, you have to have split rings on all your spoons. As you bounce the spoon along the bottom, invariably it will be striking hard against the rocks, especially where the line is tied to the spoon. To prevent excessive wear and tear at the knot, add a split ring. This also gives the spoon greater action as it hinges back and forth on the pull up and the flutter down.

As for line size, Nollar recommends 12 lb. test or less. With the lighter line, the spoon will drop faster and the fluttering effect is much more dynamic. On these heavily pressured California lakes, heavier test lines used elsewhere in the country for serious spoonin' will typically spook the fish and strikes will be fewer. Ten and twelve pound test monofilament line has minimal stretch for California spoonin' and works quite nicely.

As can be seen, spoonin' is truly a versatile all year method. Unfortunately, not enough good bass fishermen have the confidence to try it aside from deepwater winter fishing. If there are shad populations on your favorite lake, you can bet that some type of spoonin' technique will be productive. Try it -- you'll see!

Jig Fishin': Flippin', Swimmin', Bangin' and Other Secrets

For years, jig fishing has been a popular method for catching a variety of species throughout the country. These very basic looking, lead head lures have been used for decades to catch bass, trout, northern pike, walleye, and all kinds of panfish. In California, fishing a jig for bass can be an especially effective technique in the pro basser's or weekend basser's repertoire of tricks. Jigs can be fished all year long. You can swim, pitch, flip, or bottom bounce these very uncomplicated lures.

The jigs used for California bassin' are separated into two categories depending upon the kind of material affixed to the weighted hook. The Western pros divide their jig fishing into plastic and pork rind style jigs. Selection and use of these styles requires some forethought. Both "plastic" and "pork", as they are termed, have certain applications on our waters.

Plastic or Pork?

The Western pros make their jig selections based upon primarily two variables: (1) water temperature, and (2) the natural forage bait available. Many of the veteran touring pros like Jim Emmett and Larry Hopper look at the water temperature first to decide what type of jig to throw. These pros are two of the most recognized expert jig fishermen in the United States. They have been finishing high in pro tournaments for years using this type of lure. These bassers will use jigs with a pork rind trailer if the water temperature is in the forties and fifties. They will usually stay with this "pig'n jig" combination until the water temperature reaches somewhere near 65 degrees. If the water is over 65 degrees, the pros prefer a jig with a plastic skirt and trailer.

Pork is typically fished more slowly than plastic. In contrast, you can swim the plastic jig quickly and cover a lot of territory compared to slower moving baits. Plastic jigs can be deadly on actively feeding bass, whereas pork is good for more lethargic feeders.

The theory behind pork rind trailers is that they have the texture and action of a live creature, be it crawdad, lizard, snake, or salamander. The pork is practically "tenderized" in the saline solution in which it is stored. Some pros experiment further and add drops of one of the commercial crawdad fish scents to the jar to make the pork even softer and tastier. Bass pros feel that less active fish in cold water will grab and hold on to pork longer than plastic. The texture and salty taste presumably comes close to matching that of one of these aquatic animals when it is crunched by a hungry bass.

In California lakes, the largemouth bass will move up from deep water starting in the early part of the year up through late Spring. This is also the time of year that the crawdads hatch and move up into the shallows. These are near perfect conditions to throw the pig'n jig combinations with the lure matching the silhouette of the live crawdad bait.

In contrast, a plastic jig with good action can be used on any lake where the bass feed on threadfin shad. Popular jigs such as the Garland Spider and the Haddock Kreepy Krawler are certified winners, especially when the schools of shad head for deeper water. Larry Hopper notes that most of the bigger bass caught on California lakes are caught deep. Regardless of water temperature, Hopper prefers to fish a plastic jig instead of pork for deep water fishing over 20 feet. He theorizes that in comparison to pork, the plastic jigs with their wavy tail actions simulate both crawdads and shad at these depths. Thus, he feels that plastic gives him double coverage so to speak, since it can match with either of the two dominant forage baits found in California. Hopper also makes a good point in noting that the plastic jigs come in a tremendously wide array of colors in skirts and trailer tails. The serious pro likes this characteristic of plastic since it allows them to create a customized skirt and trailer jig combination.

But again, it is important to note that choosing between pork and plastic is sometimes more a matter of confidence in a particular lure than invoking a hard and fast rule. For example, it is true that most Western pros prefer to use pork when fishing in cold water, noting that under these conditions, the fish want a slow moving bait. But there are many times when I have seen a good jig fisherman throw plastic in the heart of winter and catch fish deep where pork failed to produce.

Similarly, there are top-notch Western pros that will catch bass on pork all year long regardless of warm temperatures. They simply believe that the bass will eat pork whenever there are crawdads around, which for most California lakes, is all year. Be flexible enough in your thinking to switch from time to time when one or the other type of jig isn't getting bit.

What Type of Pork to Use?

Uncle Josh is far and away the most prevalent pork rind brand sold in the country. It has become the generic name, so to speak, for pork rind baits. Few other manufacturers are making similar types of baits. For California style bassin', the most popular styles of pork rind are frogs, spring lizards, and eels. Each of these unique baits has a special application combined with a lead head jig. Let's examine each type of pork bait more closely and learn which style to use under different conditions.

Pork Frogs: Uncle Josh manufactures the pork frogs in a variety of sizes. The three most common are small #101, medium #11, and jumbo #1. Although these baits are termed "frogs", for California style bassin' this is really a misnomer. The pork "frog" appears more to represent a crawdad rather than a frog, per se.

In the Spring, the #101 Spin Frog can be teamed with a small 1/4 ounce jig. This is the time of the year when the crawdads are on the small side. Later in the spring, switch to the popular #11 Bait Frog. Match this pork with any jig from 1/4 to 5/8 ounce. The #11 is the best all-around pork bait available. It can be fished all year long, pitched, flipped, or banged across the bottom.

During the later Spring and sometimes in the Fall and mid-Winter, the bass seem to prefer a big bait that presents a large profile. This is the time to go to the #1 Jumbo Frog. Don't let the size of this bait scare you. A number of the local pros have found this large pork to be very effective on big fish pitched or flipped to thick shoreline cover. Use heavy lines (17-30 lb. test) and at least a 1/2 ounce jig in either vinyl or live rubber skirts. A magnum size bass bait like this displaces a lot of water as it slowly sinks, creating a vibration that can really call in the big fish. At lakes that are populated by the large Florida hybrids such as Vail, Silverwood, El Capitan, and Isabella, try this #1 frog for a trophy fish.

Spring Lizards: If you think the bass are looking for a super bulky bait, throw the Spring Lizard. This pork rind imitates either a lizard or salamander in the water. Pro Gary Robson likes to use this pig'n jig combination in the Spring just before the bass spawn. Robson explains that the big bass want a big bait in this pre-spawn state, and the Spring Lizard presents a bulky profile for the hungry females.

Although the lizard is seen as primarily a Spring offering since this is the time of year when these terrestial creatures tumble off the banks into the water, interestingly, this bait really excels as a good Winter lure. When the bass are down deep in cold water, tie a Spring Lizard on with a 1/2 ounce jig. Work it slowly along the bottom. The biologists note that bass will often strike a larger bait in Winter so they won't have to feed very often and expend energy. The pork lizard is a perfect choice for these big, sluggish Winter bass.

Split-tail Eels: The Split-tail Eels, #U2, #U3 and #260 are also a fairly well-kept secret among the Western pros. During the hot Summer months when many bassers put the pork rind away and switch to plastic, a few die-hard pork fishermen have been using these baits in water where you would normally use a plastic worm.

Jig fishing expert, Jim Emmett, also uses these eels for one very specific condition which makes a lot of sense. On many of the lakes in Southern California such as Hodges and Skinner, the tule growth is very thick in early and late spring. As the tules die off, or are cut down, they form a thick, heavy mat. Emmett will fish a Split-tail Eel behind a live rubber jig and gently flip this lure through the little cracks and potholes formed in the tule mat. This skinny pork rind bait will slide easily through the small openings, and will not hang up as much as a pig'n jig with a #11 Pork Frog. The black and brown patterns seem to work best with these eels.

UNCLE JOSH ORIGINAL PORK FROG

UNCLE JOSH SPRING LIZARD

UNCLE JOSH TWIN TAIL

UNCLE JOSH CRAWFROG

UNCLE JOSH BLACK WIDOW EEL

Trimming the Fat

Pro bassers disagree among themselves whether or not it is a good idea to trim the popular Pork Frogs. Some pros feel the bait is fished best right out of the jar. With the frog left in its fat, chunky state, the pig'n jig combination will slowly sink in a tantalizing fashion. Other tournament veterans are adamant about trimming and customizing their pork frogs. What are some of the little things they do to these baits to make them more appealing?

First, they will often slit the pork rind up through the center to just behind the hook opening. This gives the pork the appearance of having two, elongated swimming legs. Next, they will cut the bait across the pork pad. This, combined with the cut down the center creates a Pork Frog totally segmented into four quarters. Be careful in slicing across the pad that you don't go too deep and cut all the way through the bait. This combination of cuts makes the pork chunk very mobile with a lot of life-like swimming action.

I found that this customized trimming of the pork also has another unique advantage. I'm a strong believer in applying one of the commercial fish scents to artificial lures to make them even more attractive to these spooky California bass. By segmenting the pork chunk you can add a few drops of scent directly into the meaty part of the bait. The hinged effect of the two cross cuts has the tendency to hold the scent in a little longer than if it was simply applied to an untrimmed frog.

 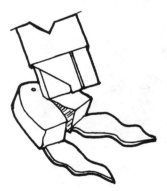 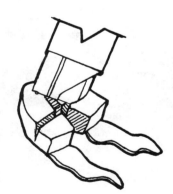

What Color Pork?

The Western pros generally agree that water clarity more than any single factor dictates what color pork rind to put on with a jig. In clear water, black, brown and purple will all work in solid combinations, e.g. a black skirted jig with a black pork rind trailer. But also, in clear water try purple and brown pig'n jig combinations. Mix and match these two colors of jigs and pork. They are very effective on clear water California lakes such as Casitas and Cachuma.

If the water appears stained with a green tint to it, use black or two-tone black and chartreuse pork. For muddy water, brown and orange, black and orange, or black and chartreuse pig'n jig mixtures seem to work best.

Here are a couple of other secret tips the pros use to come up with the "hot" pork rind colors. If you find crawdads in the lake that have taken on a greenish tint, you can come up with a fairly close custom pork color to match this natural tone. Buy some of Uncle Josh's orange colored "Spotted Craw" pork which is basically light brown with orange spots. Add some green commercial dye to the bottle and let it sit for a while. The dye will penetrate into the orangish-brown base and result in a mottled brown-green piece of pork. This color pork teamed with a brown skirted jig can be absolutely dynamite when green shelled crawdads are in the lake.

You can also take solid white pork rind baits and dye them a variety of colors. Depending upon how much concentration of the dye you use, you can come up with a wide range of your own personal custom shades. As I've been saying all along, it really pays to experiment with bait selection in fishing California lakes. Rather than always showing these leery bass the same pork rind baits day after day, add a little color to the pork and try something new.

Jig Skirts and Other Trailers

It is also important to take into account the skirt material itself in selecting the proper jig. For example, Gary Robson does not just simply use a pig n'jig combo for water under 65 degrees. His selection methodology is much more precise than that and it obviously has paid off in terms of his tournament success. When the water temperature falls to 45 degrees or below, Robson just doesn't opt for pork, but rather matches the pork rind trailer with a deer hair jig. Very few recreational anglers or pro bassers have caught on to this little secret, but it really works. The old, bucktail style jig is very responsive in the cold water. With the pork rind trailer, it makes a very slick, streamlined and quiet bait going into the water. This is an excellent lure to use on Northern California lakes such as Shasta and Oroville for both largemouth and smallmouth bass.

As the water warms up into the low 60's, consider using a jig put together with a vinyl skirt and a pork trailer. Robson will use this material in cold water because it is more responsive than the more popular live rubber skirted jigs. The vinyl skirt flairs better than the live rubber material and creates a slow, pulsating effect at rest. This can be a sensational combination on slow-moving, finicky winter bass.

A variation of this jig has been a fairly well-kept secret among the Western tournament ranks. Local pros take a 6 inch Super Float worm and cut it in half to form a 3 inch trailer section. They then split the worm down the center and slide it on to a jig with a vinyl skirt. The "hot" combinations are vinyl skirts in purple and brown shades matched with worms in either of those same colors. This rather unique bait has been responsible for catching many trophy size bass at lakes like Silverwood and Cachuma, particularly in the cold winter months.

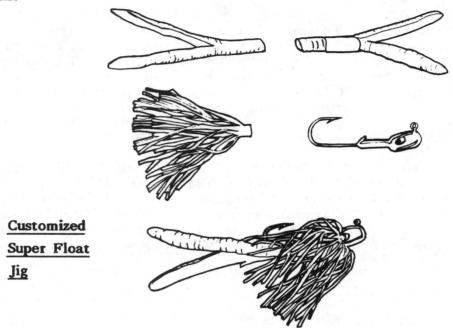

Customized
Super Float
Jig

Once the water temperature reaches the mid-sixties, many California bassers switch to either a jig with a live rubber skirt or a full plastic jig. Both the plastic and the live rubber materials are exceptionally responsive in the warmer water, generating a lot of movement even with the jig at rest. In warmer weather, the pork also dries out very quickly dangling from the rod tip making it tough and unusable. This is another reason why a lot of Western pros switch to plastic in the summer.

You can easily custom build another jig for fishing in warm water. Simply take a jig with a live rubber skirt and add a four to six inch plastic worm. With this type of lure you can fish much of the same water you would with a plastic worm, but at a significantly faster pace. This is a super bait under extremely windy conditions, or when you want to maintain maximum contact with the bottom.

There is one final little trick you can use for fishing a jig in warm water conditions. Take a plastic jig skirt such as Garland's or that made by Twin T's and match it with a #11 Uncle Josh Pork Frog. This combo works particularly well as a flippin' lure on bass rooted in the shallow cover. A popular combination is a black and chartreuse plastic skirt matched with a black #11 pork frog. In muddy water often found on lakes such as Elsinore where water ski traffic is heavy, this jig can sometimes be an incredible "secret" bait.

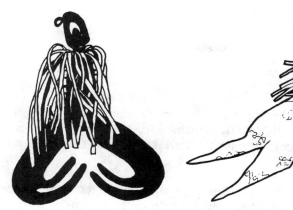

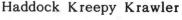
Haddock Kreepy Krawler   Pig 'n Jig(# 11 Uncle   Bobby Garland
                                    Josh Pork Frog)   Spider Jig

Jig Weights

The weight of the lead head jig can be very critical, much more than most anglers realize. Often the bass want a slow-falling bait and the fisherman is mistakenly using a jig that is too heavy. Other times, the fish are deep and the basser is not making precise contact with the bottom because the jig is too light.

Top-notch jig fishermen on the West Coast like Emmett and Hopper are very emphatic about using the lightest jigs possible. The theory is that a lot of times a heavy jig simply falls too fast and the bass have no interest in trying to catch up with it. Also, a lot of the bass lakes in California have prominent moss beds during the late spring and summer. Many bass fishermen put their jigs away - both pork and plastic - when they see the moss growth. The trick is to use a light 1/4 ounce jig head fished in the flats, coves, and shorelines that are lined with this moss. This size jig will sink very tantalizingly through the moss without picking up too much of this slimy vegetation. Be especially ready for strikes on the fall.

A 1/4 ounce head is also good for swimming a plastic jig such as the Haddock Kreepy Krawler through open water. There is usually enough weight to throw this size jig in windy conditions, and the slow fall with the swimming tail action dramatically resembles a dying threadfin shad.

Use this lighter weight lead head also with a pig'n jig combination especially when the bass want a slow-falling bait flipped in shoreline structure. You can also shake this light jig, in a way similar to shake'n bakin' a plastic worm. Here it is important to let the pork sit a little longer in the spot after it has hit the bottom. Then shake it for a few moments. This technique produces a lot of outstanding catches during otherwise tough flip bites.

If the jig is supposed to be imitating either a crawdad or shad nestled near the bottom, switch to a heavier 3/8 to 1/2 ounce head. Most of the time crawdads are right on the bottom inching around. So if the bass are clearly on this forage food, try to keep your jig in total contact with the bottom.

Similarly, in heavy shoreline cover, a light jig simply won't penetrate through the matted tules, branches, tree trunks, deadfall, brush, etc. A jig in 3/8 on up to 5/8 ounce is often necessary to get the lure down to where the bass are rooted.

Lately, the Western pros have started using jig heads weighing up to one ounce for deep water winter bassin' in 30 to 60 foot depths. In a tournament situation, the heavier jig sinks quickly to the bottom where the fish and bait are located so less time is spent out of the target zone.

It is also interesting to note that a heavier jig head can also do one other thing often overlooked in lure selection: it can make a lot of noise. For the serious flip fisherman, noise is usually a taboo. Normally, when you are flippin', you try to have the jig make as silent an entry as possible when it hits the water. But, there are times when you can actually get the fish excited with a noisy entry. Try using a little more force on the underhand lob when flippin' a heavier jig, 1/2 ounce or more, in thick cover. Often the noisy "plop" of the jig pushing through the brush or tule mat is just enough to get the bass' attention when a more subtle presentation isn't working.

Similarly, when fishing larger jigs on the bottom, the heavier weight will also produce more noise as it bangs up against the rocks and brush. This extra noise feature at depths of 20 to 60 feet can really make a difference sometimes in "calling in" the fish. Well-known U.S. Bass pro Gary Klein has taken this concept even further with the Rattlin' Weapon jig he pioneered. This live rubber jig has a built in sound chamber and rattler in the head which produces a lot of underwater commotion.

Jig Shapes, Guards and Hooks

Lead head jigs are available in a wide variety of head shapes. Along with the other components of this lure, the Western pros are very particular as to which head shape to use. The "banana" head is the most popular. It has a fairly narrow profile, falls straighter than other styles with less tumbling effect, and it is the least likely to get snagged. The "spade" head makes the bait stand up and works especially well with plastic trailers such as the Garland Spider and Haddock Kreepy Krawler. The round 3/4 to 1 ounce "football" head gets the bait down fast. This head style holds very well and kind of plows its way along the bottom.

The brushguards used on many of the jig heads are there to keep the lure from hanging up on brush, rocks and similar structure. These little innovations keep the lures remarkably weed and brush free and allow you to fish the bait where the fish live. Don't be too timid in throwing a jig with a brushguard into thick cover. Ninety percent of the time you will bring the jig in without hanging it up.

STYLES of JIGHEADS

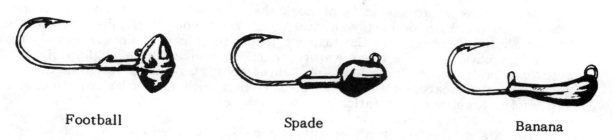

Football   Spade   Banana

Brushguards are made from a variety of materials and the pros themselves are divided as to which work best. Jigs with guards made from polypropylene fiber work well. The fiber is soft, moldable, and totally collapses on the hookset exposing a lot of hook for maximum penetration. Stiffer, plastic "Y" guards perhaps are a little more weedless, but are also somewhat more susceptible to breaking if mishandled.

The nylon bristle guard is also very popular but some pros complain it is too stiff. The trick is to cut them back so that the bristles extend just barely past the hook, then flair and bend the bristles back and forth a little to unstiffen them somewhat. A lesser known brushguard is one made from a light wire loop. This is an excellent guard but not too many commercial jigs are made with it. Most wireguard jigs are hand-made by the pros themselves.

TYPES of BRUSH GUARDS

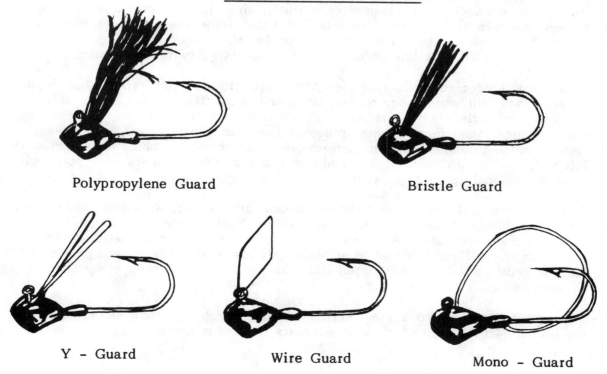

Polypropylene Guard   Bristle Guard

Y - Guard   Wire Guard   Mono - Guard

Also be selective as to the style of hook that the lead head is molded around, whether you purchase or cast your own jigs. When you are fishing clear lakes such as Shasta, Cachuma, or Casitas, use jigs with thin wire hooks. These hooks appear less obvious in the clear water and match well with the lighter jigs often used under these conditions. A lighter hook also allows for a slower fall. One other feature of the wire hook is that with minimal sharpening, it provides for excellent penetration on the hook set.

When you are pitchin', castin', or flippin' the jig into dense cover, use a heavier gauge, forged hook. These hooks were made for vicious, back-breaking hook sets with 20 to 30 pound test line. A good 3/0 to 5/0 hook is recommended for fishing in this super thick cover.

Tips and Tricks

The Western pros that are successful tournament fishermen realize that jigs produce many quality fish in California bassin' contests. Although certain methods (spit shottin' for example) produce a lot of barely legal, 12 inch tournament fish, many of the accomplished pros rely upon jigs for their large "kicker" fish. Time after time, you will see split shotters weighing in five fish limits that total between 6 and 8 lbs. Then along comes the guy who has been chucking pork all day with just 3 fish that weigh over 10 lbs. This scenerio is repeated regularly in the California tournament scene.

Many of the top Western pros will rely upon jigs primarily as a flippin' lure. As was mentioned in the chapter on worm fishing, flippin' keeps you in the strike zone 90% of the time. So many of these tournament anglers want to keep a bigger bulky bait in this zone as they hunt for the larger fish. Jigs in either plastic or pork fit this bill perfectly when such large baits are needed.

Other pros prefer to make more lengthy casts with the jigs rather than flippin' them. They will work long, rocky points and drop-offs, steep canyon walls, or shallow brushy flats with this lure. Sometimes they will want to make a cast that is longer than most flippin' presentations, but shorter than, say, a long cast to some prominent target. Here quick underhand "pitches" are needed. Pitchin', if you can envision it, combines some of the elements of flippin' with more traditional run'n gun casting.

The pro pitches the jig as quickly as he can, allows it to sink somewhat, maybe gives it a few "shakes", then quickly swims it back to the boat and fires off another underhand cast. A lot of territory can be covered with this technique, and a high speed casting reel is an absolutely essential piece of equipment. Pitchin' works well in brushy weed lines, rocky banks, and even along shady canyon walls.

The pros can't seem to agree whether or not to fish jigs on a slack, or on a tight line. One school of thought suggests that it is essential to keep maximum tension in the line to feel even the slightest strike. Other pros think just the opposite and prefer to fish jigs on a slack line. After they feel the strike, they reel in the slack and then quickly set. Here the reasoning is that the fish is more likely to really inhale the jig if it encounters minimal resistance. This is very similar to the way that most good plastic worm fishermen fish. The secret is, don't drop the rod tip as low as you might with a strike on a plastic worm. Instead, keep the rod at about 10 o'clock which will allow you to pick up the slack fairly quickly.

Larry Hopper passes along another technique he has designed for tournament level fishing. He calls this "bangin'". Hopper will take a heavy 5/8 ounce jig and fish it straight down above steep banks and ledges. He will either cast the jig or let it fall vertically into deep water. If he casts, he waits for the jig to fall off the side of a ledge, then quickly puts his baitcasting reel into free spool and lets the jig fall straight to the bottom, shaking it, and using a little doodlin' action. The erratic movement plus the noise of the heavy lead head banging into the rocks and bottom structure excites the bass into striking the jig presented in this unique vertical fashion.

Conclusion

To become a well-rounded bass fisherman or a competitive angler on California lakes, it is imperative that you learn a few jig fishing tricks. Jig-fishermen continually put larger, quality fish in the live well than those using plastic worms, cranks or spinnerbaits. Usually these simple lures represent bigger natural baits such as crawdads and mature shad. Thus, it is reasonable to expect larger fish to home in on these bigger lures.

When I asked renowned jig fishermen, Jim Emmett and Larry Hopper, what the average recreational basser does wrong when using jigs, these two Western pros had several precise points to make.

.   The pros say you must learn to set the hook hard – and they emphasize **hard** – on anything that feels unusual in either the sinking or retrieving of the jig.

.   Secondly, recreational bassers have a tendency to fish jigs too fast. Slow it down a little when using these baits. You should get better actions and more strikes.

.   Finally, Emmett and Hopper provide perhaps the best insight as to why more weekend anglers don't succeed with these simple jigs. They buy them in sizes that are too heavy. Try to stay with 10 to 15 pound line, a fairly stout rod and learn to use these lures by starting with 1/4 to 3/8 ounce models.

Spinnerbait Fishin': Lead'n Blades

If you need to cover a lot of territory quickly and you have exhausted yourself crankin', a spinnerbait may be your next best alternative. "Lead'n blades" or just "blades" as these lures are sometimes termed, are an all season bait in California. They can be casted and dragged through all types of brush and cover without hanging up. They can be pitched, jigged, and even flipped at times. There are a wealth of spinnerbaits on the market today in all shapes and sizes. Good spinnerbait tossers in the West realize that results with this lure do not come by chance. Careful understanding of how there baits are made and what the different components do under certain conditions is essential to becoming a successful blade fisherman.

Anatomy of a Spinnerbait

Blades: Shape, Size and Color. Spinnerbaits are made from three basic blade patterns, each with its own unique characteristics and application. The Colorado style balde is very round in shape and generates the most torque when pulled through the water. This blade will displace the most water which results in the greatest vibration and a distinctive "thumping" action. The narrow Willow-leaf blade yields the most flash and turns the fastest. Because it is so long and thin, it works best in areas with thick moss or grass where it will hang up the least. The Indiana blade falls somewhere between the Colorado and the Willowleaf. It is often used in conjunction with one of the other two, forming a tandem bladed bait.

Interestingly, if you examine any of these three basic blades you will also find differences in how deep they are cupped or concaved. Spinnerbait blades that are cupped deep will produce the most throbbing action and vibration underwater. Sometimes this is best to "call" the fish, in stained or muddy water. Blades with a shallow cupped surface come through the water with less vibration, and might work better in quiet, clear lakes. Often, the pros note, the novice basser thinks he should change the blade size, when all he has to do is change the cup of the blade and leave the size alone.

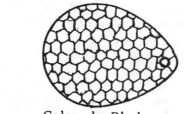

Colorado Blade

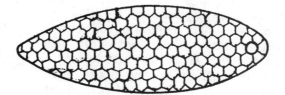

Willowleaf Blade

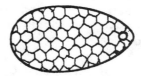

Indiana Blade

Spinnerbait blades come in a variety of sizes, with the most popular ranging from small #2 up to a large #6. If you decide to construct you own spinnerbaits, keep in mind that these blade sizes are not exactly standardized. The size graduations and the corresponding numbers vary among the blade manufacturers. Thus, you could purchase a #3½ Colorado blade from one maker, and the same size blade from another manufacturer might be labeled #4.

And make no doubt about it, blade size can be critical. A blade that is too large will have a tendency to tangle up with the wire frame on the fall. A blade that is too small won't stabilize the lure enough. A rough rule of thumb is to match a ¼ ounce lead head with a #2 to #4; a 3/8 to 1/2 ounce, with up to a #4 blade; and a 5/8 ounce to a large #5 Colorado or Indiana blade. These are the most popular combinations used on the West Coast.

Recently, Roland Martin, one of the most celebrated pros in the country, divulged that he had been using a remarkably large spinnerbait blade to catch some really "hawg class" bass. Martin uses a magnum sized #6, #7 or #8 blade with this spinnerbait. It is usually rigged tandem with a smaller #4 or #5 Colorado blade followed by the larger #6 to #8 Willowleaf trailer. Because this blade is so large, it must be matched with a 1/2 to 5/8 ounce jig head to counterbalance the torque. I'll talk a little more about this unique spinnerbait shortly.

You must also be selective as to what type of finish or color of blade to use with your spinnerbait fishing. As a general guideline, nickel blades are best under bright sunlight. Copper, red or chartreuse painted blades are better with overcast skies or very stained water. Gold or brass colored blades fall somewhere in between.

Blades with a smooth finish present a more subtle flash. Sometimes this is very critical in getting spooky, less aggressive bass to strike a spinnerbait. Blades with a hammered finish give off greater flash with all the light refracting from the little dimples or indentations on the blade surface. The light striking this kind of blade is erratically bent in all directions, producing the extensive flashing effect. This can be a good option for more aggressive fish or in stained or muddy water.

There are a lot of inexpensive spinnerbaits on the market. The Western pros emphasize that for the most part they are a poor investment particularly with regard to the blades on these baits. Cheaper spinnerbaits utilize blades made from low grade steel. These blades will usually rust once they are nicked. Better quality spinnerbaits made by maufacturers such as Turnabout, Haddock, Eagle and Strike King use blades made from durable brass. Quality copper blades must also have a lacquer finish or they will soon tarnish. Although it is tough for most anglers to always know if they are getting top quality in a spinnerbait, there is one little tip worth noting that might help. Usually, cheaper spinnerbait lures will weigh less in identical head and blade sizes than will well made blades. Again, this is because the better lures use heavier, longer lasting brass-based blades.

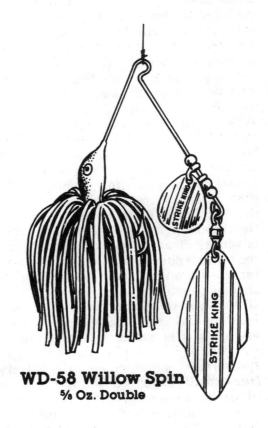

WD-58 Willow Spin
⅝ Oz. Double

Frames and Swivels: The wire frame to which the blades, skirt, hook, and lead head are affixed actually greatly affects the overall performance of the lure. This feature is very often overlooked. In the South, spinnerbait manufacturers have historically made their lures using thicker diameter, heavy wire frames. The main advantages to these heavy duty frames is that they require minimal fine tuning, are exceptionally durable and can be dragged through very heavy cover. However, the one distinct disadvantage to these frames is that the heavy wire restricts vibration from the blades.

Because the California lakes do not typically have so much dense shoreline cover, the Western pros prefer a smaller diameter wire in their spinnerbaits. To be precise, the pros look for spinnerbaits with a **tapered** wire frame which combines strength and durability. This frame also allows the blades to spin with less drag and resistance resulting in a lure with optimal vibration. Keep this regional variation in mind, particularly if you order some spinnerbaits by mail from the South. It is very possible they are made from the heavier wire frames which are not your best bets for the deeper California lakes.

Also, some wire frames for comparatively similar size lures extend back further toward the hook than others. There is a reason for this. A longer wire generates more vibration and consequently can often aggravate the bass into striking on the retrieve. But some pros want a shorter wire frame that offers less vibration on the fall and works better as a subtle lure. The good spinnerbait fisherman will keep both types handy for some serious California style bassin'.

Better quality spinnerbaits will use good swivels to which the line attaches. Although many pros prefer nothing less than a spinnerbait with a ball bearing swivel, there are many who believe that this is not that important. The addition of a quality ball bearing swivel definitely adds to the retail price of the lure.

One unique regional innovation was designed and manufactured by longtime California pro Fred Borders. As a former U.S. Bass Angler of the Year, Borders knows how to make a spinnerbait sing. Many of his fellow pros complained that too often they would cast their bulky spinnerbaits and they would invariably tumble or cartwheel on the cast, resulting in a fouled bait. To the professional tournament angler, time is money. Thus, having your lure continually foul can often be a costly situation.

Borders designed a series of unique spinnerbaits with a patented roller in front where the line attaches. This little roller bushing allows the bait to be free without any line restrictions on the cast, fall and retrieve. The entire lure can therefore vibrate tremendously. In addition, the bushing eliminates the stress at the knot found in traditionally designed spinnerbaits. This is because on these lures, the line is tied to the roller and not the wire eye formed by the frame. Thus, there is no line fray and only minimal stress on the wire frame itself.

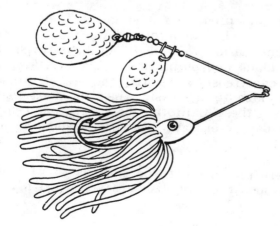

TurnAbout Spinnerbait

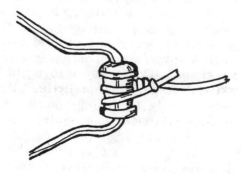

Roller Bushing
Enlargement

The Turnabout models will also not butterfly in the air, allowing the pro to consistently make foul-free casts. Although this lure is somewhat more expensive than other spinnerbaits, pro bassers throughout the country have added it to their tournament boxes.

Skirts and Trailers: As with jig components, spinnerbait fishermen have their choice of basically vinyl, rubber or plastic skirts. Some pros favor vinyl because it flairs best, but it doesn't have as much pulsing affect as rubber skirts. For the most part, spinnerbaits with vinyl skirts have slid in popularity in past years though they still work well, especially in cold water. I might add that vinyl does soften up in summer and it certainly can be used for warm water spinnerbait fishing. Even less common are blades with plastic skirts. However, some California bassers still use a spinnerbait with these skirts on clear lakes that have dominent shad populations. You might consider replacing the skirts on a few of your favorite style blades with plastic jig skirts in smoke sparkle or salt'n pepper patterns. Match them with a nickle blade(s). This can be a real "sleeper" when the fish are feeding on schools of threadfin shad.

Most of the Western pros opt for spinnerbaits with either flat or "breathing" rubber skirts. The flat rubber is best illustrated by the type of skirting material found on the old standby Hula Popper surface lure. The pros like the flat rubber because it has a very seductive swimming or undulating movement when pulled behind blades. The breathing rubber skirt is made from fine, rubberband-like strands which results in sensational pulsation when combined with the blades. A final consideration is the so-called "pro-model" skirt that features a combination of flat and breather rubber strands layered together. This is your most expensive spinnerbait skirt.

Whatever skirt material you select, always make certain that the skirt is actually **reversed** before you use the lure. Some manufacturers of the cheaper blades are not concerned with whether or not the lure works. They will not package the spinnerbait with the skirt reversed because they feel it has less shelf appeal to the novice angler. Manufacturers that cater to the serious basser will package their blades with reversed skirts. The reversed effect gives the bait greater action with the skirt flaired and pulsating.

With regard to color choice, many Western pros keep it simple. They like white skirts for clear water, chartreuse for stained. An intermediate color gaining in popularity is a chartreuse and blue combination. On really dark, overcast days, you might want to try solid black or black and purple mix. Black/yellow, green/yellow, blue/white, orange/brown and chartreuse/white patterns are all productive at times. Don't get into a rut by sticking to the basic white or chartreuse skirts. Experiment a little. Remember these California bass get conditioned very quickly to seeing the same lures day after day. Give them something new to look at once in a while.

As for spinnerbait trailers, the Western pros seem to be split as to whether or not they are necessary. I tend to believe that the fish are attracted to them at times. I don't think they are that essential for spinnerbait fishing on shallow-feeding, aggressive bass. But on deeper, more sluggish fish, they add another strike-inducing dimension to the lure. If you are using one and the fish seem to be biting short, nipping at the tail of the trailer, you can always shorten it up or remove it completely.

Plastic trailers are the most popular. You can use plastic worms cut back to the sex collar, Garland Spidertails, Haddock Kreepy Krawlers, or Mr. Twister Twin Tails. Pork rind bass strips also work quite well, particularly in colder water. I've seen trailers produce in a variety of colors. But day in and day out, white for clear and chartreuse for stained water are the overwhelming favorites.

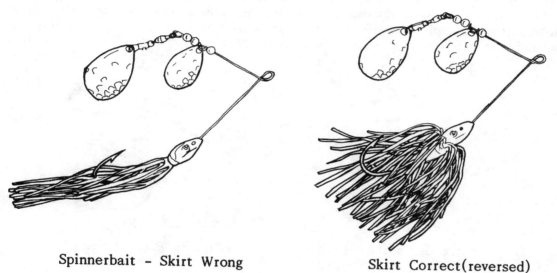

Spinnerbait - Skirt Wrong   Skirt Correct(reversed)

Single or Tandem Blades?

This is probably the main decision you will have to make in picking which spinnerbait to use. There are some broad generalizations that can be made which can serve as a general guideline for selecting this style of lure. Assuming that blade size is kept approximately equal for a single and tandem model, then there are certain features to each style that can be noted:

To begin with, tandem models fall more slowly than single blade spinnerbaits. Usually the tandem spinnerbaits also have a longer wire frame than single spins. The skirt will tangle less with a tandem blade. This is because the extra blade and the longer wire make for a better balanced, more stable lure, with the skirting material situated far away from the main components of the spinnerbait.

Next, the addition of that extra blade to the longer wire frame also allows the tandem spinnerbait to be retrieved more slowly than the single blade models. The tandem spin gives off more vibration and flash than the single blade, yet maintains good stability when retrieved slowly. The front blade actually acts to counterbalance the rear blade in this type of lure.

The single blade spinnerbait, although less popular than the tendem, nevertheless is an important weapon in the pro basser's lure assortment. The single blade can be retrieved relatively fast. But more importantly, these spinnerbaits make for an excellent "fall" lure. I'll expand upon this concept a little later.

Some pros firmly believe that a tandem spinnerbait is most suited for clear water. In contrast, the single is supposed to work best in dirty water. Other pros believe in the exact opposite. The bottom line is that all too often **both** models will work equally well in either clean or muddy water. Again, it pays to be a little experimental with this type of bait.

Single Blade Spinnerbait

Tandem Blade Spinnerbait

Spinnerbait Techniques

As I mentioned at the start of this chapter, spinnerbaits are an all season bait you can carry in your tackle box. But, there are some sophisticated techniques designed by the Western pros for this lure that are worth learning. You have to understand how these methods work if you really want to become a master with "lead'n blades".

Fishing "On the Fall": Some of the California bass lakes will have bushes, boulders, dock pilings, downed timber and similar shoreline structure that is very suitable for a spinnerbait. The key is to make your cast **well beyond** the visible structure. As you retrieve the lure, let it sink just before it bumps the submerged object. You don't have to give the blades any slack line per se. As a matter of fact, all you have to do is lift the rod, bringing the lure toward you, then drop the rod again when you reach the structure. This creates a modest amount of slack line which allows the lure to slowly sink. This is similar to the "lift-and-drop" procedure most bassers use to crawl a plastic worm along the bottom. It is often on the "fall" that the bass attack the blades. Be alert, because you have to swing instantly when you feel that characteristic "thump". A second too long delay and the fish will spit out this bulky lure.

Expert spinnerbait fishermen like Fred Borders prefer to toss a single blade model when fishing the lure as a "fall bait". The secret is to use a spinnerbait with a single, larger-than-normal blade. Borders notes that the bass in many California lakes hold very tight to what little shoreline structure there is. This specialized single blade bait will helicopter down to those fish holding tight, generating a tremendous amount of flash and vibration and quite often a jolting strike.

There are some other variations to this "fall bait" presentation that are definitely worth mentioning: jiggin' and yo-yoing the blades.

Jiggin' Blades: Many veteran bass pros have found that they could also use a spinnerbait similar to a plastic or pork rind jig. The place to try this technique is along the points and major underwater ledges on your favorite lake. Graph these spots and be particularly alert for any indication of bass suspended off these points or along the breaks. Suspended fish are perhaps the most nerve-racking experience the pro encounters. He can see the fish with his electronics, but they simply won't bite. Why this happens isn't quite clear. It's been theorized that everything from a dramatic weather change, fluctuations in water levels, to post-spawning recuperation can put the bass into this suspended mode. Make no coubt about it, this is a tough condition to fish.

Occasionally, a medium weight spinnerbait casted over the point, then pulled out to deeper water works on these stubborn fish. Let the spinnerbait sink far enough down to the strike zone to where the suspended bass are located. Then slowly retrieve the blades in that "lift and fall" motion through the suspended fish. Occasionally you will get one to strike, but the bite will probably be just a little "tick" in the line or at best subtle pressure. Be ready to swing!

You can also fish blades in a more traditional jigging fashion by using a heavier lure with a short arm and a larger blade. This combination fished **slowly** and deeply can often be very productive on big, lethargic winter fish. Interestingly, the few Western pros that use spinnerbaits in this manner prefer large, hammered chrome blades with dark black, brown or purple skirts. These are the same colors that are popular for Pig'n Jig fishermen chuckin' pork rind jigs during the cold winter months. Fish this type of heavier 1/2 to 5/8 ounce spinnerbait with a stout rod and heavier 14 to 20 pound line. The object is to "plow" through the heaviest cover in water down to 30 or 40 feet, trying to draw a reaction strike from big fish holding deep.

Yo-Yoing: Another rather seldomly used trick is to work the spinnerbait in deep water as you would with a spoon. Medium sized blades, usually in chrome with white skirts, are the preferred combination. Let the lure fall straight down vertically over the spot. When it reaches the bottom, use long, gentle lifts on the rod to get the blade turning, then drop the rod to let the bait fall. Amazingly, be prepared to get some pretty solid strikes all the way down to 50 feet. This technique is termed "yo-yoing" and is very similar to that used to catch saltwater species such as yellowtail and albacore tuna.

Magnum Willowleafs: I mentioned how top pro Roland Martin let the secret out about this magnum-bladed spinnerbait some years ago. I still find most recreational bassers to be somewhat intimidated by this bait. Those large #6 to #8 Willowleaf blades cast an awesome silhouette dangling from the end of a rod on California lakes - expecially to the guys using 6 pound test and little 4 inch worms. But be assured, this lure is a genuine "hawg hunter" in this part of the country as well as in the South.

It takes both strength and perserverance to fish it. I recommend a bait casting reel filled with 14 to 20 pound test line, and one of the heavy duty, long 7 to 7½ foot trigger grip style rods. There are really two tournament strategies you can employ in using this bait. You can throw it all day hoping to get only a few strikes, but knowing that 90% of these hits will be quality fish. Southern pros will do this a lot with this lure and buzz baits for example, figuring that they need only five good strikes to win the tournament. Or, you can use more productive methods such as wormin' to catch a five fish limit or smaller bass, then throw the large Willowleaf blade, searching for a "kicker".

There is no question that this lure can really wear you out. It generates a lot of flash and vibration and hence, a great deal of resistance on the retrieve. It does run quite weedlessly and literally "bulldozes" its way through the heaviest brush. It too can be fished "on the fall". I have seen this unique jumbo lure work on both Florida hybrids and the smaller Northern strain bass in a wide variety of lakes. The strikes are usually strong and vicious rather than subtle "ticks" or pressure. If you have the heavier rod needed to fish this lure, I highly recommend it, particularly in the Spring.

Flippin' the Blade: Of all the things that can be done with spinnerbaits, this is probably the least known and most rarely used. But believe it or not, there are times, especially in the Spring, when you can catch fish gently flippin' a blade into shoreline cover. Allowing the spinnerbait to fall through cracks in the tules, or flippin' them into thick brush and deadfall can often be a surprisingly good alternative to more traditional flip baits. Blades are very weedless and they have that nice, exposed hook that allows for a strong hook set. If you try this method use either a large single spin or, better yet, a twin-spin. The twin-spin, which I'll talk about shortly, is an excellent fall bait and less vegetation will hang up the dual blades. It is a bulky bait to flip but can often produce larger quality fish from this cover.

"Matties" or Tail-Spins: These lures enjoyed their greatest popularity many years ago as a favorite among the Western pros. Tail-spinners or "Matties" as they are known locally, will probably be found in a few tackle boxes to-day. It is too bad, because this simple spinnerbait can be very productive, es-pecially for the beginning basser.

Tail-spinners are actually lead-headed jigs with a swivel slipped over the hook and a small to medium sized spinner blade attached. The skirt material is usually a reversed vinyl, with purple, black, brown, silver, char-treuse and white the best colors. You can actually convert any vinyl-skirted jig to a "Mattie" by adding the swivel and blade to the hook. Haddock lures still markets these in-expensive spinnerbaits in California.

Haddock Killer(Tail Spinner)

Tail-spinners are terrific little baits in 1/4 to 3/8 ounce when you are into school fish that are actively feeding. You just simply cast out and retrieve similar to the way you would fish a crankbait. But this lure also has tremen-dous, overlooked versatility. You can fish it deep as a fall bait, or it can be yo-yoed. A stop'n go presentation through suspended fish often generates strikes. Give the reel four or five quick turns through the strike zone, stop and let the "Mattie" sink for a second or two. Repeat this retrieve all the way back to the boat. Or, fish the tail-spins like a jig in cold weather along points and drop-offs. I have also used these lures in very shallow, muddy water, pitching them very gently into and around the brush with good results. You can add a brush guard to make the tail-spinner fairly weedless, or fish it with an open hook.

One subtle trick that a local pro at Lake Casitas once passed along to me adds a little more appeal to these simple baits. Take a plastic worm and cut off about 1/2 or 3/4 inch of the wider part of the bait. Take this little worm chunk and thread it on to the hook before adding the blade and swivel to the skirted jig. This gives the tail-spinner a more attractive mid-section particu-larly with a piece of brightly colored plastic along the hook shank. Transparent red, purple, or chartreuse worms work really well to dress up these uncompli-cated lures.

Twin-spins – A Lost Art: Along with the Matties and the California grizzly, the twin-spinner has pretty much reached extinction in the Golden State. Many years ago, when the spinnerbait craze just started to catch on, most of the sales in California were made in these bizarre-looking twin-spin models. Lures such as the Shannon Twin Spin and Bomber Bushwacker enjoyed tremendous popu-larity here in the West. These funny-looking baits that resembled some kind of insect with feelers produced a lot of trophy catches up and down the coast from Clear Lake in the North, to Isabella in the Center, and Lake Henshaw in the South. One popular technique was to use chest waders and make long casts with these vibrating blades into brushy flats and stickups. These lures were soon replaced by the single and tandem blade models with the "V" style frame popular today.

It is interesting for fishing historians to track the rise and fall of a particular bait. Perhaps one of the reasons twin-spins lost popularity was due to their propensity to get fouled on the cast with those dual "feelers" often tumbling erratically and wrapping into the line. Too many times, some of these hot lures from yesteryear get retired prematurely. The twin-spin is a good case in point.

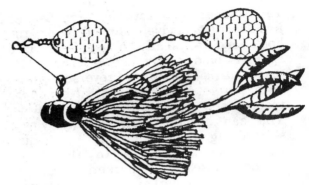

Haddock Twin-Spinner

This lure is a state-of-the-art fall bait if fished properly. Use the lift-and-drop retrieve. Those pros that still throw them recommend a large 1/2 to 5/8 ounce head, and medium sized, nickle finished, Colorado blades with a reversed vinyl skirt in dark colors. The real tip is to use either a #11 or U-3 Uncle Josh pork rind trailer with these baits.

Fish the twin-spin over deep rocky ledges or through underwater brush. You might even let it fall vertically down submerged tree trunks. It is imperative that you watch for strikes on the fall. A majority of the fish that hit this bulky, vibrating, flashing intruder are going to do it while it is sinking. Again, a stiff rod with heavier line is crucial in getting a good hook set.

Twin-spinners are still sold by a few of the local and national spinnerbait manufacturers. During the winter doldrums, if you get tired of fishing the standard pig'n jig set up, switch to a twin-spin tipped with a pork trailer. You can bet the fish haven't seen one for some time and the results may be surprising!

Conclusion

Spinnerbaits have to be a staple item in any serious basser's tackle box. They are truly a year 'round bait. However, many anglers make the mistake of throwing and retrieving them too shallowly. That is, most fishermen always fish the spinnerbait in sight, slightly below the surface. Try to develop more versatility with these lures. The spinnerbait can be fished through a variety of strike zones, not just shallow. Learn to fish blades more as a fall bait, letting it seductively drop into little pockets of cover. Finally, be very aggressive with spinnerbaits. They are remarkably weedless and rarely get hung up. Too many novices make the error of being overly timid with these lures. Don't throw them only next to visual cover, throw over and through it. You can definitely fish blades where the fish live!

Grubs, Darters, Gitzits and Other Subtle Baits

This chapter is about some unique methods used by the Western pros to lure hook-shy California bass. Sometimes an ultra subtle presentation is necessary. For years, many pros resisted using these baits in big league tournaments with the belief that they fish too slowly and tend to catch only smaller fish. To some extent, this is true. But as the lakes experience more pressure, any technique that produces has become worth considering.

The one thing all of these methods have in common is the use of particularly light monofilament. When the bassin' gets super tough it is time to resort to 4 to 8 pound test lines and small, scaled-down baits. These subtle offerings can often mean the difference between a full limit of bass or being blanked when traditional techniques fail.

Most of the baits referred to in this section can be presented very nicely with a medium light spinning reel and a six to seven foot rod. Many pros claim that they have a better feel for these small lures and light line with a spinning out- fit. As I'll discuss, the strike is often nothing more than some mushy pressure and a quick hook set is imperative. Other serious bassers simply do not feel comfortable with this set up. For these fishermen, one of the lightweight, palm- size baitcasting reels provides a suitable alternative.

The reason these subtle baits work so well is very easy to understand. First, they are fished with fine diameter line that is hard for the fish to see. Second, many of these lures are commonly rigged with small 1/16 to 1/4 ounce jigheads. This forms a bait that very closely resembles the size and shape of much of the threadfin shad found on these lakes. Finally, this combination of small lure and light line allows the angler to impart a tremendous amount of **action** to these subtle baits. Often less aggressive bass will just get so irritated that they can't pass up striking these dancing and darting little morsels. The subtle baits can be divided into four basic categories: (1) P-heads and darters, (2) grubs, (3) tube baits, and (4) mini-spinners. Fishing these lures requires a different technique for each grouping.

P-heads and Darters

These are basically miniature jig heads made to fish with small plastic trailers. The "P-head" is so termed for the round pea-sized 1/16 to 1/8 ounce lead head used with this method. You can purchase these jig heads separately and then select a matching plastic trailer. The best combinations include 2 to 4 inch curl-tail plastic worms, although there are times when a larger, 6 inch model works very well.

These jig heads come with or without a barb behind the lead head. On thicker-bodied, plastic worms such as Reds, Culprit, Mr. Twister, and Manns, use a P-head with a barb to keep the worm trailer from sliding down the hook. If you prefer

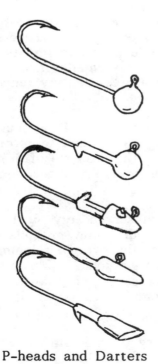

P-heads and Darters

Paddle-Tail Worm on P-head

Curl-Tail Worm on Darter

Split-Tail Grub on P-head

Curl-Tail Grub on Darter

to use one of the 2 to 4 inch spaghetti-thin worms such as Cato, Teazer or Flutter-craft, use the P-head without a barb, otherwise the barb will have a tendency to protrude through the thinner plastic with these baits. The P-head jig is meant to be fished open-hook style without a weedguard of any sort. You will be surprised at how amazingly weedless these little jigs will fish.

Darters are similar to P-heads in weight but are molded in sleeker, more aerodynamically-shaped heads. Darters receive their name from the way they dart back and forth as they sink on the cast or are twitched back on the retrieve. In contrast, P-heads fall in a straighter fashion without as much of the darting effect. It is best to carry both of these little jig heads in your tackle box as the bass will often prefer one action over the other.

When you fish P-heads and darters be sure to keep your eye on the line - this is critical. So often, the bass will inhale these subtle baits as they are sinking following the cast. The strike is often nothing more than a quick little "tick" or a jump in the line. Immediately wind in the slack and set the hook. You have to be on your toes here for if you are a second too late, the bass will spit out the little jig.

P-Heads and darters can be fished back to the boat with a variety of retrieves. Sometimes just a moderately slow grind works. Other times a stop'n go is effective, with strikes occuring as the lure is stopped and begins its fall. These baits can also be shake'n baked or doodled vertically below the boat. I cannot emphasize this enough: stay alert and be ready to swing on any unusual pressure.

Often, in retrieving P-heads and darters, you might see your line go very slack all of a sudden, or it may appear to be moving off to the side. This is a sure sign that a bass has picked up the jig and is either swimming in with it or parallel to your boat. Quickly pick up the slack and set!

P-heads and darters are a bonafide year 'round bait. I have seen many tournament-sized 12 inch "keepers" come to the scales with these lures. I have also witnessed some genuine 10 pound class trophies taken with these minuscule lures off of ledges in the Winter. I have also used these baits extensively while guiding because they are excellent producers in the hands of raw beginners. Not only do they cast well with spinning tackle, the exposed, open-hook results in a lot of catches that might not be made with a traditional Texas-rigged worm.

Be prepared to switch off with regard to trailer size in using these lures. Sometimes, for example, the fish want a P-head or darter with only a 2 to 3 inch plastic trailer. This can be especially true when the fish are suspended or feeding on small shad. Other times, if the fish are eating crawdads, a thick-bodied 4 or 6 inch worm trailer is probably best. Quite often the bass will root in the thick moss beds and a P-head or darter dropped down in between the vegetation can be absolutely deadly!

A few more tips: use smoke and clear patterns if you suspect the fish are working the shad. Smoke sparkle, smoke/purple, smoke/blue, smoke/red, plain smoke and salt'n pepper are solid choices. For a crawdad imitation, earth tone browns with blue and green neon stripes, brown and black, motor oil, and especially purple with red and blue flake trailers match well with these little jigs.

Take the time to sharpen the jig hooks. Although these hooks are made from fine wire you will find that your set-to-catch ratio will improve by putting a needle-sharp point on them. Also, keep constant tension on the retrieve. This is very important. These are small hooks you are using here and it doesn't take much for the fish to throw them. Once you set the hook and start the retrieve, the slightest amount of slack may result in a lost fish. Keep the line tight, wind it in a smooth, steady action and avoid erratic, jerky retrieves.

Plastic Grubs

These soft baits have been a real "sleeper" in California for some time. Pro bassers have enjoyed a lot of success using grubs elsewhere in the country. But it has only been in recent years that the Western pros have picked up on these lures.

The most popular grubs in California bassin' are fat, single-tail versions. The five inch Twin-T's and the four inch Fluttercraft grubs are regional favorites. These curly-tail baits can be fished in a variety of ways. The most common is to fish the grub on a 1/8 to 1/4 ounce P-head or darter jig. Fish it exactly as you would with a worm trailer, again watching for strikes on the fall and for pressure bites.

Single-tail grubs, interestingly, can also be fished with a basic Texas rig. This method has produced good results in alpine, cold-water lakes such as Silverwood and Shasta where the bass primarily feed on shad, and are deep in winter months. A Texas-rigged grub fished slowly along the bottom can be very effective during this time of the year especially when the fish prefer a bigger bait.

Two other techniques that illustrate the versatility of these curly-tail lures are also worth mentioning. Lake Skinner in Riverside County has an excellent population of Northern-strain largemouths. Threadfin shad are overwhelmingly the dominant forage food for these bass. P-head and darter-rigged four inch worms work all year long at Skinner. But, there are times when the bass seem to want a big shad-imitation, fished **slow**. A curly-tailed grub fished with either a Carolina or split-shot set up is just the ticket. Use larger 3/0 to 4/0 hooks to embed into these fat grubs and swing hard to drive the hook home.

On this same lake, if the water level is up, the bass move into the tule banks. Although plastic worms and pig'n jig combinations often produce results, a real hot tip is to flip one of these grubs. The best technique is to rig the grub Texas style and peg the bullet weight with a toothpick. When the shad have been pushed deep into these tules, a grub flipped into this cover can be absolutely sensational.

Fat, double-tail grubs are used primarily as jig trailers often matched with a plastic skirt. There are times however, when this bait will also work flipped or with a small darter or P-head. The double-tail grub has a lot of tail action and will displace more water and create greater vibration than single-tail models. Haddock and Mr. Twister also make small twin-tail grubs. These lures were originally designed for crappie, but can be very effective on bass when light lines and subtle baits are in order.

The straight-tail.fat 2 or 4 inch grub is traditionally what has been fished in other parts of the country for largemouths, smallmouths and Alabama spots, alike. In California, the pros seem to favor the larger, curl-tail patterns, however there are times when a super slow presentation is necessary. The simple, single-tail grub could be a good bet here. It can also be split-shotted, but the best over-all method is on a superlight, 1/16 to 1/8 ounce P-head. This can be an excellent lure for coldwater fishing. Another tactic is to jig there grubs vertically over touchy, suspended bass.

Manns' Sting Ray Grub in a wide variety of sizes and colors is a bonafide producer. A California variation of this bait is Haddock's Split Tail Grub with the rear section split into four tiny, separate tails.

Haddock Split-tail Grub

Manns Augertail Grub

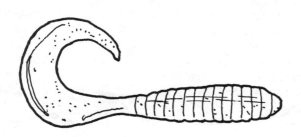

Fluttercraft Grub

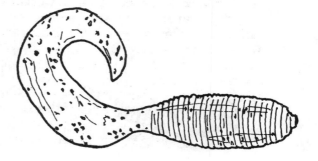

Twin-T's Salty Grub

Your best choice of colors in fishing any of these fat-body baits would be to stay in basic shad-colored patterns. Smoke, smoke/sparkle, clear/sparkle, salt'n pepper, and silver are very effective. Grubs in green, blue or purple flake some-times produce exciting results when shad patterns fall. Although this color does not enjoy wide-spread popularity, a light, watermelon-colored grub(kind of "icy"-green) can be a real sleeper bait, particularly on spotted bass and deepwater largemouths.

The Scrounger is another subtle bait that enjoys quiet respect among some California pros. This little curl-tail grub is unique due to the way it is rigged on a P-head with a patented soft plastic lip. The manufacturer used this lip to give the grub an incredible oscillating action. On the San Diego lakes, the Scrounger can be a true secret weapon on surface crashing bass. Local pros will make long casts into the frenzied fish with this lure on a spinning outfit with 6 pound line. A straight, steady retrieve just below the surface seems to work best. The con-stant thumping and vibration given off from the plastic lip often generates strikes from these boiling fish when nothing else works. Fish the Scrounger in silver or smoke/sparkle patterns in 1/16 or 1/4 ounce models.

Another specialized bait designed for California's high-pressure lakes is known as the Reaper. Not quite a grub or a plastic worm, the Reaper most closely resem-bles a minature eel. This lure was originally another well-kept secret among the elite pros who fish those tough, trophy San Diego lakes. This bait should be fish-ed with either a small 1/16 or 1/8 ounce P-head or split-shotted, using a #2 worm hook. Split-shotting is my favorite technique. The strike with this bait is some-times so subtle yet so vicious. Let me explain. The first indication you may get is a slight "tick" in the line when you split-shot the Reaper. Stop and pause for a second, but stay alert. It is often at this pause when the bass eats the bait so hard it nearly yanks the rod out of your hands! The best I can figure is that the Reaper looks like a very slow fluttering shad. The bass makes a slight move on the bait, then when it senses it has crippled the bait(the pause period) a vora-cious strike follows.

Use the Reaper primarily in shad patterns. However, an unusual solid chartreuse with black flake color also works. Use this color in the Reaper when you fish stained water. Try this unique bait. It should prove to be productive in almost all California lakes.

Scrounger

Reaper Eel

Tube Baits

Western bass pro Bobby Garland has designed an entire series of tubular baits that have become fantastic weapons on the tournament trail. These phenomenal soft plastic lures can absolutely save the day under the toughest conditions.

The hallmark model in this collection is known as the "Fat Gitzit". This is nothing more than a small, 3 inch, hollow plastic tube with the last inch cut into a number of tiny tentacles forming a squid-like tail section. The Gitzit can be rigged in one of two ways. You can take a 1/16 to 1/4 ounce P-head or darter jig and run it inside the tube which is sealed off at the head. Push down on the plastic to force the Jig's hook eyelet to pop through(see diagram). Or, you can use a similar size jig head with a barb on the shaft and slide the Gitzit over the hook as you would with any plastic jig trailer. The barb will keep this tube bait from sliding off the jig head.

Mini-Gitzit

Skinny Squid

Fat Gitzit

Other tube baits in this series are the smaller baby Gitzit and a longer, thinner lure called the Skinny Squid. It is a good idea to carry some of all three of these tube baits, since the bass often key in on one over the other.

Tube lures are the epitome of subtle bass baits. They have to be thrown on light line and fished **very slowly** to get the maximum effect. They can be used in a manner similar to a P-head or darter, with many strikes occuring while the lure is slowly sinking. Pressure bites are also quite common as the bass just some-times suck on this bait. Weedless models are also sold in the Fat Gitzit version, making this lure an excellent flip bait. Watch for the slightest movement or "tick" in the line, or any unusual pressure when flippin the Gitzit. If in doubt, swing and set.

Take time to examine these baits closely in the water and to observe the type of action you can impart with just the slightest twitch of the rod tip. Their se-ductive darting, swaying and falling motions can generate strikes all year long under the most dismal conditions. Tube baits match well with the shad schools and can be fished all the way down to 60 feet when the bait is deep. Keep in mind that it will take some time for the lure to sink.

In the Spring, when the bass are on the nests or in shallow brush, the Gitzit acts like a wayward crawdad often aggravating the fish into an explosive strike. Similarly, when the bass sometimes root deep in the thick of summer moss beds, tube baits can excel at bringing these fish out to bite. Here, the trick is to look for an opening in the moss then gently cast the bait just slightly beyond the hole. Ease it to the edge of the moss and then with a single twitch, let it fall into the opening. Big bass laying in these moss beds simply can't resist annihilating these seductive intruders. Although these lures are usually fished with an open hook, they are remarkably weedless.

Smoke/sparkle is far and away the most widely used color in these tube baits as it obviously closely resembles a threadfin shad. Clear/sparkle, blue/sparkle, and black/sparkle also work. The real sleeper color is the blandest of all - plain smoke. I have often caught both largemouth and smallmouth bass on smoke Fat Gitzits when the fish were puddlin' around lazily, feeding on shad when nothing else was working.

If the fish are eating crawdads along rocky ledges, in the shallow brush, or in the thick moss, there are a variety of colors that will work with these baits. The favorite for a crawdad imitation is smoke/red flake. There have been periods, for example at Lake San Antonio, where the summer moss is very extensive and this color Gitzit produced consistent results for days at a time. Sometimes, if the natural crawdad coloration is green, try a Fat Gitzit in a green/orange flake, motor oil/red flake, or a green/brown combination.

Three other little tricks are worth mentioning with the Fat Gitzit. Many pros feel that bass will more readily strike a lure with a painted eye than a bait without one. I have experimented using a plain smoke/colored Fat Gitzit and P-head with an eye painted on the jig. I seem to get improved results with this combination. The painted eye distinctly shows through with the jig inserted into the clear plastic and must represent, even more closely, a natural shad.

Another tip to try is to fill the Fat Gitzit up with one of the commercial fish attracting scents. The thick, hollow tube body will hold the scent for quite a few casts, and will leave a very tantalizing "vapor trail" around the lure as it darts from side to side. The Gitzit is usually selected by the Western pros when the bite is tough. Adding the scent to this natural cavity only increases the overall appeal of this bait on these heavily pressured lakes.

Lastly, keep a Gitzit rigged on a medium light spinning outfit when top-water fishing in the Golden State. Often bass will teasingly slap at a big stick bait like a Zara Spook, or strike short on a buzzer. When this happens, instantly pick up your spinning outfit and fire off the next cast to where the strike occurred. Many times, the Gitzit irritates the bass into making a more aggressive attempt at the lure on this follow-up cast.

Mini-Spinners: Overlooked Baits

There are a variety of minature lures which utilize a spinner blade in their design and are really overlooked by the weekend basser. Many of these lures have been charaterized as trout or panfish baits. A few of the Western pros use these lures under very tough conditions to produce outstanding results.

One such bait is the solid lead tail-spinner that was actually designed for bassin'. These lures are made from a small slab of lead(usually chrome plated) with a small spinner blade affixed to the tail portion. Manns Lil' George and the Spin-rite are classic examples. These lures can be cast a long way with hardly any wind resistance. When the bass are in a feeding frenzy, crashing the surface for shad, these tail-spinners can be dynamite. They also work jigged vertically in deep water and through schools of suspended bass.

Manns Lil' George   Rooster Tail   Blakemore Roadrunner

A variation of a mini-spinner is the Blakemore Roadrunner. This little lead jig is molded in the shape of a horsehead with either a maribou feather or live rubber skirt body and a tiny spinner blade attached below the head. Many fishermen think that the Roadrunner is nothing more than a crappie jig. Again, a few pros know differently. Fish this little mini-spinner the same way you would a P-head or darter. When the bass are feeding on shad, this is a very simple bait to use in the hands of a beginner. There are times when the white maribou version can be exceptionally productive with light lines on surface feeding fish.

Finally, this last tip comes from Western pro Dave Noller, who is an authority on the San Diego lakes. Noller, like many of us, frequently encounters the large schools of surface-crashing bass at lakes such as Sutherland, Hodges and Otay. Rather than being frustrated by the churned up commontion, he does something unique. Working the perimeter of these schools, Noller will throw a white trout spinner like a Roostertail or a Shyster to induce these bass to strike. I have tried this technique myself and it really does work at times. These little spinners put out a tremendous, tight vibration in the water and seem to excel when the shad are very small.

Conclusion

This chapter, perhaps more than any other in this book, illustrates what it takes to consistently catch bass in California. Armed with a spinning outfit, light line and a handful of subtle baits, the recreational angler can often fish circles around the pro who persists in using the 15 pound line and the traditional baitcasting rigs. These lures are **finesse** baits and require much forethought in their proper selection. You must also be constantly alert and extrmely patient in using these lures - they usually are most effective when fished **slowly.**

Smallmouths and Spots

Most of the bass caught in California lakes are either northern strain or a hybrid mix of the northern and Florida species. However, on certain lakes there are two other bass species that provide a unique fishery, i.e. the smallmouth and Alabama spotted bass. Unlike their northern or hybrid cousins, these two species require some distinctively different techniques in lure selection and presentation.

California Smallmouths

Smallmouth bass have been introduced into a variety of California waters and rivers. At lakes such as Trinity, Shasta, Almanor, Nacimiento, San Antonio, Oroville, and Cachuma, these bass capture a significant portion of the bass angler interest. Although smallmouths do not grow as large as northern and Florida's (a five pounder is a true trophy), many pros feel their tenacious fight is the best of all the bass species.

The smallmouth bass has certain characteristics that clearly distinguish it from other bass. Their coloring is usually a distinctive bronze or brownish tone highlighted with prominent vertical markings. The upper jaw of this bass does not extend beyond the eye as with the largemouth strain. In contrast to the largemouth bass, smallmouths spawn earlier and in deeper water. They spawn in 60 to 70 degree water in late April or early June and build their nests at 3 to

20 foot depths. Smallmouths also orient to different terrain than their northern and hybrid relatives. Northerns and hybrids seek out a lot of brush, boulders, trees, tules, deadfall, and similar shallow structure. These bass use this type of cover for ambush points from which to attack the forage bait. In contrast, smallmouths can be found on gravel bottoms, broken rock, and deeper rocky reefs. So, be prepared to fish smallmouths a little bit deeper and in rockier areas than largemouths.

Both smallmouth and Alabama spotted bass have one major characteristic in common -- they both feast on crawdads in their natural habitats. This heavy crawdad orientation dictates to a significant degree the proper lure selection and methods used to catch these scrappy fighters.

Smallmouth Lures and Techniques

The first thing to do in smallmouth fishing is to scale down in tackle and lure size. These fish are often found in clear water environments and can be very touchy feeders. Veteran Western pros like Don Iovino and Larry Hopper fish many tournaments in these dominant smallmouth lakes and are in unanimous agreement that 6 to 8 pound test is a must if you are going to seriously fish these bass.

Next, be prepared for a lot of soft pressure bites. Although the smallmouth may strike a bait viciously, they often are very selective feeders. Sometimes, they will just mouth the bait before really eating it. This will even occur occasionally with crankbaits, not just plastic worms, grubs, or jigs. You can be crankin' the plug when all you feel is some mushy pressure rather than the jolting impact that you expect from largemouths.

On this note, crawdad patterned crankplugs can be very effective for smallmouths. Many of the local fishermen believe any crankbait is good for smallies as long as it has a red belly. The smaller Rebel plugs such as the Deep Wee R, the Storm Wiggle Wart, and the Rapala Fat and Shad Raps will all work. Smaller shad colored patterns can also be productive.

Small pig'n jig combinations are also very effective bait for these bronzebacks. Look for jigs with super fine rubber skirts. Small pork rind trailers such as Uncles Josh's #101 Spin Frog are excellent. Brown jigs matched with brown pork is the best overall combination. Smallmouths will have a tendency to peck at the pig'n jig more than largemouths. Let them actually pull on the jig more than you normally would to insure that they have really eaten the bait before setting the hook. As an alternative, use the vinyl skirted jig with a Super Float worm trailer. Purple and brown combinations are best.

Bobby Garland's Fat Gitzit fished with 1/16 to 1/4 ounce heads is also a top producer for California smallmouths. The pros favorite colors are smoke with red flake, chartreuse, and a chartreuse and clear combination in this little tube bait. For spoonin', the ole' standby Hopkins #075 3/4 ounce chrome is a solid choice.

Crawdad-colored worms, especially in the 4 inch custom hand-poured earth tones can be sensational smallmouth baits. Not enough anglers use these small worms teamed with subtle presentations for the bronzeback population. A case in point occured on a summer trip to lake Almanor. I had been fishing the Sierras for trout, and decided to try Almanor's famous smallmouths for a few hours before dark one day. The landing operator informed me that the bite had been miserable in past days, with mostly small sub-legal fish being caught on live crickets. Veteran lake regulars were fairing no better with the standard array of crankbaits and larger worms.

Fortunately, I had packed away a handful of 1/8 ounce P-head jigs, some split-shot, hooks, and a few dozen of my favorite hand-poured worms in "San Diego" shades of brown/neon blue, brown/crawdad, brown/shad, and brown/smoke. I started working some flats in fairly clear water at about 20 feet, slowly crawlin' P-heads with 4 inch straight-tail worms. After I realized I was getting ultra-soft pressure bites, I started sticking some beautiful 2 to 3 pound smallmouths on these little baits. Then I switched to split-shottin' a 4 inch brown/black Superfloat, tail-split of course. Additional fish were caught on this combination.

Finally, don't leave your spinnerbaits and crappie jigs at home when you are heading into smallmouth country. Scaled-down spinnerbaits in 1/4 ounce, with smaller blades and little grub trailers can be dynamite on these fish. The single best overall color according to the pros is a white spinnerbait with white and chartreuse skirts and nickel blades. You might also try some of the popular trout spinners on the bronzeback community. Roostertails, Mepps, and Shyster spinners can all work at times, especially with light lines in clear water. Small 1/16 to 1/8 ounce yellow and white maribou crappie jigs can also be productive fished behind a float near submerged structure.

Spotted Bass

Alabama spotted bass are noticeably very fat and chunky compared to other species. They also have distinctively different markings from other bass found in California. The "spots" that characterize these bass are found on the sides of the fish. The lateral band is a series of short blotches. Below the lateral line the scales have dark bases that form the lengthwise rows of small spots. Similar to smallmouths, "spots" or "footballs" as they are termed, do not have mouths extending beyond the eye like largemouths. However, unlike the smallmouth, spots do not have any vertical bars on their sides.

Spotted bass also spawn deeper than their Northern cousins in water 4 to 6 feet deep. Pure northern strain largemouths prefer water less than 4 feet for spawning. Spots have been planted in a variety of California lakes including

Shasta, Isabella, Millerton and San Vicente. The fishery I want to really focus on however, is at Lake Perris in Riverside County. This lake is the only lake in California that is populated purely by Alabama spotted bass without any other bass species sharing the water. It is a recognized trophy fishery with the current world record spot coming from Perris, weighing a whopping 9.06 pounds.

Dave Nollar is considered the foremost authority on this lake and the feeding habits of the spotted bass. Nollar points out that spots are very unique in contrast to other bass in the way they predominantly orient to the lake bottom. They are simply not as structure-oriented as northern and Florida strain largemouths. Nollar is emphatic that you won't catch spots unless your bait is making contact with the bottom. This is the very key to consistently catching these bass. Like the smallmouth, spotted bass feed extensively on crawdads. As a matter of fact, on lakes where both species abound, look for them to be found mixed together on the rocky points.

The best time to fish for trophy spots is mid-December through mid-January. These are very much a school fish, and the females will congregate tightly in a given area. This is the time just prior to the annual spawn when the bigger fish are moving up. Later in the spring, the fish will be somewhat more scattered.

Of all the bass found in California waters, the spotted bass tend to move most rapidly from one area to another. Nollar notes that an entire school of these fish can come through quickly in a given area and you can load up if you are there at the right time. He recommends that rather than runin'n gunnin' from one place to another, it is best to rotate between 3 or 4 key areas where the fish are known to congregate. Patience is a virtue when fishing for spots. You simply have to have the confidence that a school will move up to a particular location on the lake and sit and wait them out.

Spots can be caught on crankbaits in both crawdad and shad patterns. The Bagley DB-III in Tennessee shad finish is a local favorite at Lake Perris. The current world record from this lake was caught on a white spinnerbait, another popular offering. But the best artifical baits are those that slowly hug the bottom. Pig'n jig combinations in browns and blacks work well. Better yet are plastic worms and grubs in interestingly enough -- green patterns. For some reason, the spots at Lake Perris really turn on to the green worms and grubs.

The 4 inch Super Float worm in "mean green" and the Manns Sting Ray and Haddock Split-tail grub in watermelon color have been consistent producers. Work these lures slowly and methodically. There is every indication that record breaking spotted bass remain to be caught in this lake.

As the Department of Fish and Game experiments with further plants of "spots" in other waters, give pro Nollar's special techniques a try. What works at Perris, should also prove to be fairly effective in other spotted bass habitats as well.

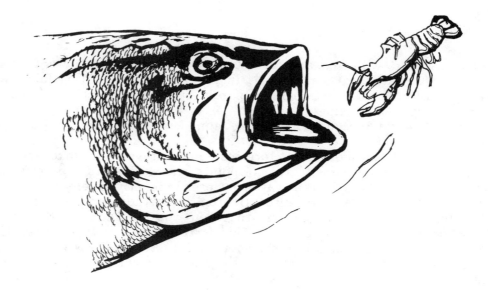

Live Bait Fishin': Things That Swim and Crawl

Most pro bass fishermen in the United States fish primarily with artificial lures. Nearly all of the governing professional organizations, including the two largest -- B.A.S.S, and U.S. Bass -- have restrictions against using live bait. The reasons behind this provision are really two-fold. First, it is felt that the fish have less of a sporting chance against live bait than with artificials. Second, some bass caught on bait are often hooked deep, which if handled improperly, can cause serious damage to the fish.

Almost all bass tournaments practice the ethic of "catch and release", whereby the fish are kept alive in aerated live wells then released after weigh-in. This sporting and conservation measure is tough to implement with deep-hooked bass caught on live bait. For competitive tournaments, too many of these fish would not survive throughout the day, until weigh-in time.

I know of some professional bassers who, although they regularly fish in money tournaments, will sometimes use live bait during non-competition, recreational outings. There are some lakes, for example Lower Otay in San Diego County, where live bait is practically the only way to catch bass during certain times of the year. Some fishermen -- recreational and pro alike -- just want to catch fish. They may also dream of a trophy bass for the wall.

Here again, live bait is going to account for many of the fish caught in California over 8 pounds, especially the Florida hybrids. Similarly, for numbers of bank fishermen and families in pleasure boats, live bait fishing is sometimes the only way they can fairly compete with the pro and his $20,000 rig.

Thus, it is not the aim of this book to pass judgment on anyone regarding whether or not it is sporting to use live bait for catching bass. This author will take a stance, however, against the rape of many of these pressured waters by so-called "sportsmen" that use live bait either wontonly or illegally.

Some lakes, for example, do not allow live crawdads for bait. The lake management feels that too many trophy-sized females in the Spring are susceptible to this bait, which if not restricted will soon deplete the bass fishery. But, so often I have seen pro bassers in hi-tech boats not only fish "dads" at some of these lakes, but even more illegally, lay out a "chum line" of 30 to 60 crawdads in front of their boats! Some of these guys get off the lake in the Spring with 5 fish stringers totaling over 40 pounds! Then they have the audacity to say they caught them on artificial lures. Using live bait legally to catch that one trophy fish is one thing, fishing for 40 pounds of "meat" is another.

Similarly, the people who insist on using other restricted baits to catch bass can pose a serious threat to the overall ecology of these precious waters. The usage of commercially purchased goldfish introduced illegally into lakes can create havoc in the long run. A few of these small aquarium fish get free from the hook (or worse yet, are dumped in after a day's fishing) and the lake is soon being overrun by a foreign gold fish population.

These junior members of the carp family feed on small plankton and organic debris which has settled to the bottom. This is the same diet that sustains young bass fry. Thus, these prolific, colorful fish can soon interfere with the established food chain on a good bass lake and potentially overrun the gamefish population.

If you like to fish live bait, then please make certain to check the restrictions at each individual lake here in the Golden State. To be caught using an illegal bait even in unintentional violation of the rules, can be a very costly mistake. Fines can be steep. As with all the artificial lures I have discussed, there are some interesting little secrets you may find helpful in fishing live bait here in California. Let's see what some of these are by outlining the different choices of bait available.

Night Crawlers

Without a doubt, the night crawler is overwhelmingly the most popular choice for live bait fishermen in California. These magnum-size worms are available from a wide variety of sources. They can be purchased at tackle shops, sporting goods stores, markets, convenience stores, gas stations, drug stores, and of course, at most lake concession stands. Be selective when you purchase a box of these jumbo baits. Occasionally, an unscrupulous bait wholesaler will "salt" the container with only a few large night crawlers. The box may contain one dozen worms, but only two or three are large, healthy specimens. The remainder are small, more immature baits. If you are going to fish bass with 'crawlers, then use the largest ones you can find. Have the clerk either empty the carton into a tray or finger through it yourself to make sure you are getting good, large crawlers. Keep these worms fresh by storing them in a cool ice chest.

The biggest mistake I see fishermen making when they fish 'crawlers is to use hooks too large and to wad the bait four or five times on to the hook. This "gob of worms" effect may work with red worms for catfish or trout, but it really ruins the potential of the 'crawler when fishing for bass. Night crawlers should be handled gently and hooked once through the sex collar. The trick is to then re-embed the point of the hook into the worm to make it almost totally weedless. This is very similar to the way you rig a plastic worm Texas-style.

Fish the 'crawler on 6 to 8 pound line with a medium action spinning rod. The least amount of weight you use, the better it will work. The object is for the bass to feel the smallest amount of resistance when it picks up the bait. Small BB-sized to #5 shot will suffice. Crimp it about 12 to 18 inches above the 'crawler. Sometimes, an interesting variation is to slide the shot all the way down to the eye of the hook, and fish the 'crawler like a miniature lead head jig. Use a #6 to #8 bronze, long shank, baitholder hook.

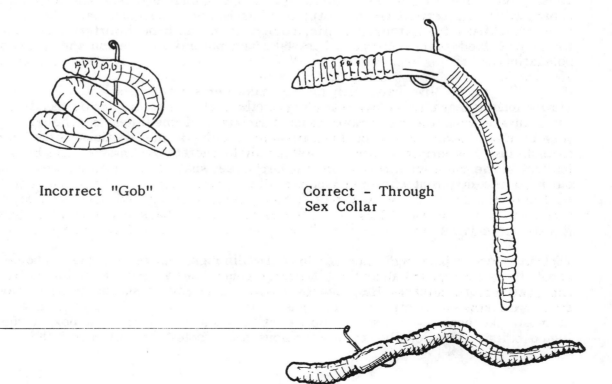

Incorrect "Gob"

Correct - Through Sex Collar

Another preference is to use no weight whatsoever and simply "fly-line" the bait. Here you have to make a delicate lob cast and watch the 'crawler gently sink to the bottom. Be prepared for a strike on the sink which may appear as a little "tick" in the line. Whenever you fish bass with "crawlers, let the fish run somewhat after that first strike. Rather than letting them peel line off the reel in free spool, fish with the reel engaged in gear. But, when you feel the strike, quickly point the rod tip down toward the water. This creates a modest amount of slack. Let the fish "have some pipe" as it begins to swim with the bait. When the line is perfectly tight, swing and set.

Occasionally, the 'crawler can be suspended through moss and weeds by using a small float about 3 feet above the bait. This will also work sometimes as a way to drift fish the 'crawler in shallow water. The bobber keeps it from snagging all the time on the bottom.

Most of the good bait fishermen however, prefer to work the night crawlers similar to the way you would crawl a plastic worm. They will select a likely looking bank and make repeated casts as they work along it. The best technique is to slowly "line feel" the crawler back to the boat (or uphill if you are bank fishing) occasionally pausing. This is a much more productive method than "still fishing" a stationary bait, since so much more water is covered.

Crawdads

Many experts concur that the next world record largemouth bass weighing over 22 pounds will come from California. It most likely will be caught on a live crawdad. These freshwater crustaceans have to be ranked as the number one bait for trophy-sized bass -- Florida, northern, Alabama, spotted, and smallmouth alike. 'Dads, as the locals refer to them, are a relatively easy bait to fish and are not quite as menacing as they look.

They can be purchased at bait stands at lakes where they are legal. Or, for the more adventurous, you can try to catch your own. Look for a small pond, shallow slough, or drainage ditch at night and there is a good chance you will find some 'dads. The most popular way to catch them involves some angling finesse in itself. Tie a piece of raw liver to the end of a line. The crawdads will soon latch on to the meat, and then you can slowly drag them in. They will usually hold onto the liver all the way to the bank, refusing to let go of their tasty feast. Firmly grab the 'dads along the middle of the back between your thumb and index finger. This keeps your hand away from those vicious little claws.

Crawdads should be stored in a shallow container with water not much deeper than about three fourths the height of the largest specimens. Put some lettuce into the container to serve as feed for the 'dads. This will also keep them away from each other.

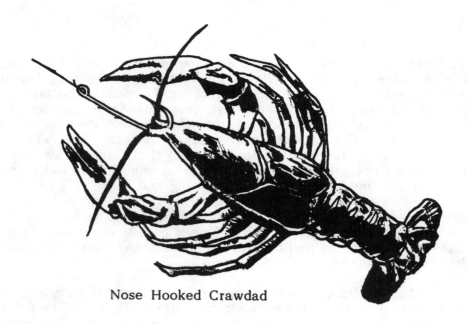

Nose Hooked Crawdad

Crawdads or "clickers" molt or shed their shells throughout the year. If you can find one in the "soft shell" stage -- you've got a winner! The hard shell 'dads will certainly work, but allow the fish to run with them longer. The bass will usually crush the hard shell 'dad, back off to see if it is dead, then inhale the rest of the bait.

You will also find that the 'dads range in colors from bright red to orange, to mottled green and brown. The best baits tend to be the smaller to medium sized ones ranging up to 3 or 4 inches in length. You can use the larger "mag 'dads", but I recommend clipping off the claw sections with a pair of needlenose pliers. The bass will more readily strike these larger baits if they do not have to engage in combat with those two large pincher claws.

A lot of traditional literature tells the fishermen to hook crawdads through the tail section. Although this may work, the preference on the California lakes is to drive the hook though the nose section. You have to be careful in hooking the 'dad in this area and a gentle lob cast is crucial. But, the benefit is that the bait can swim with minimal restriction and there is only a small amount of shell to drive the hook through on the set.

Local bait fishermen are split as to what is the best hook to use. Some prefer a larger, long-shank, baitholder hook in sizes #6 to #1 depending on how large the 'dad is. Others like a super strong, yet very short shank bronze saltwater live bait hook. These are the same hooks used for fly-lining anchovies. #2 to #1/0 are the recommended sizes. Whichever hook style you decide on, fish the 'dads with a medium action spin or baitcasting outfit with 10 pound test line. You will get more strikes with this lighter line. Surprisingly, sometimes you won't get any with much heavier line even though you have a primo natural bait tied on.

Most of the bass I've seen caught on crawdads have been quality, kicker-sized fish. Let the bass run the line out somewhat after the initial strike. You have to be patient, since the fish may make a few passes at the 'dad before they finally decide to devour it.

Shiners and Shad

Shiners are one baitfish that can also make for a good meal to a hawg-sized bass. Golden shiner minnows are members of the cyprinid family of fish. Their closest relatives are carp and goldfish. These forage fish can be purchased at certain lakes where they are allowed as legal bait. At San Diego lakes such as Otay, Hodges, and Sutherland, they account for a lot of wall-hanger bass in the Spring. Some local anglers prefer to catch their own shiners directly from the lake they are fishing. They feel the natural shiners are much hardier than the commercially raised variety and will thus last longer.

The way to catch your own shiners is to find areas around the shoreline and the docks where there might be some shade. Use a #18 gold treble hook and fish it like a snag lure, casting and twitching it. Believe it or not, shiners will often strike the gold treble hook without any bait. Other times, a small amount of dog food, stink bait, bread or dough will help. The key is to use ultralight monofilament on these touchy little minnows. The locals scale all the way down to 2 pound test line.

Shiners can be kept in a minnow bucket or an aerated boat live well for many hours. It is important to keep the pump on at all times circulating fresh water into the well. A small battery operated portable pump can be attached to a bait bucket as a suitable alternative for the bank or boat fisherman.

The shiners typically sold at the lake are divided into small, medium or large sized. The largest specimens rarely exceed 10 inches in length. The larger the shiner, the more it will cost, varying about one or more dollars difference per dozen between each size. These are not cheap baits to use, and you should learn to fish them conservatively.

Use medium action spin or baitcasting rigs and 8# to 12# monofilament. The smaller baits can be fished with a #8 to #10 bronzed saltwater bait hook. Go up to #4 to #6 for the medium shiners and #1 to #1/0 for the largest minnows. You can fish shiners in one of three ways.

The most popular method is to run the hook through both lower and upper lips and run'n gun with the bait. Use no weight at all, or use up to a #3 split shot. Cast the shiner to a likely spot on the bank near visible cover. If the bait doesn't get bit instantly, reel it in and fire off another cast. This can be expensive unless you catch quite a number of the shiners yourself. You should figure each bait to last only 3 to 4 casts as it takes a beating being tossed so frequently. But, the hot shiner fishermen like this type of fishing, because they can cover so much more of the lake looking for that one trophy fish.

The other two ways to fish shiners are to fly-line them in open water; or, to rig them below a bobber and still fish them near the tules, rocks and shoreline brush. This is very similar to shiner fishing in the South, only using much smaller baits. These methods are much slower than the run'n gun technique, but they do produce and conserve on the bait. For this type of fishing, it is better to hook the shiner once through the back below the dorsal fin. The bait will thus live a lot longer this way and swim fairly unrestricted.

The strike in shiner fishing can be deceiving at times. The secret is to acquire a sense of what it feels like when the shiner is lazily swimming with free line. When all of a sudden that sensation stops and you feel a kind of "dull" pressure, there is a good chance the bass has the bait. Gather up the slack and swing. When these California bass hit the shiners, they will not always run with the bait. So be prepared for any unusual feel at the end of the line.

A few lakes permit you to use dipnets to catch your own threadfin shad. These forage minnows are not as sturdy as shiners and won't last as long in a bait bucket or live well. However, when they are schooled in tight "meatballs" as they are termed, you can literally net hundreds in a short amount of time. Fish shad similar to the way you would work a shiner in open water. Use either a bobber or flyline with a very small split shot and hook the shad through the back. Allow the bass to run with the bait a little, then swing hard. Lighter lines in 6 to 8 pound test work best when using shad for bait.

Mudsuckers and Waterdogs

Neither of these two baits are indigenous to the freshwater lakes of California. The mudsucker is a baitfish similar to tropical gobies and is found in coastal tidal flats. The waterdog is not a "fish" per se, but rather the larval stage of the tiger salamander raised commercially outside of California. Both can be purchased at local bait shops during certain times of the year. Mudsuckers are the cheaper of the two, with supplies of waterdogs usually being fairly limited.

The way to fish these baits is basically the same in either case. Run your hook lip-to-lip, then fly line the bait weightless or with a medium sized shot. Use a long-shank bronze baitholder hook ranging from #4 to #1/0 depending on the size of the bait. You may want to consider fishing mudsuckers or 'dogs with your casting reel in free spool or with the bail open on your spinning reel. These are big, free-swimming, bulky baits, and it is best to let the bass have a fairly good run with them before setting the hook.

Both of these baits should be kept in a fairly shallow receptacle with only 2 to 3 inches of water. Some bait chuckers like to line the bottom of a plastic tray with lettuce or sea weed for the mudsuckers. They seem to stay calmer in the shallow water as they root into the vegetation. If kept moist, mudsuckers can actually live out of water for 6 to 8 days.

Crickets and Grasshoppers

These two insects are the least used of the bass baits mentioned in this chapter. Crickets are sold commercially in little wire cages, particularly in the Lake Shasta and Lake Almanor areas where they are dynamite on smallmouths. For a while, as a matter of fact, this bait was so deadly on the bronzeback population at Shasta that there was a moratorium on their usage. They are now legal to fish again as of this writing.

Grasshoppers must be caught by hand in open fields and meadows. A professional butterfly net is a necessary piece of equipment for the serious 'hopper hunter. You can make an improvised net very cheaply by stretching a woman's nylon stocking around a coat hanger frame and taping the wire to an old broom handle. Few bass fishermen use 'hoppers for bait, but they definitely can be productive, especially on alpine lakes. A lot of times anglers fishing at higher elevation lakes that have both trout and bass populations, inadvertently tie into bass while fishing 'hoppers for trout.

Both crickets and grasshoppers should be hooked just behind the head with a small #6 to #10 bronze, long-shank, baitholder hook. You can fish either with a small lead shot worked off the bottom. The best set-up however, is to use a float about three feet above the insect and just let it drift along the bank in the current. Light 6 to 8 pound test line is recommended.

Conclusion

As you can see, there is a wide menu of natural baits that can be used to catch California bass. For some recreational bass fishermen who have only a few weekends a year to fish, live bait can sometimes maximize their chances for a productive day. But, please keep in mind that if you use bait, you can still release your fish. As was stated, some bass caught with natural bait will not survive being released unless they are hooked in the lip or around the mouth. But, gut-hooked fish can also be returned to the lake if you cut the line and leave the hook in the bass. The natural body enzymes will soon dissolve the embedded hook.

Avoid fishing bait in the Spring. Those big females need every chance we can give them to reproduce. You might also keep a camera handy, and begin to practice "catch'n release" while still having a nice record of your accomplishments for that day. This is a very delicate fishery here in California. Whether you are a diehard bait fisherman or a seasoned tournament pro, every effort must be made to manage these waters and preserve them for future generations of bass fishermen.

Bass Fishing Clubs and Pro Tournaments

Once you have started to do some serious bassin', you may decide that you want to learn even more about this sport. There is probably no better way to do this than to get together with other frustrated fanatics and compare notes. Bass fishing clubs and professional tournaments are good places to both commiserate with, and learn from fellow bassers.

Club Fishing

Most bass clubs in California are affiliated with one or more of the larger bass fishing organizations. They usually have one meeting and a separate tournament each month. Tournaments are almost always held on Saturdays as single day events. Occasionally clubs will schedule some two day contests ending on Sunday. These are usually held on lakes some distance from the club's home base.

Bass clubs vary in size from small groups of a dozen, or so anglers, to clubs boating rosters of over fifty members. Some clubs have the reputation of being "high profile" organizations, preferring to recruit only the most dedicated, "hard core" weekend bassers. The monthly tournament is often the focal point for this type of club where the members can put their skills to the test. Other bass clubs stress more camaraderie and put less emphasis on tournament fishing. Still, other clubs try to combine both fellowship and a high level of competition at their events, stressing a great deal of sharing of technical knowledge among members.

Most bass clubs try to recruit an equal number of boat-owning and non-owning members. If certain courtesies are followed, this has a very good reciprocal effect for both groups of anglers. The boater benefits from having the non-boater as a tournament partner because he then has someone with whom to split expenses. The costs of towing a bass boat, running it at high speeds, paying lake use permits, launching fees and possibly motel expenses adds up quickly. It definitely helps to split these with a fellow club member.

In turn, the non-boater (usually the less experienced angler) gets the chance to fish from a hi-tech bass fishing machine, piloted by a veteran basser. The bass fisherman who does not own a fancy bass boat may learn a lot from fishing club tournaments as a non-boater. The cost of such an on-the-water "seminar" is very cheap compared to what a veteran teaching pro would charge.

Most tournament rules at both the club and pro-circuit levels require that the boater and non-boater have an equal chance at fishing from the front of the bass boat. However, it is up to the non-boater to request the "front seat". This provision was made so that the partner in the back seat would not be relegated to fishing behind the boat owner all day. For some types of bassin' -- for example, crankin' and spinnerbait fishing -- the person in the back seat is often at a clear disadvantage. Many fish caught on these baits result from reaction strikes. Put simply, whoever casts first to that particular fish, will most likely be the one to get bit.

Thus, the unsuspecting novice sometimes can't figure out why the pro in the front is catching all the fish when they are using identical lures. This is known in tournament circles as being "backseated". A good basser with a sense of professional ethics will usually position his boat at such an angle so that both fishermen can have a good shot at the fish. Or, he may invite the back seat partner to stand up front near the bow and fish together with him. Many non-boaters will actually prefer to have the boat owner run the front and the trolling motor if these little courtesies are extended to them. They figure, "He's the veteran, I'll let him take me to the fish and show me what to throw." But by the rules, the non-boater clearly has the right to run the trolling motor and fish wherever he wishes for one half of the tournament day if he feels he is being backseated.

To select tournament fishing partners, all the names of the boat owners wishing to fish in the upcoming tournament are placed in one hat at the club meeting, and non-boaters in another. Each boater is then matched up by random drawing with a non-boater for the upcoming tournament. This is termed a "draw" tournament. Each entrant then fishes during the prescribed tournament hours to try to accumulate the largest five fish limit possible. Live wells in the front and rear of the boat keep each participant's catch segregated. Should you be so lucky as to catch five bass before weigh-in, you may then keep fishing and cull your smallest fish, always trying to keep the five largest. Winners are determined by whoever weighs in the heaviest string of fish. All bass are weighed and returned to the lake. Penalties are assessed (usually a two ounce deduction) for each dead fish brought to the scales. Stiffer sanctions are leveled against those weighing in a short, sub-legal bass.

You can find out about joining a bass club in a number of ways. A lot of club members hang out at the local bass pro shops to exchange tips and share in the latest gossip. Many of these fellows would be flattered if you asked them about their clubs. The shop owners also know about a lot of club activities in their area, and they will often be able to refer you in the right direction.

Fishing publications that cater to the serious recreational or professional bassin' man also publish club news and information on how to join. Most of these periodicals are also available at your local bass pro shops. Representatives of such Western organizations as WON Bass, West Coast Bass and the California Fishing Association, regularly advertise and set up display booths at outdoor recreational shows. They also have some of their teaching pros occasionally conduct bassin' seminars at certain locations. All of these people have knowledge of bass fishing clubs throughout the state. Most will try to give you some direction on how to contact the right kind of club for your needs that meets near you.

Most clubs have a trial initiation period, whereby they can check you out and you, them. Usually, they will invite you to fish as a guest in a few draw tournaments, and then each party can decide if this is the right club for the prospective new member.

Many of today's most successful touring pros started fishing for money and prizes at the club level. You can envision the clubs as fuctioning similarly to a semi-pro system or minor league farm team for the big time tournaments. If you think you might want to someday fish these more prestigious events, club level fishing can often serve as an excellent training course in preparing you for the "big time". Make no doubt about it, there are many, many club fishermen who could fish very competitively at the upper echelon of the pro ranks if they had the time or finances to afford these circuits.

Regardless of your level of expertise, or whether or not you have fished many club contests, you can still actually take a shot at certain high-level pro tournaments if you have the money and time to do so.

Fishing the Pro Circuits

The three major organizations staging draw-style tournaments in California are WON Bass, West Coast Bass, and Redman. Almost all of these groups put on an open circuit consisting of four or five different tournaments culminating in a qualifying fish-off for the grand prizes -- sometimes up to a six figure payout. These circuits are "open" to anyone that has the entry fee money to lay down.

As a matter of fact, many full-blown novices enter these tournaments not so much with the idea of doing well; but rather, in the hope of drawing a well-known touring pro as a boater-partner, figuring to get one of the finest on-the-water seminars possible under tournament conditions at a very reasonable price (the cost of the entry fee). The entry fees range from $50 up to thousands of dollars. The payouts increase in proportion to how steep the entry fees are and how large a field of anglers participates in the event.

The rules for sharing expenses and control of the trolling motor and front seat are the same as with most club tournaments. The length of the event can range anywhere from one day on up to a whole week with a given number of practice days included. The highest finishers after the circuit is finished then qualify to participate in even higher stakes, usually in the form of a fish-off.

Tournament promoters also stage other contests that are by invitation only, usually to the recognized top-ranked pros in the area or the nation. The various organizations devise ranking systems similar to those used in golf and tennis for the top-money winners in the sport.

Another form of tournament bassin' that is gaining in popularity is known as "team fishing". In this situation, you actually enter the tournament with a partner and you can fish an entire circuit of events together. There is no "draw" involved at all in this type of contest. The team gets to weigh in a combined total of ten bass. It doesn't matter who caught what or how many. You are working as a team and every effort must be made to help your partner catch fish.

Entry fees for these team contestants are usually very affordable, typically under 100 dollars per team. Naturally, the cash payouts are not as lucrative as the draw tournaments. But promoters do put up some excellent merchandise awards including fully-rigged bass boats for the winners of the most prestigious team tournaments.

Unlike other professional sports, there are only a handful of "pros" that actually make a living from tournament bassin'. Even at that, some of this income comes from product endoursements and personal appearances, not just from prize monies. This situation will likely improve as the sport becomes more sophisticated. Television revenues from large-scale tournaments along with corporate sponsorships will certainly add a lot of dollars to be shared among the pro ranks. Still, if you are serious about becoming a full-time bass pro, realize from the start that this is a very humbling sport. All too often, the guy that gets "hot" today and wins a few tournaments, slides from the top when the fish don't cooperate tomorrow. You have a better chance as a professional lineman controlling a shifty running back than you do as a bass pro trying to control the unpredictable little green fish!

California Bass Lakes

This section provides a rundown of 36 of the premier bass fishing lakes in California. Although there will always be oversights whenever attempts are made to compile such lists, I've tried to pick the lakes both in terms of their angler popularity and/or the good quality of their bass fishery. No doubt, there are arguably other lakes that could have been included if space had permitted. The information gathered comes from a variety of reliable sources. Much of the description is drawn from personal, firsthand experience. In addition, lake landing operators, professional guides and veteran Western pros have been consulted.

A map of each lake listed has been included. These are rough representations of the waters and are no substitute for good topographical maps of a particular lake. High quality topographical maps can be obtained at your local bass pro shop. In addition to the maps, I've included an overall description of the lake and the bass fishery, the best areas to fish, the right time to go, and finally, the tips and tricks that have produced at that lake. Additional current information can always be obtained from local lake authorities, tackle shops, marina operators and field reports found in any of the popular weekly outdoor tabloids.

Almanor	Folsom	Lower Otay
Amador	Havasu	Pardee
Berryessa	Henshaw	Perris
Cachuma	Hodges	Piru
Camanche	Indian Valley	San Antonio
Casitas	Irvine	San Vicente
Castaic	Isabella	Shasta
Clear	Lopez	Silverwood
Colorado R.(Blythe)	Morena	Skinner
Don Pedro	Nacimiento	Sutherland
El Capitan	New Melones	Trinity
Elsinore	Oroville	Vail

Also, there is a section on bass fishing in the California Delta. Although not actually a lake, it is a unique and productive bass fishery.

And finally, there is a chapter entitled "Special Bass Lakes" that profiles four more bass catching opportunities. It starts on Page 232.

. Big Bear   . Mead

. Davis   . Mojave

Lake Almanor (Map-p.126)

Located about 3 1/2 hours from Sacramento. and about 30 miles from the town of Quincy in Plumas County, Lake Almanor is one of the true jewels of the eastern Sierras. This lake is known for its tremendous chinook salmon, rainbow, and brown trout fishing. But, what a lot of anglers living out of the area fail to realize is that this lake offers fantastic smallmouth fishing!

Almanor is a relatively old lake by California standards, formed in 1914 when a power dam was built on the north fork of the Feather River, and adjacent meadow land was flooded to create the lake basin. The lake is a good size body of water, measuring 13 miles long and up to 6 miles wide. Almanor is a fairly shallow lake, with the deepest water rarely exceeding 60 feet. It is a beautiful alpine lake, offering a magnificent view of nearby volcanic Mount Lassen from practically any place on the water. There are numerous resorts, marinas, campgrounds, stores, and tackle shops that dot the lake, along with fleets of rental boats.

Areas to Fish: The smallmouth bass at Almanor are usually found in rocky areas or shallow flats where there are submerged rocks, tree stumps, or stick-ups. Along the dam and the eastern shore would be a good place to start looking for Almanor's bronzebacks. The mouth of Bailey Creek and the rocky points on the western side of the lake are also popular smallmouth haunts.

The fish will move up into the shallower, 4 to 12 foot water in the early morning and evening, then retreat to the 15 to 30 foot depths during the day.

Best Times: Smallmouth fishing is best in the late Spring through the Summer months at Almanor. The fish are not particularly active when the water temperature drops considerably in the Winter. Night fishing is also allowed on this lake, and can be particularly productive during those "dog days" of Summer.

Tips and Tricks: The smallmouths at Almanor average from about 1 1/4 to 2 1/4 pounds. A 5 pound fish would be considered a real trophy. What they lack in size, they make up with their aggressiveness. The bronzebacks here feed on natural forage baits found in the lake: crawdads, and a small anchovy-like, baitfish known as the pond smelt. Lures resembling either of these baits can be exceptionally effective.

Small pig'n jig combinations with either #101 or #11 pork trailers will work. Black and brown shades are best overall, but also try copper or dark brown jigs during the Spring spawning period. A local favorite is the Fish Hawk jig sold at bait shops on the lake. Crawdad-pattern crankbaits, especially the Rapala Shad and Fat Rap series are also productive. Another hot ticket is custom, hand-poured plastic worms four inches long in typical earth tone patterns. Use 1/8 ounce P-heads and split-shot rigs with these small baits.

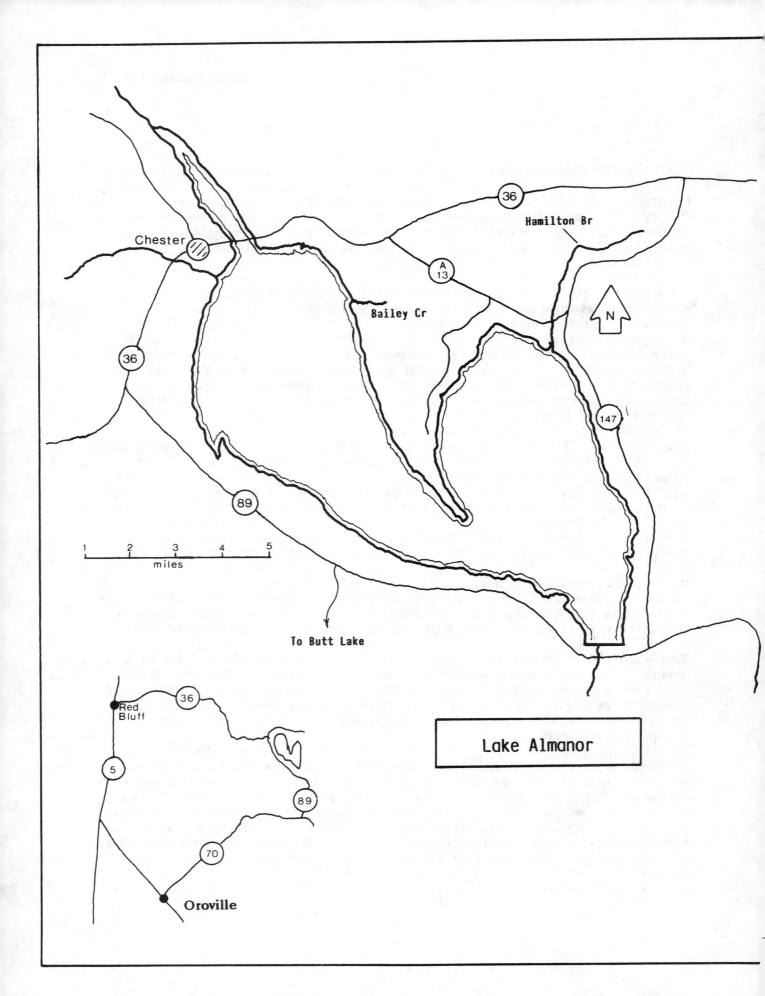

36

Hamilton Br

Chester

A
13

Bailey Cr

N

36

147

89

1 2 3 4 5
miles

To Butt Lake

Lake Almanor

36
Red
Bluff

5

89

70

Oroville

Also, try two other subtle presentations on Almanor's bronzebacks. Sometimes a white or yellow crappie jig fished behind a float can be very deadly. Many bank fishermen will use this method quite effectively on these high elevation smallmouths. Similarly, small P-heads or darters teamed with smoke or watermelon-colored grubs will catch these fish as they retreat midday to deeper water.

For surface activity, either in the morning, at sunset, or at night, use a lure that most closely resembles the pond smelt. A smaller #7-S or #9-S floating Rapala minnow twitched, jerked, or ripped should fit the bill.

Almanor can also be a good lake for the bait fisherman, and especially those fishing from the shore. Crawdads caught from the lake along with a fly-lined night crawler will always tally up a significant share of bronzebacks. Crickets fished below a float, either still fishing or drifting, can also drive the smallmouths into a frenzy but be prepared for a lot of small fish. Use light, 6 to 8 pound test lines and work the bait along the rocky banks for your best chances to catch these scrappy fighters.

Lake Amador (Map - p.128)

Amador Lake has a tremendous array of facilities and services to offer the bass fisherman and his family. Excellent camp sites, R.V. hookups, bass boat rentals, dock tie-ups, a full-service marina, tackle shop, hot showers, and guide services are just some of the amenities you will find at this Northern California lake. In addition, there is no water skiing on this lake.

To get to Amador, drive about 40 mies northeast of Stockton. Take Highway 88 north and turn off on Jackson Valley Road. The lake usually opens January 31st and closes the Sunday after Thanksgiving.

Amador is a very small lake, encompassing only 400 surface acres and a little over 13 miles of shoreline. Don't be deceived by the size of this lake, for as the saying goes, sometimes good things come in small packages! Amador proves this adage to be true as it is a genuine trophy bass fishery for this part of the state.

Florida-strain largemouths were stocked initially at Amador in 1970 then again in 1973. From this initial plant, a fairly nice hybrid population has emerged. Today, there are quite a few fish caught over 6 pounds and a number brought to the scales topping the 10 pound mark. Bass over 15 pounds have already been caught at Amador, and there is the possibility that bigger fish are yet to come.

Areas to Fish: Amador is layed out with a series of long creek arms channeling off from the main lake. The lake is supplied only by runoff water and is not a particularly deep lake. The water typically gets fairly cold in Winter, and quite warm in Summer. The best areas to fish are the Jackson and Rock Creek

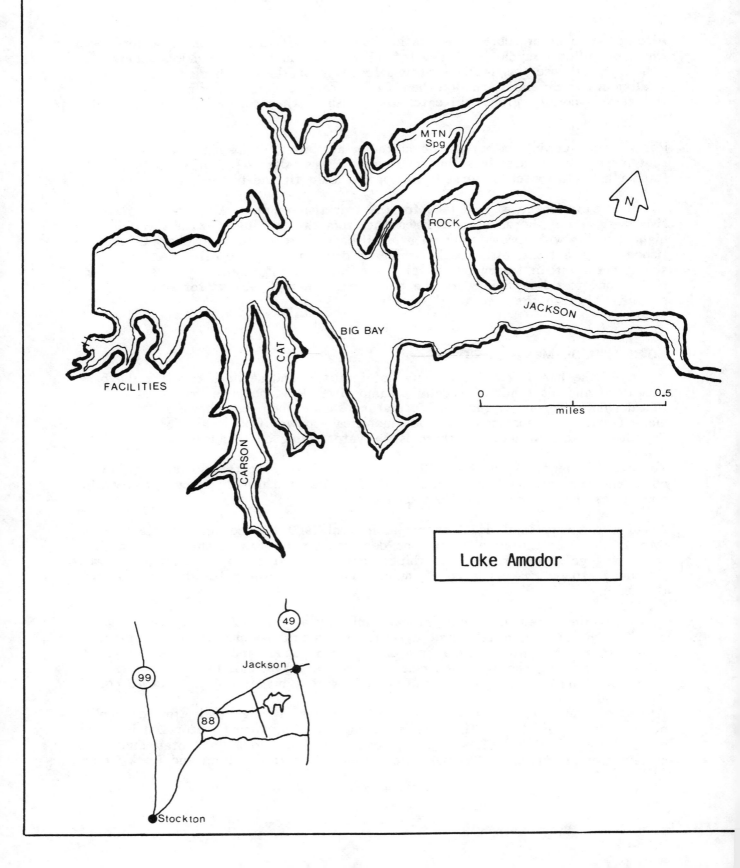

MTN Spg

ROCK

JACKSON

BIG BAY

CAT

FACILITIES

CARSON

0   0.5
              miles

Lake Amador

99   49

Jackson

88

Stockton

arms. The bigger trophy fish seem to come mostly from the Jackson Creek area in the Spring. The shoreline drops off rather quickly. Fish these drop offs in about 10 to 15 feet of water. Work the backs of coves, and along and across the major points. There is a lot of brushy structure along with occasional deadfall.

Best Times: The Spring is without question the best time to fish bass at Amador, especially if you are looking for a wall-hanger fish. Locals like to fish the lake when the water is fairly clean with minimal spillage draining in from rain and runoff. The spawning period lasts for about six weeks and accounts for a lot of the trophy-sized bass.

Amador offers a very unique opportunity not found on many California lakes -- night bass fishing. In the late Spring, all the way through July and August, the bass will move up into shallow water, sometimes only two feet deep at night. The key is to time your trip to correspond with a full moon. This is when the Amador bass really turn on. The bass bite otherwise is fairly typical -- early morning, then at sunset. During the midday period, the action is pretty slow. Thus, the full moon phase adds an extra bonus period to this fishery.

Tips and Tricks: If you manage to take advantage of Amador's night bite, bring an assortment of surface plugs. Floating Rapalas and Rebels twitched and jerked will work. Small prop baits such as the Heddon Tiny Torpedo in clear, frog, or white/red combinations have been productive, along with the old standby, the Arbogast Hula Popper. Plastic worms and pig'n jig combinations in dark patterns will also get bit when the bass move up shallow at night.

During the day, the bass seem to be oriented primarily to bottom-bouncing baits. The pig'n jig accounts for some nice trophy fish, using standard black, brown, and purple #11 Pork Frogs and matching live rubber skirts. Plastic worms fished Texas-style in black, purple and dark motor oil green are local favorites. During the Spring, be sure to try some additional surface action in the early morning in the backs of coves.

Bait fishermen may also find Amador to their liking. Many fish over 10 pounds have been caught by anglers walking the banks. Fly-line a live night crawler threaded on a #6 baitholder hook for the best bait combination.

Lake Berryessa (Map - p.130)

This is one of California's largest lakes, spanning a whopping 20,000 surface acres when it is full. Berryessa is nestled between Sacramento and San Francisco, twenty miles from the picturesque Napa Valley wine country. The lake is over 25 miles long, up to 3 miles wide, and drops to 275 feet at its deepest spot. The shoreline is dotted with numerous marinas, resorts, and all the facilities the bassin' man could possibly require.

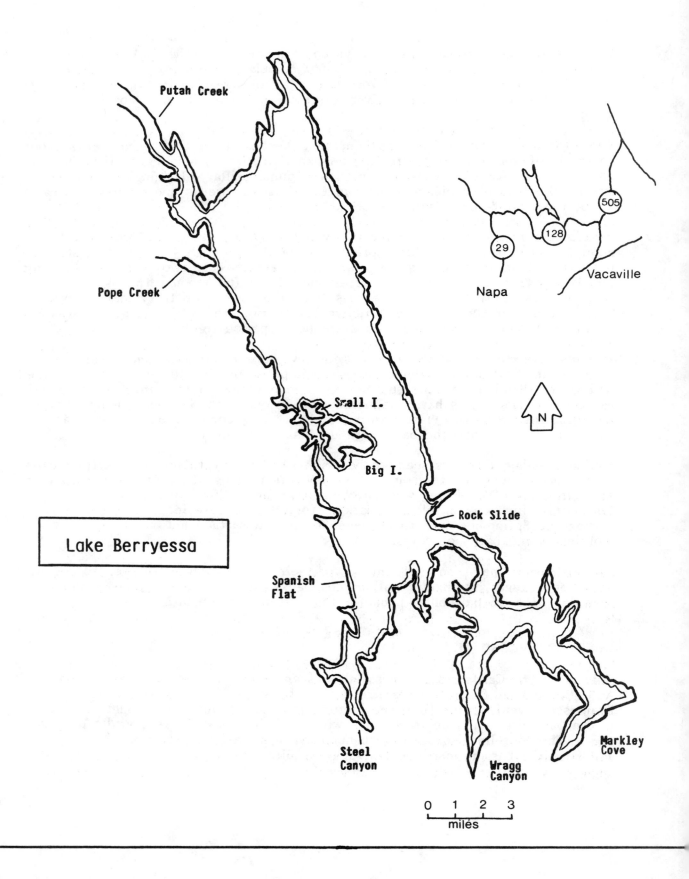

Putah Creek

Pope Creek

Small I.

Big I.

Rock Slide

Lake Berryessa

Spanish
Flat

Steel
Canyon

Wragg
Canyon

Markley
Cove

Napa

Vacaville

29

128

505

N

0   1   2   3
miles

Berryessa produces about an equal catch of northern-strain largemouths and smallmouth bass. There are also a few jumbo-sized Floridas cruising around and a small minority of Alabama spotted bass. The smallmouths average about 1 1/2 to 3 pounds, while largemouths over 10 pounds have been caught.

Areas to Fish: The lake has recently received a good supply of water from past Winters and is close to full capacity. The smallmouths prefer rocky areas -- boulders, long points and gravel bottoms, such as those found in the Pope Creek arm of the lake. The island near Spanish Flat and the rock slide on the east side of the lake near Skier's Cove also have historically been good smallmouth areas. The largemouths are less selective and can be found in a variety of brushy areas around the lake. There have been a lot of grassy meadows flooded with the recent increase in water level, and these flats will hold largemouths from Spring through Fall. Concentrate on fishing the smallmouths in rocky areas in 8 to 10 feet of water, the largemouths in brush-lined banks and flats in 3 to 8 foot depths.

Best Times: Mid-Spring and Fall months seem to be the best times to take advantage of Berryessa's bass fishery. Look for the bronzebacks to move up shallow in the early Spring sometimes feeding around the smallest little trickle streams that empty into the lake. By later Spring, these fish, along with the largemouths, will move into the larger creek arms such as Putah Creek to spawn. You might try to wade or tube fish in some of these shallow areas in the coves and on the flats. This is not done too often here and could be very productive for the basser otherwise stuck on the bank.

Tips and Tricks: The Berryessa bass populations feed on crawdads and threadfin shad. Occasionally, you can see large schools of shad boiling to the surface with sea gulls picking at the baitfish. Crankbaits in siver foil finish and Tennessee shad patterns work well, along with the popular models of crawdad-colored plugs. You might also keep a few chartreuse-colored cranks handy for this bass population.

Surface action can be good in the Spring, both late and early in the day. A #11-S floating Rapala fished on a twitch or jerk retrieve will produce. Other popular surface baits are the Arbogast Hula Popper and the Smithwick Devil's Horse. Use light colors such as yellow or coach dog in the morning then switch to dark patterns like frog or solid black in the evenings.

Plastic worms, particularly in brown or purple tones, also catch their share of fish. In addition, don't overlook the flip bite in the willows along the banks. A 3/8 to 1/2 ounce pig'n jig of brown, purple, or black mixes will work. Spinnerbaits in white or chartreuse should also be tried.

The bait fishing at Berryessa can be outstanding. Crawdads and nightcrawlers will usually be a good bet for both largemouth and smallmouth bass. A lot of anglers like to fish small shiner minnows on a #6 baitholder hook for trout and panfish. Fished behind a float drifting or with a small split shot fly-lined, these minnows also put a lot of nice-sized bass on the stringer. This method can be very productive during the heat of the Summer at Berryessa.

Lake Cachuma (Map – p.133)

For sheer scenic beauty it's hard to beat the mountainous setting of Lake Cachuma. Located 25 miles north of Santa Barbara, it is over 7 miles long. It has over 3200 surface acreas and a lot of accessible shoreline. Because it is a reservoir for drinking water, no bodily contact with the water is allowed at this lake. It can be pretty much a year 'round bass fishery. There are both northern strain largemouths and smallmouths in Cachuma, although a strong majority of the catch are northerns. Northerns over 10 pounds have occassionally been caught, usually on live crawdads. The lake has great facilities, extensive campsites, boat rentals and so forth.

Areas to Fish: The coves at Cachuma always seem to hold some fish. Cachuma Bay and Santa Cruz Bay are the two most popular. Usually during the Spring, one or the other of these coves is put off limits to be used as a spawning sanctuary. These coves are thus opened up on alternate years during the Spring. Both coves have pretty good moss and aquatic plant growth during the Summer and Fall. Bass will lay under and along side the vegetation. Some expert casting is needed to fish the little pot holes in the weeds. The cliff area near the mouth of Johnson Bay is also productive for bass holding deep and comprises a good crankbait spot. Similarly, to the right of the landing in Martini Bay, you will find numerous submerged boulders that provide cover for both northerns and bronzebacks. Finally, down by the narrows and Arrowhead Island to the east, there are a lot of rocks and some deep drop-offs. These can serve as good smallmouth cover.

Best Times: Cachuma can be productive year round. Summer is toughest with the heat and increased boater traffic. Spring is fairly good and there is usually a pretty prolific bite in the Fall. Bass can also be taken here in the dead cold of Winter, particularly with deepwater techniques.

Tips and Tricks: Cachuma is one of the best jig fishing bass lakes in California. The pig'n jig consistently produces results at this lake. Browns and purples are the preferred colors. Without fail, also use the brown and purple vinyl skirted Super Float jig here. This bait has been a killer on both smallmouths and northerns for many years, especially in cold water.

Plastic worms in 6 inch lengths fished Texas-style will also take fish. As with jigs, purples and browns match well with the native crawdad forage. Other good color schemes are smoke/goldflake, smoke sparkle/copper flake, and salt'n pepper. If you see a lot of bass fry, throw the Heddon Zara Spook in baby bass finish. This bigger top-water bait also works at Cachuma. Brown or white skirted buzzbaits are definitely effective fished aggressively into the weeds

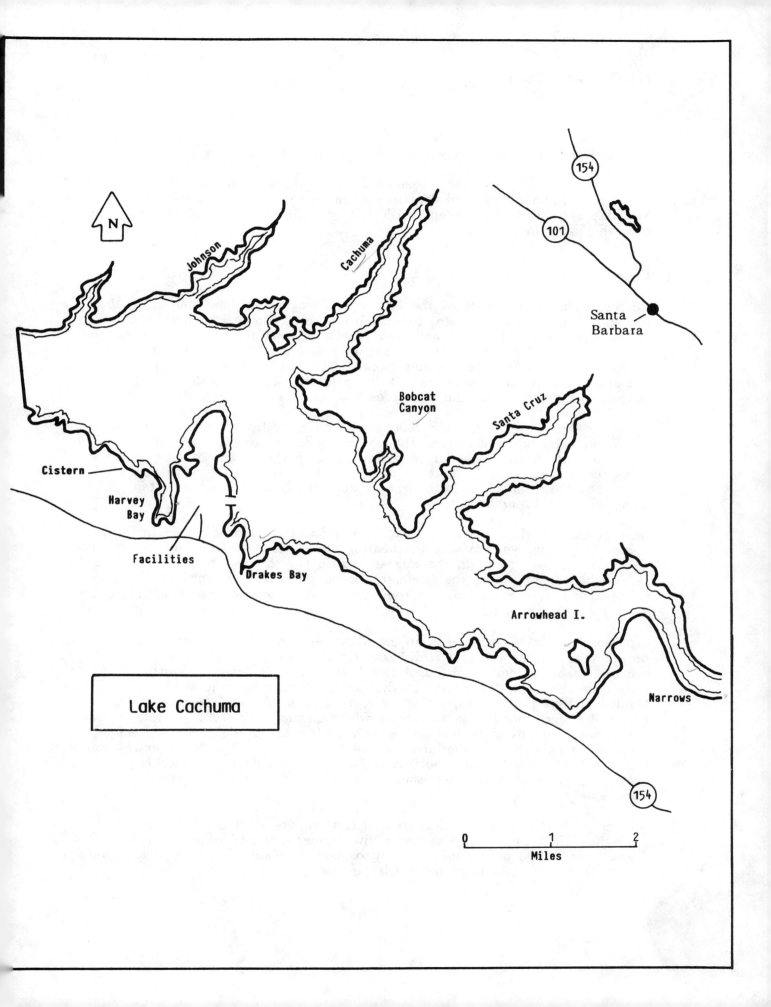

N

Johnson

Cachuma

154

101

Santa
Barbara

Bobcat
Canyon

Santa Cruz

Cistern

Harvey
Bay

Facilities

Drakes Bay

Arrowhead I.

Narrows

154

Lake Cachuma

0   1   2
        Miles

and stickups found on the backs of coves at this lake.

Bait fishermen will have their best chances fly-lining a live nightcrawler on 6 pound monofilament. Crawdads also account for some of the larger Cachuma bass. But, day after day, more keeper fish will be nailed with 'crawlers, especially with the light line.

Camanche Lake(Map - p.135)

Resting right in the heart of the Mother Lode country, Camanche is another one of those modernized complete, full-facility lakes. Along with the marinas, tackle shops, general stores, and boat rentals, a separate concession even has tennis courts and horses for rent. The lake is open all year long and water skiing is heavy during the summer months. Camanche provides a lot of recreational opportunities for people living in the San Francisco Bay and Sacramento areas. The lake is just east of Lodi, off State Highway 12.

Areas to Fish: There are over 7600 acres and 60 miles of shoreline to fish on this lake. The north shore and the northeast banks near China gulch are good spots to try. There are a lot of grassy areas in the lake and largemouths and smallmouths can be found here. Camanche also has a small population of Alabama spots, and they can often be caught in the slightly deeper water often schooled along with the bronzebacks.

Best Times: April and May are excellent months to fish bass at Camanche. School is not out yet, so vacation boating traffic is reduced. This is also the time for the bass to begin the migration into the shallows to spawn. There are fish to be caught during the Summer, though the bite is somewhat tougher. By October and November, look for the bass to be more cooperative until the cold, Winter weather sets in.

Tips and Tricks: Camanche is an excellent lake for plastic worm fishing. Most of the regulars use the standard Texas rig on 8 to 12 pound lines. Split-shottin' hasn't gained much popularity here, but it is certainly worth a try. It is best to match the worms to the dominant crawdad coloration. A red with black bloodline pattern is popular. Mr. Twister makes their 6 inch straight and curl-tail Phenom models in this color which should work well. Other, regional, hand-poured brands in both 4 and 6 inch models are available in this unique red/black combination. Similarly, any of the commercial or hand-poured worms in crawdad tone browns will be effective here. Brown/black, brown/blue, brown/orange, rootbeer, brown/smoke, and brown/shad are good colors for Camanche.

Staying with the crawdad orientation that is so prevalent at this lake, brown pig'n jigs are very good. Use brown live rubber matched with brown #11 pork frogs. Brown and purple mixes are also good jig choices. In the colder water, switch to solid brown vinyl skirts with matching frogs. Don't overlook shad-

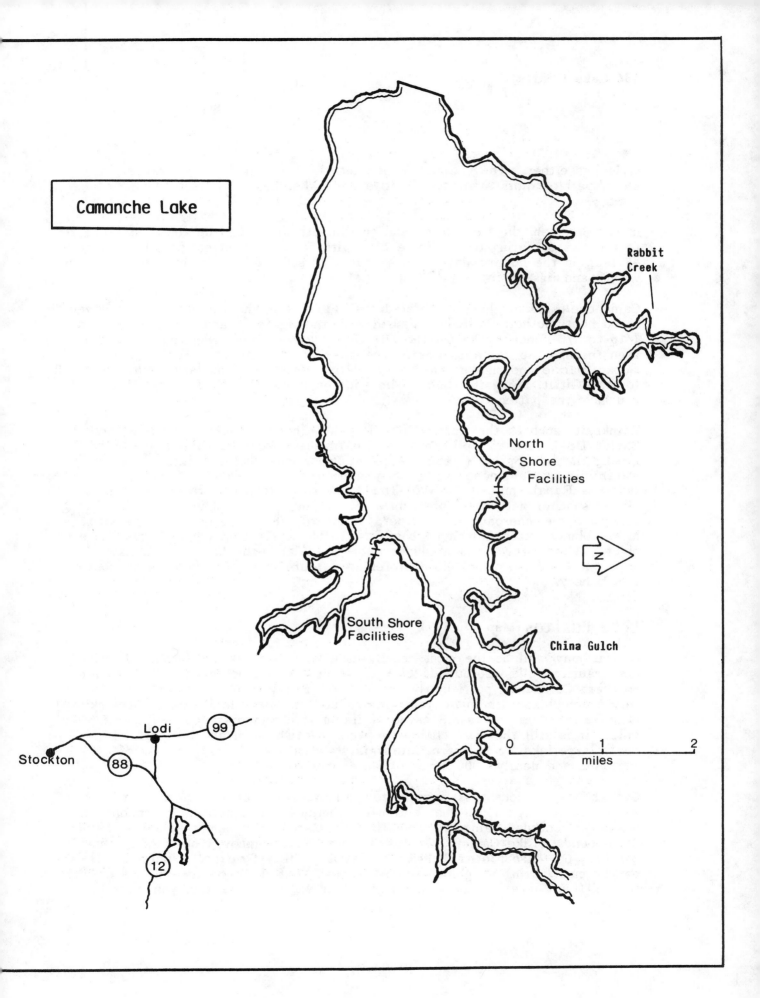

Camanche Lake

Rabbit
Creek

North
Shore
Facilities

South Shore
Facilities

China Gulch

N

Lodi
99
Stockton
88
12

0   1   2
                miles

style jigs either. The Garland Spider and the Haddock Kreepy Krawler in clear/sparkle colors are very effective here when the bass start feeding on shad.

In the Summer, the bass, large and smallmouth alike, can be found in 17 to 20 feet of water during parts of the day, with some fish retreating all the way to 45 feet on the hottest days. These bass can still be caught, but stay with the worms and jigs to fish them deep.

Camanche's bassers have discovered the "Fat Gitzit Phenomena" that has swept throughout Southern California. Fished with the lighter 6 and 8 pound lines and 1/16 to 1/8 ounce jig heads, the Fat Gitzit works well during the Spring and even through the warm Summer. The most popular colors used here are smoke/sparkle and smoke/blue flake. Both bronzebacks and largemouths will fall for the Gitzit. Fish this bait shallow in the grass or even down to 45 feet if you have the patience.

Crankbaits such as the Rattle Trap, Rapala Fat Rap, Bomber Model A, and the Bagley DB-II in shad, foil, and crawdad finishes also take their share of bass. During the late Spring through the Fall, you might also luck into a good top-water bite at Camanche in the early morning or late evening. The locals like to twitch a Rapala minnow or walk-the-dog with a Heddon Zara Spook in silver glitter shad or with the more subtle Storm Chug Bug in phantom black. Don't forget your spinnerbaits here either. Standard 3/8 to 1/2 ounce white with nickel blades catch Camanche bass. Bait chuckers should try the usual faire of nightcrawlers, crawdads and shiner minnows. Camanche has a solid bass population and more and more professional tournaments are being scheduled for this fishery.

Lake Casitas (Map - p.137)

Casitas may well be the most heavily-used lake in all of California. Resting in the beautiful hills just outside of Ojai, Casitas draws boaters from all over Southern California, particularly Los Angeles and Ventura Counties. It is a very scenic lake with many campgrounds and excellent facilities. Water skiing is not allowed at Casitas. Because of its short distance from Los Angeles (78 miles) it is still the first choice for weekend fishermen and campers. It is a fairly large lake by Southern California standards with over 30 miles of shoreline and nearly 3000 acres of water when it is filled.

Casitas lures serious bass anglers from all over the world in quest of that world record largemouth that authorities believe swims here. The second largest bass ever recorded came from this lake in March 1980, and weighed an astounding 21:3 pounds! Like Castaic, Casitas has a thriving rainbow trout fishery that can bulk up these Florida hybrids in just a matter of years. Numerous fish are caught each Spring weighing over 10 pounds. But don't be fooled, this can be a very difficult lake to fish with its gin clear water. Here too, you must be

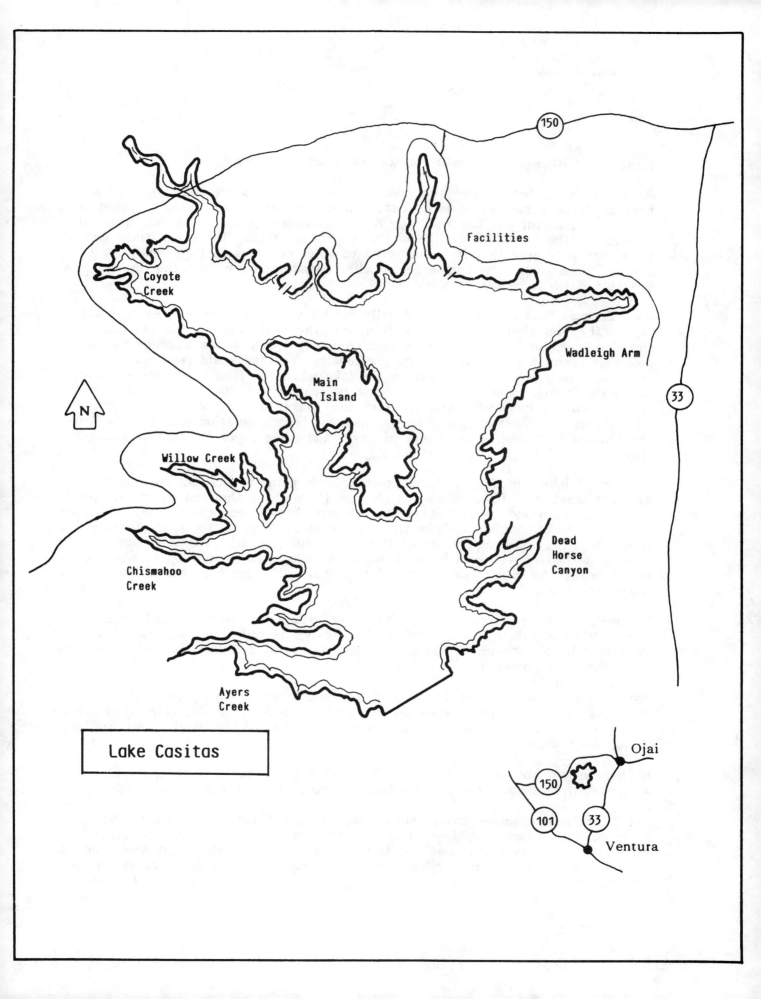

proficient with light line, subtle baits and a lot of finesse.

Areas to Fish: Just outside the main launch ramp there are some rock piles that have produced a number of large fish.   These will show up on your electronics as prominent structures.   The Wadleigh Arm is always a good bet in the Spring in addition to the Deep Cat and Dead Horse Canyon areas.   The main island can often be a very good spot, but it is subjected to a lot of pressure from bass, trout and cat fishermen.   The submerged smaller islands and the buoy line by the dam are also viable locations to work.

Best Times: Casitas is an exceptionally good late Winter and very early Spring lake.   The best times begin in the first few weeks of February all the way to the first week of April.   The lake is particularly tough in the Summer and then picks up again in late Fall.   If you are looking for that world record fish, then without question, try to get to the lake when the first warm rains fall in the early Spring.   The rain creates a lot of feeding activity and the big females will momentarily move up from deep water to feed in the shallower points and ledges.   During the Spring spawn, Casitas' bass population will migrate into the shallow flats and in the backs of coves and some super red hot days are in store!

Tips and Tricks: In the Spring, split-shottin' is going to account for the greatest number of fish.   Work the shallow flats where the bass are feeding on crawdads.   Four inch worms in rootbeer brown, brown/neon green, brown/neon blue, purple/red flake, and smoke/blue flake are popular patterns for split-shotters. When the wind comes up, many of the locals will just drift the split-shot rig behind the boat.   A 4 inch brown/black Super Float worm split up to the sex collar, makes for a very seductive offering that will float high above the submerged brush.

Be ready to throw on big bass crashing the surface for shad or small trout. Larger #7-S Rapala Fat Raps and Bagley DB-II's in foil finish are solid choices. Then switch to a #5 or #7 Rapala Fat Rap in crawdad finish and crank the flats when the wind comes up.

Jigs are also good lures at Casitas.   Purple and brown pig'n jig combos work well, but use vinyl skirts instead of live rubber.   Also, vary this combination with a brown or purple Super Float worm trailer behind the vinyl.   This has been a well-kept secret here.

If there is any top-water activity to be found, use either a floating Rapala or a silver glitter shad Zara Spook in the flats and in the backs of coves.

Finally, if you're set on hawg hunting, nightcrawlers and live crawdads are going to catch many trophy-sized bass at Casitas each Spring.   In this clear water, you will need light line and lots of patience.   The Deep Cat area, the Wadleigh Arm and the rock piles near the launch area are popular spots for live bait fishing.

Castaic Lake (Map - P.140)

This is one of the most popular recreational lakes in the state. Located 45 miles north of metropolitan Los Angeles, Castaic plays host to hordes of water skiers, pleasure boaters and of course, bass fishermen coming from all over Southern California.

Castaic is actually divided into two bodies of water: the main lake and the after bay. The main lake is about 2500 acreas divided into a ski and a fishing arm. Fishing is permitted in both arms, but water skiing is allowed only in the designated ski area. The afterbay is only 180 acres, with no powerboats allowed. You can launch a bass boat in the afterbay, but you can only use your electric trolling motor.

The lake has numerous facilities including camp grounds, grocery stores and tackle shops, marinas and snack bars. The launching ramps are excellent and can accommodate many boats at one time on the main lake. However, a word of caution about Castaic. The winds here can be very treacherous. Sometimes, the lake ranger will close the lake to boat launching early in the morning due to weather reports of impending wind. Other times, the patrol boat will ask boaters to leave the lake quickly as the afternoon winds become too strong. The winds can generate dangerous wave action and difficult conditions in which to put your boat back on the trailer.

When the weather permits, this can be an outstanding bass lake, populated primarily by Florida hybrids. Many bass in double figures are caught here each year with fish up to 18 pounds the current record. Because the lake is heavily stocked with rainbow trout, there has been some speculation that a potential trout-eating, world record bass over 22 pounds may be lurking at Castaic.

Areas to Fish: Depending upon fluctuations in water level, Castaic sometimes has excellent shoreline brush, other times it's a lot of rocky banks. The bass will hang around these steeper rocky walls, particularly those in the water ski arm in the early morning and later afternoons. The longer, rocky points and ledges in the fishing arm seem to always hold some fish, along with the buoyline area at the far end of the ski arm. During the colder weather months, the bass will frequently move up from deep water during the day, particularly in the fishing arm. Look for the shallow, sloping, red clay banks to retain radiant heat longer and thus, providing a place for some crawdad activity. One trick is to anchor your boat tight to the bank, cast out and fish uphill with a jig or a worm. The banks of coves traditionally are good during the Spring spawn on this lake.

Best Times: Castaic is remarkably a good lake during the late Fall and Winter, and of course, during the Spring. This water is subject to tremendous pressure throughout the Summer from all the pleasure boaters, skiers and recreational fishermen. Fish can be caught during the Summer months, but you often have to

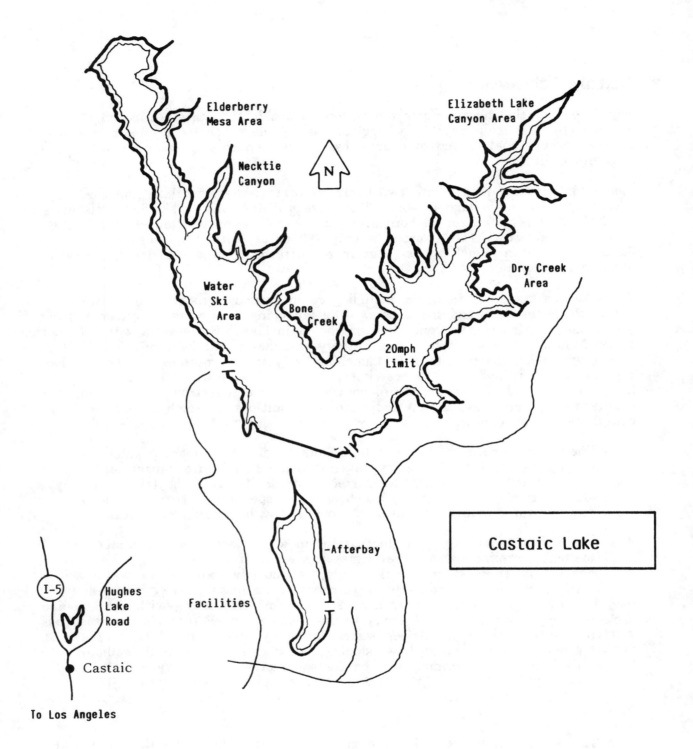

Elderberry
Mesa Area

Elizabeth Lake
Canyon Area

Necktie
Canyon

N

Water
Ski
Area

Bone
Creek

Dry Creek
Area

20mph
Limit

Castaic Lake

-Afterbay

I-5

Hughes
Lake
Road

Facilities

Castaic

To Los Angeles

really fight for space. Save Castiac for the colder months when other lakes have shut down.

Tips and Tricks: Because of the heavy lake usage, you must really become an expert with the subtle baits at Castaic if you want to catch fish. Probably the best method is split-shottin' with 6 pound line and small, custom, hand-poured worms. Four inch worms in cinnamon/blue, black/shad belly , brown/crawdad belly, and smoke sparkle/black flake will get bit with a split shot rig. Be prepared to fish these deep -- up to 70 feet! Sometimes it is even better to throw a two-inch hand-poured worm or a Reaper in smoke sparkle patterns. P-heads and darters will also take fish with small worm trailers in earth tone colors or with salt'n pepper grubs. Similarly, Fat Gitzits in smoke/sparkle and Haddock Kreepy Krawlers in the same shades are effective when the bass follow the schools of shad into deep water.

Doodlin' off the underwater ledges and spoonin' along the points are excellent methods during the Winter months. Four inch hand-poured worms in browns, purples and shad tones in either paddle or curl-tail models are the ticket. For spoons, the Hopkins #075 in chrome, Kastmasters in 1/2 ounce silver, and Haddock Structure Spoons in blue anchovy are proven winners.

Crankbaits such as Rapala Fat Raps and Bagley's DB-II in shad and crawdad finish account for quite a few Castaic bass along with a #11 or #13-S Rapala minnow ripped along the shoreline.

Bait fishermen would do best working rocky points and sloping banks with live nightcrawlers, again, fished with light 6 pound monofilament.

Clear Lake (Map - p.143)

Stretching out with over 100 miles of shoreline, Clear Lake is the largest natural lake in California. Located three hours north of San Francisco, Clear offers a full-service range of accomodations from campsites, marinas, tackle shops, markets and over 240 resorts. It also offers one of the finest bass fisheries in the state.

Clear is not a very deep lake, with lots of shallow, rocky, and brushy banks, extensive tule growth and many grassy areas. Some pro bassers compare this terrain with that found on typical lakes in the South. The lake is open all year long and 24 hours a day. It has been only recently that bass fishermen have taken advantage of these hours, with some night tournaments producing spectacular results during a summer full moon. For the most part however, nighttime bassin' has been overlooked here.

Many large-scale pro-tournaments are annually scheduled at Clear because of its fertile waters. The bass are primarily northerns, but more and more lunker-class Floridas are showing up at the scales. The lake record is over 14 pounds, but commercial rough-fish fishermen have found Floridas topping the 17 pound mark in their nets.

Areas to Fish: Locals feel the Horseshoe Bend and State Park areas are by far the best spots when the bass move in to spawn.   Konocti Bay, Soda Bay, the Redman Slough and County Park are also considered prime bass hangouts.   During the summer, locals crank the creek channel and the drop-offs in the Narrows and Horseshoe Bend areas.

Best Times: The spawning period at Clear usually occurs from the first of March, with the fish orienting toward the tules and other shallow banks all the way through mid-June.   This is the best time at Clear.   However, locals persist in bringing in nice stringers in the heat of Summer and in the Fall when a lot of other fishermen have given up on the lake.

Tips and Tricks: The bigger fish from Clear have traditionally been taken on plastic worms fished Texas-style.   Lake regulars keep their worm selection pretty simple here -- blacks and purples in 4 and 6 inch lengths.   Occasionally, a little silver or red flake included with these two colors adds a little spice to the bait.   Flippin' the tules also produces a good share of fish.   Pig'n jig combinations in the basic black, brown, or purple mixes will work. Interestingly, you might also try to flip a spinnerbait into these tule banks when the water is very stained.   A little extra "flash" can sometimes bring Clear's largemouths crashing out of the tules.

During the Fall, a surface film of algae scum can cover a lot of shallow banks at this lake.   Bass will still be resting under this film, looking for shade. The hot tip is to throw a buzzbait right into the thickest scum and be prepared for a vicious strike.   Similarly, work white or chartreuse buzzbaits during the midday Summer heat.   This has been a very effective warm weather method.

Clear Lake bass also seem to be rather sentimental in their top-water preferences.   "Oldies but Goodies" like the Arbogast Hula Popper and Jitterbug, Creek Chub Injured Minnow, Smithwick Devil's Horse, and floating Rapalas are on the "can't miss" list.

Because of the heavy concentration of crawdads in the lake, crankin' is also a worthwhile technique to try.   Rapala crawdad-colored Fat Raps in #5 and #7 sizes, along with the Rebel Deep Wee-R, Bomber Model-A, and broken back Rebel in the same finish are favored.   A bluegill-colored crankbait with a little blue/green shading is also a good bet.

Baitfishing on this shallow lake can also be very productive.   Crawdads and nightcrawlers are first on the menu.   Shiners fished behind a float will also catch fish.   A natural forage fish in Clear is the silverside smelt.   Bass will gorge themselves on this bait.   They can be netted from the lake, but are overall, a very fragile bait to fish live.   If kept with proper aeration, try one with a small #6 baitholder hook fished underneath a bobber.

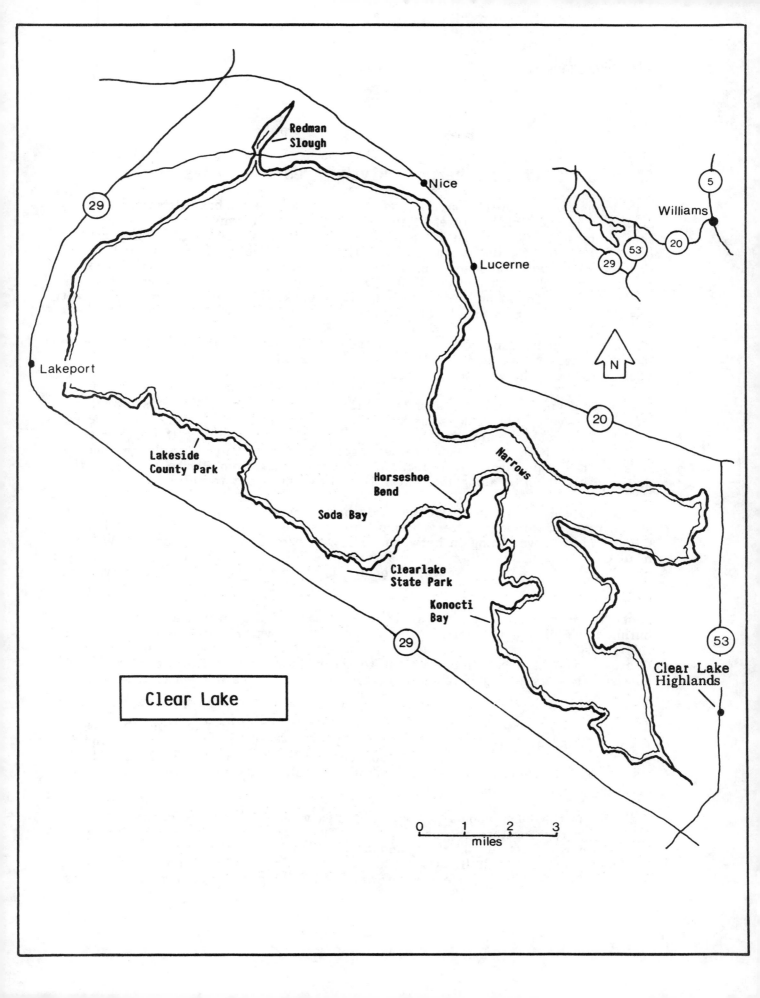

Colorado River (Palo Verde - Blythe Area) Map - p.145

This immense waterway comprises one of the most unique bass fisheries found anywhere in the Golden State. Situated along the California border at the southernmost portion of the state, this section of the Colorado River is also one of the most fertile bassin' spots in California. The river snakes for endless miles, with the banks lined sometimes with massive tule growth, other times with thick brush and deadfall. Occasionally, there will be steep canyon walls to throw to, along with hidden lakes or backwater pockets known as "pretty water", plus numerous small coves off the main river channel.

Navigation can be dangerous along this stretch of the Colorado River. There are many sandbars to watch for, plus the current can always be a factor in setting your boat the right way for fishing.

The most popular facility is a small rustic landing, known as Walter's Camp. Here you have a fuel dock, some primitive campsites, a small store and a decent launch ramp. Make sure you have all your tackle when you get there. Walter's is technically part of the Palo Verde Lagoon, a long 15 mile plus slough that runs off the main river. It is located almost an hour from Blythe to the north and is over 40 miles along the water from Lake Martinez to the south.

Areas to Fish: You have basically two choices here. First, you can stay in the slough and fish around Walter's Camp, motor some 10 miles north to Mitchell's Camp and fish everything in between. Or, you can veer to the right of Walter's, head east and quickly move into the main river channel. Now you have the choice of fishing either north or south, depending upon how many miles of river you want to run.

Best Times: Walter's and the areas on this part of the river are excellent during the Fall and the early Spring. Because the water does not get that cold this far south, a very decent bite can also materialize as early as January or February when the bass root in tight to the shallow cover. However, for consistently outstanding catches of northern bass, it is hard to beat this area in the Fall.

Tips and Tricks: So many serious bassers make the 5 hour trip from the Los Angeles area to Walter's Camp for one primary reason: it is an absolute flippin' paradise! The water rarely gets much deeper than 7 to 8 feet in the slough itself. The combination of thick deadfall and tule banks make for endless miles of potentially good flippin' water.

Pig'n jig is the most popular setup. Fish heavy duty 1/2 to 5/8 ounce live rubber jigs to penetrate the dense brush. There are many 5 to 8 pound class bass along this part of the river, and they typically lay in very tight, deep in the center of the deadfall. Use brown or black jigs tipped with #11 or #1 Pork Frogs. Black and brown are the favorite colors for pork. But also, try a black

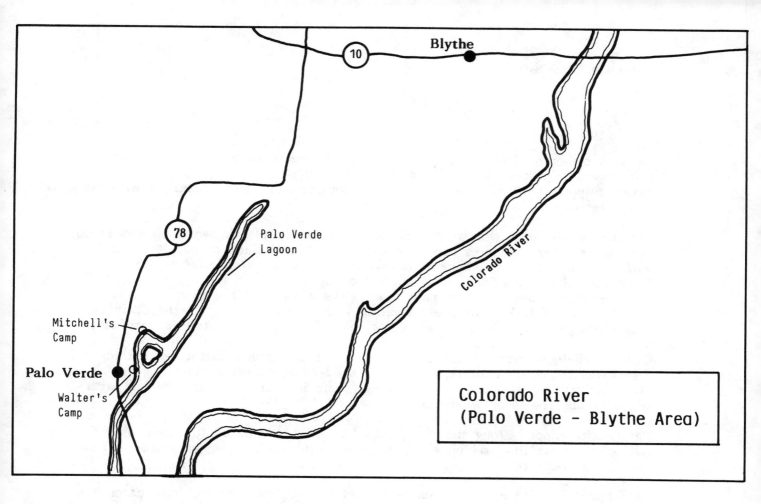

Blythe

10

78

Palo Verde
Lagoon

Colorado River

Mitchell's
Camp

Palo Verde

Walter's
Camp

Colorado River
(Palo Verde - Blythe Area)

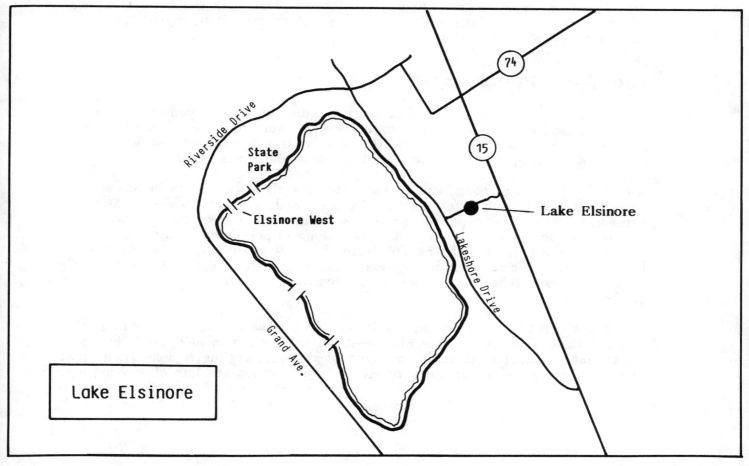

74

Riverside Drive

State
Park

15

Elsinore West

Lake Elsinore

Lakeshore Drive

Grand Ave.

Lake Elsinore

jig with either a black/chartreuse or solid chartreuse pork chunk when the water is exceptionally stained. A 5 fish limit over 30 pounds is a real possibility here. Flippin' pork along these banks is not for the timid. Gear up with 30 pound test!

Sometimes, the bass will want a sleeker bait, and a plastic worm flipped in both the deadfall and the tules can be great. Use brown/black or purple Super Floats with the tails split or a 5 inch Gatortail worm in black/chartreuse tail. Sometimes a small 4 inch worm flipped on lighter line is the hot ticket, particularly in coves off the main river. The all-around top river color is purple with red flakes for these smaller 4 to 6 inch worms. In the Spring, a brown/orange plastic lizard is a solid choice if the pig'n jig fails to produce.

Other techniques work in these backwaters. P-heads and darters with thick 4 or 5 inch plastic worm trailers, along with shad-colored crankbaits are good alternatives. Occasionally in the Spring, some nice fish can also be had with white or chartreuse spinnerbaits.

Fat Gitzits flipped along the tule banks have also accounted for some nice fish. Along this same line, rig up a salt'n pepper grub with a pegged sinker and flip it through these tules. They work!

Zara Spooks, white or black buzzbaits, and floating Rapalas will also catch some bass from time to time down here. Try them especially in the early mornings to the right of Walter's Camp near the concrete structure, or in any of the backwater coves off the main river.

Lake Don Pedro (Map - p.147)

This is one of Northern California's largest bodies of water, spanning nearly 13,000 surface acres when at full capacity with over 160 miles of shoreline. The lake is located 49 miles from Stockton. It is a typical river-style lake, over 26 miles long, with numerous spidery coves and creek inlets.

Don Pedro has a full complement of services for all water sports including fishing, swimming and water skiing. You may even want to consider renting a houseboat for a more extensive bassin' vacation, staying right on the water. The lake is open all year long and night fishing is permitted. This has not become that popular for the bassin' fraternity here as it has, for example at Lake Amador. Most nighttime anglers work for crappie. But you certainly might want to chuck a bass lure or two if you decide to sample the night bite on these panfish.

Don Pedro can be a tough lake, but it does have good numbers of northern largemouths. There are a few Florida-strain bass mixed in along with just a smattering of smallmouth activity. Most of the bass angling is done from boats and there are a wealth of coves to select from. There are lots of wooded coves,

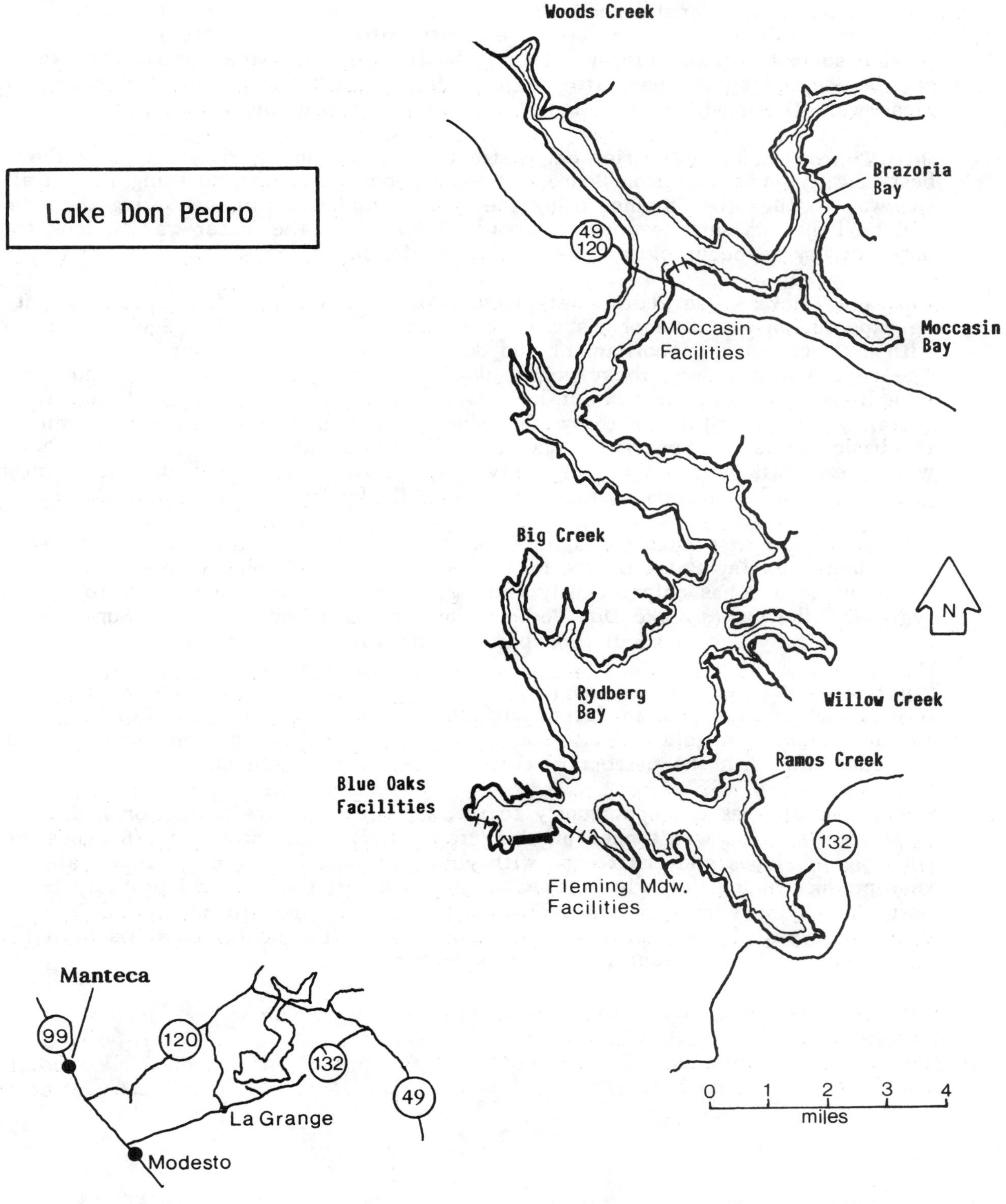

Woods Creek

Brazoria
Bay

Lake Don Pedro

49
120

Moccasin
Facilities

Moccasin
Bay

Big Creek

N

Rydberg
Bay

Willow Creek

Ramos Creek

Blue Oaks
Facilities

132

Fleming Mdw.
Facilities

Manteca

99

120

132

49

La Grange

Modesto

0   1   2   3   4
miles

rocky points, creek channels, grassy areas, boat docks and fallen timber.

Areas to Fish: Big Creek, Woods Creek, Willow Creek and the Ramos Creek arms have all been traditionally good places to try for bass at Lake Don Pedro. There soon will be Christmas tree reefs artifically planted in the lake to provide some additional brushy spawning habitat for the largemouths. The reefs will be located by the dam area in Jones Bay and off the points at Fleming Meadows. These will be excellent fish-holding areas in the future.

Best Times: Lake authorities emphasize that March and April are clearly the best bassin' months at Don Pedro. However, locals continue to bring fish in all the way through the Summer using the right techniques. In the Spring the fish will be from the surface down to about 12 feet. As the water warms, look for bass activity to occur closer to the 20 foot depth.

Tips and Tricks: Don Pedro's largemouths prefer a variety of baits. As might be expected, a lot of emphasis is on crawdad imitations. Lake regulars spool up with 8 to 12 pound monofilament and do a lot of wormin' primarily Texas style. The multitude of coves, rocky points, docks, and grassy areas are all conducive to a little worm crawlin'. Four inch baits are the preferred length here but certainly don't hesitate to throw the larger 6 or 8 inch models. For wormin', the basic colors are bonafide winners: black, brown and purple. A fourth choice would be a dark motor oil green. Try some of the thicker-bodied baits in either straight or curl-tail versions made commercially by Reds, Culprit and Manns.

When it comes to crankbaits, again, crawdad-colored lures are most often used. The smaller Bagley Balsa B is a local favorite. Another plug I believe was discontinued and has only recently returned to production also appears to have a regional following at Lake Don Pedro. This one is called the White Super Cedar and is made by Poe, a small crankbait manufacturer.

For top-water action, work the lake over in the early mornings and evenings. Interestingly, one of the preferred surface baits is the #9 or #11 Rapala floating minnow in gold finish. You can work this bait with a spinning rod and 10 pound line with the customary twitch, jerk, or rip techniques.

Finally, don't miss the opportunity to throw some spinnerbaits at Don Pedro's largemouths. You won't need anything fancy here. The standard 3/8 ounce white with nickle blades and chartreuse with gold or nickel blade combinations are very productive, particularly in the Spring. Bait fishermen would probably be best off staying with a live nightcrawler fly-lined in and around all the different types of cover at Lake Don Pedro. Bank fishing for bass has been pretty much a tough proposition at this rather expansive lake.

El Capitan Lake (Map - p.150)

Tucked in about 30 miles east and north of San Diego near the town of Lakeside, "El Cap", as it is known locally, is one of the smallest big bass fisheries in the state. At its maximum capacity -- which is rare due to seasonal water demands -- the lake has only 1100 surface acres and a sparse 15 miles of shoreline. But this is one of the lakes in the famous City Lakes group that is managed especially as a trophy fish factory. El Cap is only open three days a week and operates just from March through October. In this way, the bass fishery in particular receives a rest and recuperation period from all the pressure it gets the other eight months. Water skiing and body contact with the water are not permitted.

El Cap has minimal facilities. Launching can be restricted to one boat at a time. Be prepared to wait in line, especially if the water level is very low and the ramp is hazardous. There is no camping at this lake, but there is a small concession where boats can be rented and live bait purchased.

Although this lake is "primitive" compared to many in the north with their mega-services, the rustic facilities are worth putting up with after you sample the bass fishing! The lake has Florida hybrids and they can be very selective feeders. But be persistant. Many fish over 10 pounds are caught here annually.

Areas to Fish: If the lake level is low, the banks lining the main channel of this canyon reservoir are the best bet. There are numerous rocky and brushy spots and small coves along this stretch of the lake on both the east and west sides. The northern end of the lake usually gets too shallow, with a lot of mud and silt. However, if the lake level is up, this area can produce an excellent flip bite in the various trees, stumps, and brush piles. The dam arm is the most rocky and can be productive if you anchor outside of visual rock piles, working either a plastic worm or live bait.

Best Times: March and April are overwhelmingly the choice times to fish bass at El Cap. Those first two or three weeks after the lake opens can be absolutely sensational. Remember, the fish would have been rested for over 4 months and are starting to move up shallow during this time.

Tips and Tricks: El Cap is a bassers dream in terms of its versatility of patterns that work year after year. Wormin' is probably the local favorite. A Texas-rigged worm crawled across the bottom in the slow, line-feelin' tradition always accounts for some trophy fish. Shake'n bake worms in the brush and along the rocky banks. Both 4 and 6 inch styles will work. Use the same baits for split-shottin', especially in the backs of coves and in the flooded flats. The split-shot worms will slowly rise and fall over the light weed growth. Top colors include: brown/neon blue, brown/black, smoke sparkle/chartreuse tail, smoke/blue flake, purple/chartreuse tail, black/chartreuse tail, and orange/green bloodline. Both hand-poured and injection molded varieties are fine. Scale up to 8 or 10 pound test for all the wormin' techniques. The bass

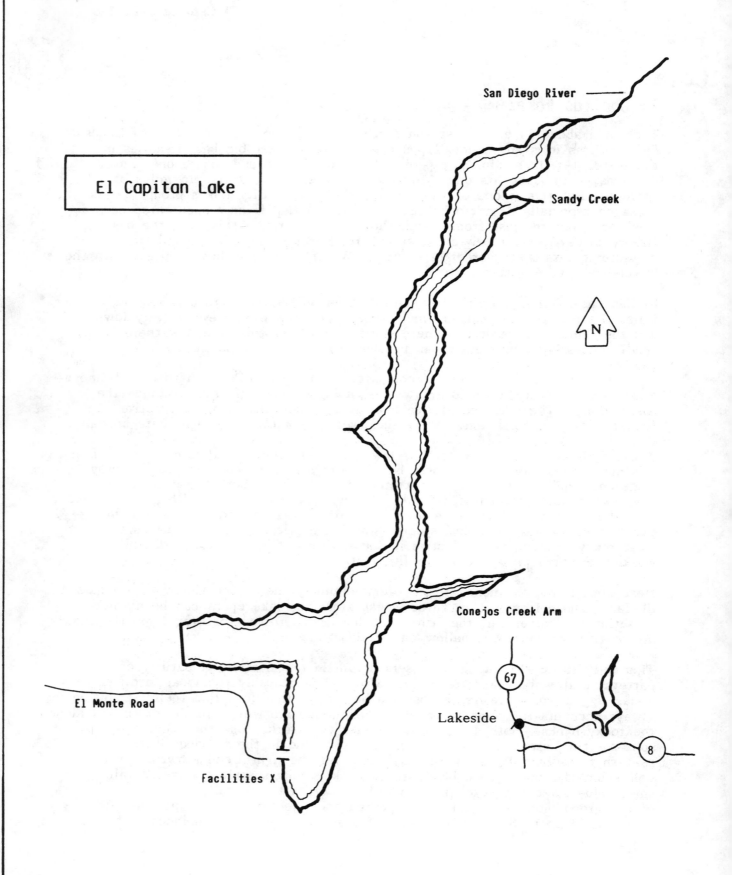

El Capitan Lake

San Diego River

Sandy Creek

N

Conejos Creek Arm

67

Lakeside

8

El Monte Road

Facilities X

are not overly spooky in El Cap's stained water. Smoke colored Fat Gitzits and assorted grubs round out the plastic menu.

Brown and black pig'n jig combos work, especially on the bigger kicker fish. Don't think twice about using a Big bait. The #1 Jumbo Frog is a proven winner. The same goes for blades. You can get away with throwing the larger #6 to #8 willowleaf spinnerbaits here. White and chartreuse patterns are the most common colors.

Many quality fish will also hit a crankbait at El Cap. No mystery here -- Rapala Fat and Shad Raps, Bomber Model A's and Bagley DB-II's in foil and Tennessee shad finishes are best.

The surface action at this lake can also be terrific at times. Buzzbaits in brown or in white are effective. The #11-S floating Rapala is always deadly. But also, throw the Heddon Zara Spook in the glitter shad finish throughout the day as the weather warms. This large top-water plug will sometimes call El Cap's bass out from their Summer doldrums.

Bait tossers will really enjoy El Cap. Golden shiners, crawdads, and night crawlers purchased at the concession stand can be dynamite throughout the season fly-lined on 10 to 15 pound test along outside boulders. Don't be surprised if you get the strike of your life as one of El Cap's famous 30 pound blue cats decides it wants that shiner!

Lake Elsinore (Map - p.145)

Bassers in Southern California have pretty much kept this lake a secret from their brothers in the North. Elsinore is a relatively small body of water located about 35 miles from Riverside. The lake has had a varied history, having dried up completely at one time, then being flooded in recent years. Currently, the water level has dropped dramatically and there are only a few places where the depth exceeds over 25 feet.

Due to all the past flooding, there is a tremendous amount of submerged structure in this lake. There are fence lines, concrete slabs, dilapidated house frames, walls and sunken rock jetties. In addition there are lots of shoreline brush, groves of trees and a few unique palm trees that jut out from the water. Elsinore also has a decent northern bass population with many quality 2 to 3 pound fish. Rumor has it that a few Floridas have been transplanted in the lake with some fish over 10 pounds having been caught here.

There are limited tent camping areas, but you will find extensive R.V. sites, plus nearby markets and a small marina. To my knowledge there are no fishing boats for rent at Elsinore.

Areas to Fish: The best place to launch and start fishing from is the West Marina. Fish the sides of the boat channel. They are lined with large rocks and drop off at the end of these submerged jetties. As you work outside the channel, you can motor left to the State park area and fish palm trees, brush piles and underwater fence lines. This area used to be a picnic spot before it was flooded so you can sometimes find yourself casting to things like submerged barbecue pits and picnic tables. If you chose to venture to the right, you will run into groves of trees that are a favorite with local bassers. Continuing down the South shore, fish the trees and brush piles near the military academy all the way down to Rome Hill.

Best Times: Unless you can tolerate endless water ski wakes and the drone of jet boats, forget fishing Elsinore from late May through September. The recreational traffic on this lake is just too heavy. The lake excels in November and December and also in the early Spring. At these times, the water temperature has chilled down quite a bit and only the most dedicated diehard skiers will visit the lake.

Tips and Tricks: A number of methods work well at Elsinore. You can figure that there will usually be some fish to be caught up shallow flippin'. Use lighter 1/4 to 3/8 ounce live rubber jigs in brown, brown/orange, or black, and brown or black #11 frogs. Pork will produce year round on this flip bite. In the warmer water try a plastic saltwater-sized Boogie Tail in silver shad color, longer 7 inch AA worms in smoke/brown, and plastic lizards in black, blue and brown.

A lot of flip fish can also be caught here using salt'n pepper grubs and shad-pattern jigs. Both the Haddock Kreepy Krawler and Garland Spider jigs in smoke/sparkle and smoke/blue flake will flip well at Elsinore. Along this same vein, use the grubs on P-heads and darters along with Fat Gitzits in solid smoke and smoke/sparkle fished in the deep structure around the State Park and West Marina areas.

Winter spoonin' has also been a "hot" secret at this lake. Work the 20 to 25 foot depths again on that west shore with small spoons. The Hopkins No-Equal and 1/4 ounce Kastmaster in chrome and the Haddock 3/8 ounce Structure Spoon in smoke shad are winners. Some locals also fish a purple 1/2 ounce twin-spinner, fluttered down along the rock jetties and tree trunks in the Winter months. Use a #11 or #U-3 pork rind trailer in brown with this spinnerbait.

Plastic worms fished with either a Texas rig or a split-shot set up consistently catch Elsinore bass. The best colors are blacks, browns, motor oil/red flake, and any of the smoke shad patterns with flake. Both 4 and 6 inch worms will work. This water is fairly stained and the bass are not overly touchy.

Spinnerbaits have accounted for some outstanding catches of larger fish. A few locals prefer to wade the lake in the Spring and spinnerbaits will be their number one bait. Use 1/4 to 1/2 ounce blades in white, chartreuse, blue/white, and purple/black. If the water is cold or very stained, add a white or chartreuse RippleRind trailer.

Slab-style crankbaits such as the Heddon Sonic or Cordell Spot are sometimes effective in the Spring and Summer months. Other crawdad and shad-colored plugs such as the Bagley Balsa B, Rapala Fat Rap and Storm Wiggle Wart will also work. Occasionally there is some limited surface action. Cast floating Rapalas, white buzzbaits, and Zara Spooks if the bass decide to hit top-water here.

Folsom Lake (Map - p.154)

One of the largest reservoirs in Northern California, Folsom Lake is located 45 miles northeast of Sacramento. With nearly 12,000 acres to fish, the lake offers a wide variety of opportunities for both largemouth and smallmouth bass.

There are numerous boat launches around the lake, full-service marinas, boat rentals, campgrounds, and tackle shops. Private boat owners must pre-register their vessels for inspection at either the marina or Granite Bay.

The bass species seem to pretty much divide themselves between the two major forks of the lake. Smallmouths are found primarily in the North Fork, while largemouths cruise the South Fork. There are a lot of sub-legal (under 12 inch) smallmouths to be caught, so be sure to bring a Will-E-Go board to measure for keepers. The largemouths are northern strain with 2 to 4 pound fish common.

Areas to Fish: The smallmouths are going to be found on sandy and rocky banks, gravel bottoms, deeper outside structure, old underwater road beds, and at the ends of boat ramps. Largemouths will seek more prominent structure here, like brush piles, shorelines with stumps, stickups, rows of trees, and submerged weed beds. Give Rattlesnake Bar on the North Fork a shot for smallmouth action. Shift to the South Fork and look for largemouths around the Jack's Shack area and New York Creek Cove. Fish the backs of coves all the way to the upper end of the South Fork by Salmon Falls Bridge.

Best Times: Folsom is open all year, but becomes a tough proposition in the hot summer months and during the Winter. Still, lake regulars fishing deep-water tactics bring in some nice limits during these seasons. April through June are the best months as both species of bass move up to spawn.

Tips and Tricks: Plastic worms are probably the best all around ticket for Folsom's bass. Lake regulars prefer to fish these baits with not only a standard Texas rig and 6 to 8 pound mono, but also with open-hooked P-heads and darters. Three very popular regional choices are the Cato Little Bits Culprit, and P.R.O. models in 2 to 4 inch lengths. These baits worked deep (30 to 40 feet) during the hot summer months, account for some nice limits by lake regulars.

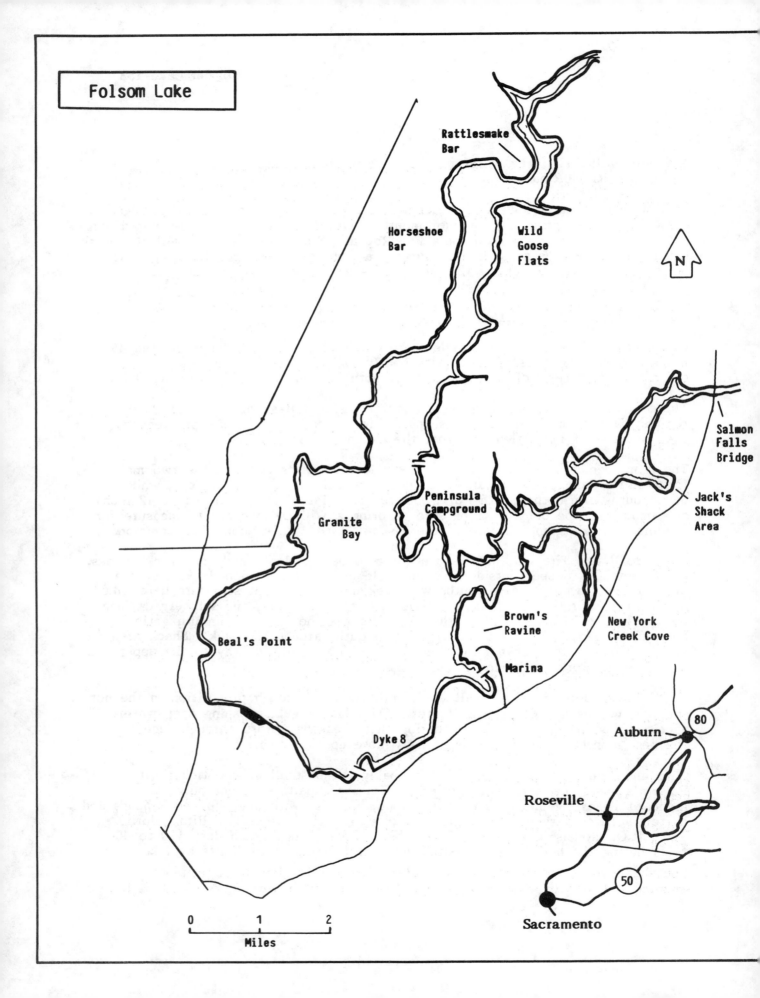

Some of the preferred colors include solid purple, black, brown, clear/sparkle, brown/red sparkle, and purple/sparkle. Fish all of these worm models in their full length when threaded on an 1/8 ounce P-head or darter. Basic pig'n jigs will also catch fish holding deep at Folsom. The #11 Pork Frog matched with a 3/8 to 1/2 ounce live rubber jig in purple, brown, or black works well.

There is a solid forage population of crawdads and threadfin shad at Folsom. Thus crankbaits which imitate these natural baits are also sometimes effective. Larger Rapala Fat Raps and Shad Raps, Bagley DBII's, and Bill Norman Deep Little-N's should be tried when the bass are on a crankbait pattern. Also, chuck these cranks in a perch pattern for a change of pace.

Bobby Garland's Fat Gitzit jigs fished on 1/8 ounce heads have also put a dent into the Folsom bass numbers. Besides the favorite smoke/sparkle color, plain smoke, rootbeer, and purple variations in this tube bait will work here.

Folsom bass will also attack a surface plug in the warmer weather. Floating Rapala minnows, Arbogast Jitterbugs and Hula Poppers, the Smithwick Devil's Horse, and the Heddon Zara Spook are all bonafide winners at this lake. Buzzbaits in assorted colors are also productive.

Some of the bigger fish caught at Folsom are going to be taken on live bait. A fly-lined nightcrawler will always account for a few, but the "hot ticket" will be a live crawdad, especially fished shallow in the Spring.

Lake Havasu(Map - p.157)

Many accomplished bass fishermen in Southern California get tired of fighting the weekend crowds, so they hitch their rigs up and head to Lake Havasu. The lake area is an immense and varied waterway lying between California and Arizona on the Colorado River. It spans over 45 miles between Davis Dam to the north and Parker Dam to the south. There are numerous facilities scattered all over the lake including resort hotels, bait and tackle shops, trailer parks, R.V. campgrounds, houseboats, tent campsites, markets, and a variety of marinas.

Havasu has a thriving largemouth population thanks in part to a 13 inch size limit imposed throughout this waterway. You really have two choices when you fish Havasu. The lake itself offers a wide variety of structure. You will find sheltered coves, steep canyon walls, broken rock, moss beds, reefs, rocky points, some trees and deadfall. If you venture out into the main river and head north, you will encounter a lot of coves, endless tule banks, deadfall, sandbars, and some steep walls. Sometimes, the "bite" can be good in the lake and off in the river and vice versa. Many tournaments are won here based on which way the pro decides to gamble -- the lake or the river.

You should bring an assortment of tackle with you for fishing Havasu. A spinning rod with 6 pound mono, a good wormin' outfit with 8 to 10 pound line, a rig filled with 12 pound test, to throw top-water plugs, crankbaits, blades, and pork, and a flippin' stick loaded with 20 pound test.

Areas to Fish: In the main lake, if the water level is up, a popular place is at the far end of the Bill Williams Arm. The bass will move into the tules up at this part of the lake. The red clay banks on both sides of the lake before you hit this arm are also good. The large flats across from and the coves southeast of Queen's Bay Resort hold fish all year long. As you motor into the main river, the coves just before and after you reach the Blankenship bend are productive. The slough or marina area at Park Moabi all the way up to the Topock Swamp can have good concentrations of fish throughout the year.

Best Times: Havasu is literally a year 'round bassin' haven. Spring is always popular for more agressively feeding fish, but don't pass up Fall and Winter in both the main lake and river. Summer can be a little tough, but if you can find sanctuary from the day cruisers and jet skiers, there are definitely bass to be caught.

Tips and Tricks: If you fish the lake, plastic worms are going to produce all season. Texas-rigs, split-shottin', and especially P-heads and darters fished on 6 to 8 pound mono will work well. There are some very clear water spots on the lake, so the lighter lines will often help. A variety of worm colors will be effective, but here are some time-tested favorites: smoke sparkle/gold, purple/red flake, brown/orange tail, black/chartreuse tail, salt'n pepper, and red/black bloodline. Six inch models are fine and these bigger worms can be rigged in their full length with P-heads or darters. This combination is particularly effective in fishing openings in the moss beds.

Pig'n jig is an excellent choice for either the river or the lake, for pitchin' or flippin'. Use brown or brown/orange live rubber matched with black, brown, or purple #1 or #11 frogs. Try some brown vinyl jigs in the colder winter months. Also, bring some 5/8 ounce jigs for tossing into the flowing current in the main river. A lot of bass are caught around the swirling eddies and where the current rips by the tule banks. A brown live rubber jig with a #25 brown Craw Frog pork bait can be dynamite. Haddock Kreepy Krawlers in smoke/blue flake, smoke/red flake, and solid silver are additional favorites.

Other subtle presentations are great, both on the river and in the lake. Fat Gitzits in smoke/sparkle, solid purple, smoke/red flake, and solid smoke can be light-lined in the lake or flipped in the river. Lake experts sometimes fish the Gitzit in the current, bouncing it along the bottom to resemble a struggling crawdad. Try a smoke/red flake model with a larger 1/4 to 3/8 ounce head and 10 pound line. Salt'n pepper grubs are also hot, fished with either a P-head or flipped Texas style.

Spinnerbaits and cranks take a lot of bass in Havasu's waters. White or chartruese blades are especially effective thrown into the river's tule banks in the Spring and Fall. Crankin' will work sometimes along these same banks. The

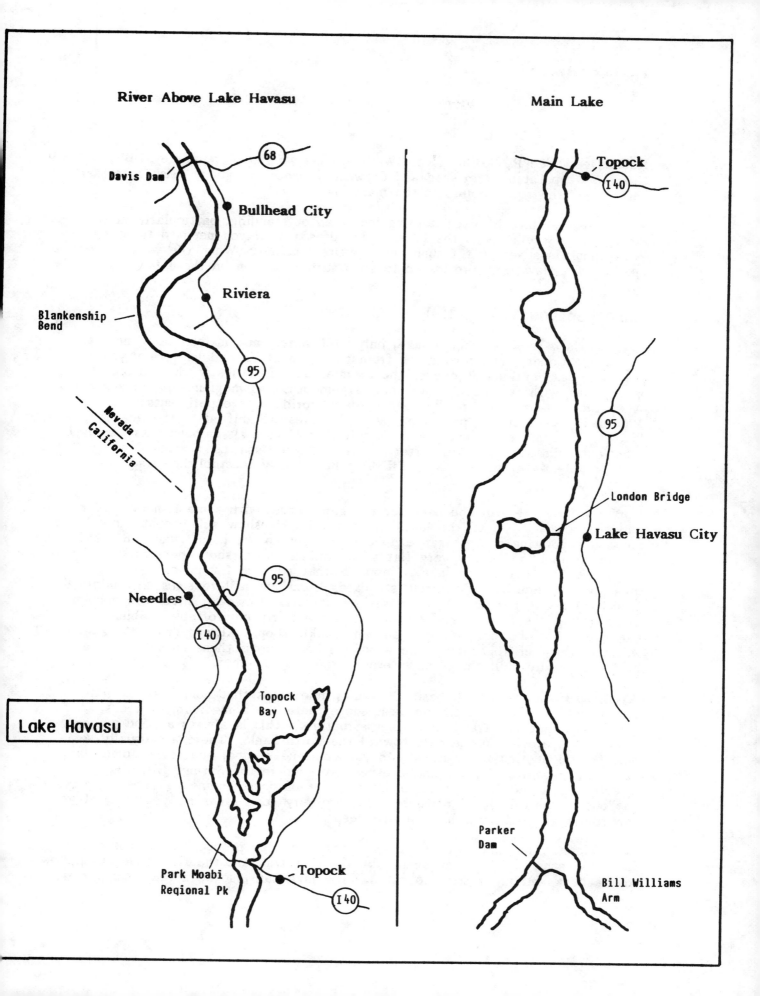

Rebel Deep Wee R, Storm Wiggle Wart, Rapala #5 Fat Rap, Bagley DBII, and Bill Norman Deep Little N in shad and crawdad finishes are good. Fish these same baits along the rocky points in the main lake.

The top-water bite is often nothing less than outstanding, particularly in the coves and on the flats in the lake. Two lures are all you need to take: the Zara Spook in silver glitter shad and a white buzzbait. When the water warms up, look for Havasu to provide some good surface action on these two baits.

Lake Henshaw (Map - p.159)

Henshaw is a relatively small lake, only 1100 acres, and is located in northern San Diego County, about 45 miles from the town of Escondido. Many years ago, the lake was heralded as one of the premier bass fisheries in the nation. It was loaded with fat, chunky northern largemouths and magnum-sized black crappie. When the San Diego City lakes began their Florida bass experiments in the 1960's, Henshaw slid in popularity as angler pressure shifted to the new trophy lakes. For some time, many anglers felt that Henshaw's famous bass fishing had practically disappeared. But after a series of good spawns, combined with fairly stable water levels, the bassfishing has clearly reestablished itself at this lake.

Northern bass are still the name of the game here, with some fish over 10 pounds caught annually. Of all the lakes in California, Henshaw will probably be the most disappointing in appearance upon first sight to the bass fisherman. The terrain around the lake is very flat with minimal visual shoreline structure. When you look across the lake, it appears that you are fishing on a flooded meadow. By Southern California standards, Henshaw still receives only minimal fishing pressure, particularly from serious bassers. However, there are enough amenities at the lake to make your trip there fairly comfortable: cabins, campsites, hot showers, a restaurant and tackle shop. Always bring along some warm clothing on this lake. The wind can howl across these unsheltered flat lands and really chill things down even during the Summer.

Areas to Fish: There are basically four prime areas that hold bass at Henshaw. To the left of the dock on the west shore there are a modicum of rocks, boulders, submerged trees, and other structure. This is always a good place to start. Fish around to the dam toward the north bank. There are usually some bass holding in this rocky area. As you continue around, you reach some flats on the east shore. These can be especially good in the Spring. Finally, directly out from the dock there are a series of deep channels. These appear to be "out in the middle of nowhere", but are very good areas all year long if you can find them and know how to fish deep.

Best Times: Henshaw is open all year and it can be productive on bass all twelve months. Spring may overall be the best time, as the fish move up shallow to the bank and are easiest to catch. The lake can also be a real "sleeper" in

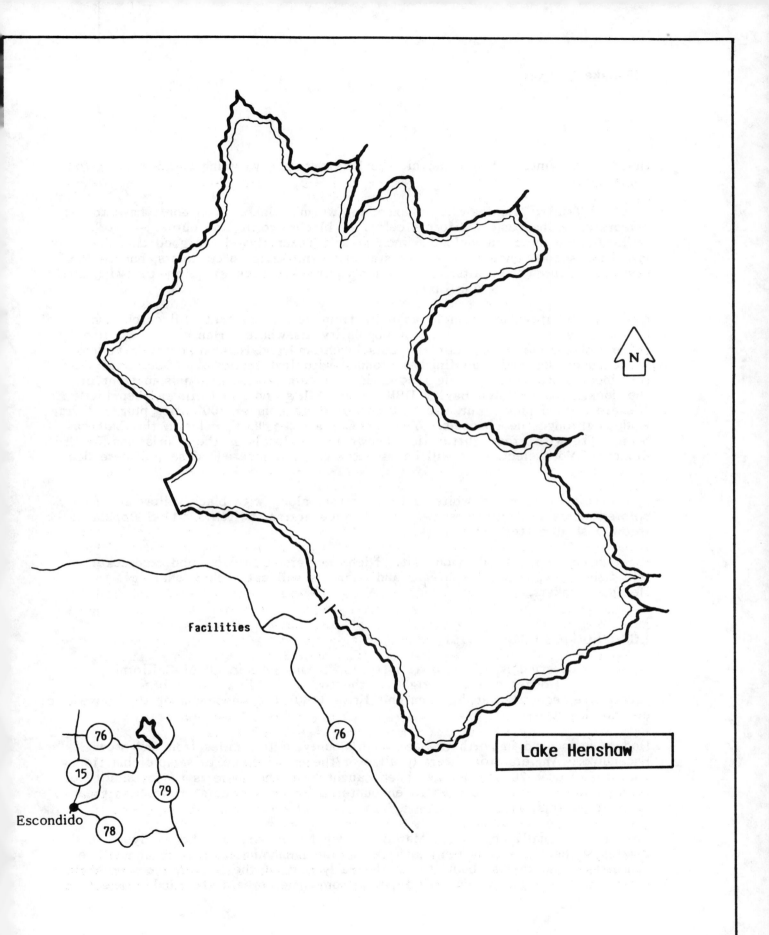

N

Facilities

76

76

15

79

Escondido

78

Lake Henshaw

the dead of Winter, if you can hit the lake during a warming trend without too much wind.

Tips and Tricks: Henshaw is an excellent wormin' lake. You don't have to get elaborate. The basic California colors -- black, brown, and purple -- work well. Simple injection-molded 6 inch models Texas-rigged are good enough. Pork is a solid second choice. You can stay with the same three colors, but don't hesitate to throw big baits. In addition to the #11 Pork Frog, try the #1 Jumbo Frog and the larger Spring Lizard.

Interestingly, there are some crankbaits from yesteryear that still catch fish at this lake, though they have lost popularity elsewhere. Henshaw's bass like the old slab-style lures. Cordell Spots in chrome and Heddon sonics in yellow, white coach dog and shad finishes produce with fast retrieves. Chuck and wind a prominent alphabet-style plug that dives deep along those channels in front of the dock. Shad-colored Bagley DBII's and DBIII's and Bill Norman Deep Little N's are a good pick. But also, get out your old Bomber 600 series plug and drag it deep through the channels. Year after year, the "hot" color in this bait has been white with green glitter ribs, known to the locals as the "Christmas Tree" Bomber. Your electronics will be essential here to locate and sit on these deep cuts.

Spinnerbaits in standard white and chartreuse, along with black/yellow and frog-colored skirts work at Henshaw. For surface action, twitch a #11-S Rapala or throw a shad glitter Zara Spook.

Big fish can also be taken on bait. Nightcrawlers, crawdads, and mudsuckers still-fished deep along the breaks and channels will catch their share of Henshaw lunkers.

Lake Hodges (Map – p.161)

When the question is asked, what is the best bass lake in all of California, recurrently, Hodges comes up right at the top of the list. More bass over 8 pounds are regularly caught from this little 1100 acre impoundment than anywhere else in the state.

Hodges is located in northern San Diego County, a few miles from downtown Escondido. Anglers from literally all over the world come to sample this trophy lake. Bass over 20 pounds have been caught here and there is the possibility of bigger fish still. Be prepared to encounter a lot of crowds at times and great pressure at this lake.

The lake is usually open from March through November, and then, only three days a week. There are boat rentals, a three lane launching ramp, bait and tackle consessions and that's about it. In the early part of the season, the weekend crowds can be astronomical in size, with sometimes over a thousand people

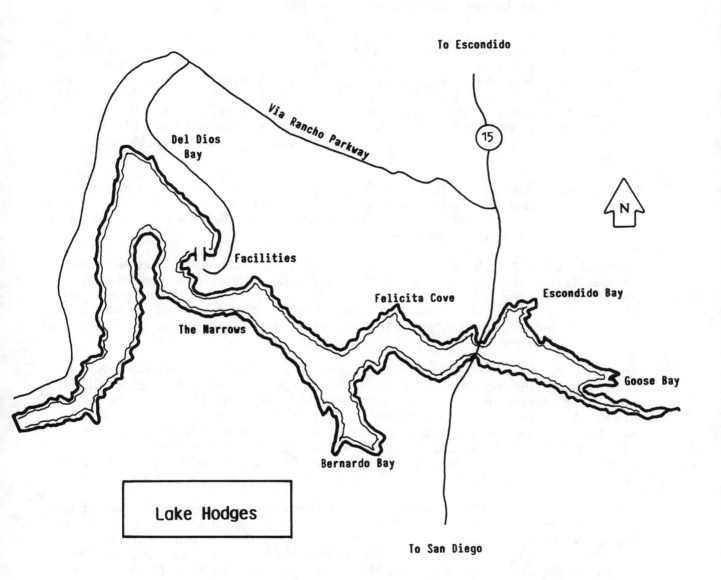

To Escondido

Via Rancho Parkway

15

N

Del Dios
Bay

Facilities

Felicita Cove

Escondido Bay

The Narrows

Goose Bay

Bernardo Bay

To San Diego

Lake Hodges

waiting in line to get started. Many bassers actually get in line to launch early the evening before the day they are to fish.

Areas to Fish: To start with, Hodges is a premier flippin' lake. There are miles and miles of tules lining its shores. When the bass have moved up into the banks, tules almost anywhere on the lake will hold some fish. If you feel comfortable fishing steep rocky shorelines, the Del Dios Arm is best on the east side of the dam. There are also numerous coves on both sides of this arm that are good bass haunts. The Narrows is also a local hot spot, as are the flats across from the boat docks. As you travel to the east to the Bernardo Arm, try the shallow coves, brushy flats and the pilings under the Interstate 15 highway bridge.

Best Times: Early Spring from March through May will be your best chance to take a lunker-class fish from Hodges. The bites and the crowds diminish by late Summer but limits can still be taken if you know the lake. Fall action can also be good with a variety of methods.

Tips and Tricks: In the Spring, flippin' is the main technique. Lake experts continually take beautiful, trophy bass on pig'n jigs. Use browns and blacks, mixed and matched with either #11 or #1 frogs. Throwing pork on to the flats or off shallow points at the openings to coves also account for some big female bruisers. Another hot tip: try some solid blue pork as a variation on this theme.

Accomplished worm fishermen will take the greatest share of fish throughout the year. Worms flipped, crawled, shake'n baked, split-shotted and doodled will all connect at certain times. Hand-poured "San Diego" earth tones are staples at Hodges, but also try black/chartreuse tail, purple/blue, purple/red flake, and red/black in these custom baits. Injection-molded worms in black/sparkle, solid red, red/black bloodline, and brown/black, and solid black Superfloats are excellent in 4 to 8 inch lengths. Reapers and P-heads in smoke/black flake are also regional favorites.

The top-water bite at Hodges ranges from frustrating to outrageous, depending upon whether the busting fish decide to eat. Throw Schurmy Shad or Kastmaster spoons, white Rooster Tails, or Fat Gitzits for a subtle approach with light line. More conventional weapons such as the Heddon Zara Spook in glitter shad or yellow can also be deadly. But don't ever go out without a #9, #11, or #13-S floating Rapala in silver/black at close reach. The quasi-topwater "twitch-jerk-twitch" technique nails a lot of big bass at Hodges with these lures.

Crankbaits and blades are also consistently good at this lake. The Rapala Fat and Shad Raps, Bomber Model A, and Bill Norman Deep Little N plugs are worth trying all season long. Stay with foil, shad, or crawdad finishes. Likewise, spinnerbaits in white, blue/white, chartreuse or chartreuse/blue are not used by lake regulars as much as they should be because they really produce. Don't think twice about throwing the bigger #6 to #8 Willowleafs either, especially in the flats.   Quality, kicker bass will bushwack these in the Spring at Hodges.

Baitfishing is an on-and-off proposition at this lake.   Crawdads, shiner minnows, and nightcrawlers do take some trophy fish each year.   But, your most consistent action will be with artificals with which a lot of Hodges' shoreline can be covered.

Indian Valley Lake (Map - p.164)

Northern California pros have kept this 4000 acre lake and its outstanding bass fishing pretty much a secret for a long time.   Indian Valley was formed in 1974. Although it is somewhat off the beaten path, those who venture there invariably return with an excellent catch.   The lake is situated about 90 miles out of Sacramento, a short distance from the more famous Clear Lake.

Indian Valley has the bare minimum of facilities, and you will not find any major resorts here.   There is however, a well-equiped bait and tackle concession, a good concrete launch ramp, campsites with flush toilets, a few rental boats, but no electric hook-ups.

The lake is absolutely loaded with every conceivable stucture and avails itself to a smorgasbord of bassin' techniques.   You will find oak trees, mesquite brush piles, lots of deadfall, rocky points, and numerous mile-long fingers to fish. Indian Valley has primarily northern strain bass with fish up to 9 1/2 pounds on record.   The main forage selection is comprised of crawdads, perch, and bluegill.   Lake authorities report there are no shad in the lake.

Best Times: March and April are the best months overall.   But, Indian Valley also kicks out consistent limits in the heat of the Summer through late Fall. Night fishing is allowed, and is definitely worth considering for summertime bass action.

Areas to Fish: The far north end of the lake is popular in the Spring.   The water is very shallow up there with numerous snags.   In the Summer, the west shore is most popular, with the east bank preferred in the Spring.

Tips and Tricks: Crankin' is a high priority tactic at this lake.   Crankbaits ranging from small to larger sizes will work.   The thing to keep in mind is to select patterns more in the panfish shades than in shad finishes.   A local favorite is the Bagley DBII in perch color with the orange belly.   The Rebel Deep Wee-R, Heddon River Runt, Storm Wiggle Wart, Rapala Fat Rap and Shad Rap in perch or crawdad patterns are also effective.

The top-water bite in the warmer weather can also be sensational at Indian Valley.   The early morning and late evening hours are typically the best times for surface action.   Floating Rebel and Rapala minnows, the Zara Spook, and the Storm Chug Bug all work.   A local favorite is the Arbogast Hula Popper in a

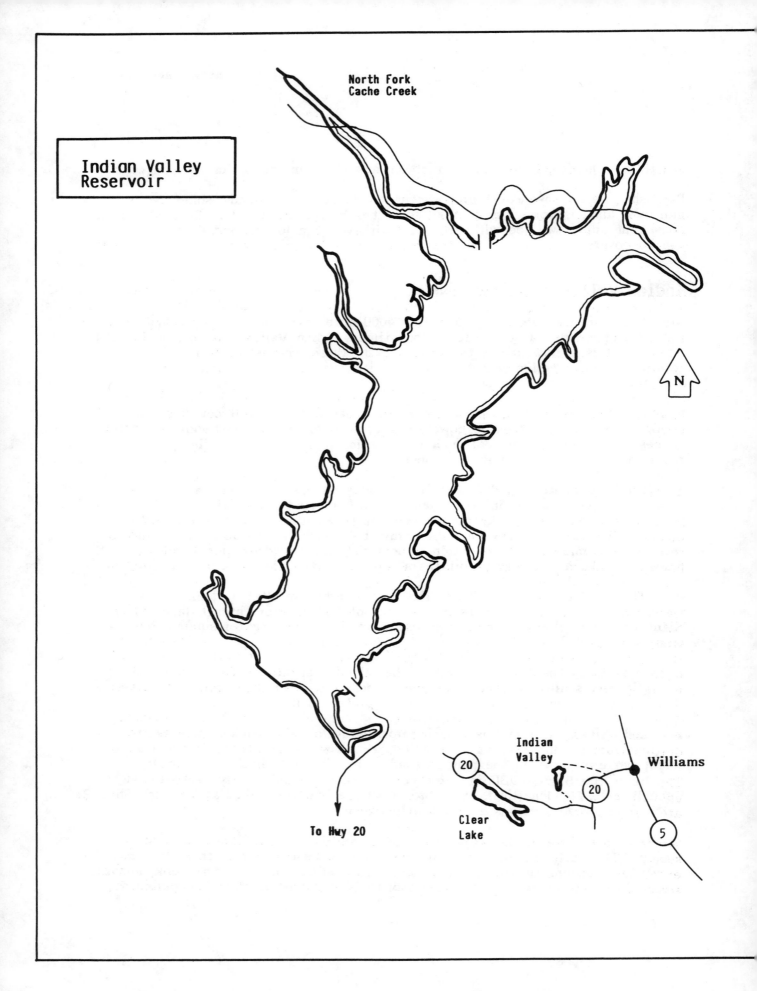

Indian Valley
Reservoir

North Fork
Cache Creek

N

To Hwy 20

20

Indian
Valley

Clear
Lake

20

Williams

5

yellow/black combination.

There can be good flippin' opportunities here along with some pitchin' action with pig'n jigs. Darker color #11 Pork Frogs behind Dusty's Bass Stalker jigs are used by lake regulars. The Garland Spider jigs in smoke/sparkle and amber/sparkle similarly can be very effective pitched along the rocky and brushy areas.

Spinnerbaits in the basic white or chartreuse models also are regularly tossed at Indian Valley's bass. Nothing fancy, just standard 3/8 ounce models, white/nickel and chartreuse/gold blades. Plastic worms should be tried all through the season. Four inch styles fished on Texas-rigs will bring fish to the well. Black is probably the number one color, followed by blue, black/sparkle, and purple.

For a change of pace, consider wading or tubing Indian Valley. Fly fishermen catch fish on popper bugs. Spinning tackle with blades, top-water lures, and worms will work fine from a float tube. Try these methods for some different action in the Spring.

Irvine Lake (Map - p.166)

Irvine has been included in this section because of its tremendous popularity among weekend fishermen who come from all over Southern California. This is a very small lake with only 700 surface acres at its peak water level. It is, however, located just minutes from the City of Orange in the Santiago Canyon area of Orange County.

Hordes of anglers visit Irvine each year to take advantage of its two incredible "put'n-take" fisheries. During the late Fall and Winter, more 5 pound rainbow trout are cuaght out of Irvine than all of the High Sierra lakes combined! In the Summer, the lake is heavily stocked with channel catfish and is open to night fishing. The lake uses a split schedule: one permit to fish in the morning until 4:00 p.m. and/or another to fish the after 5:00 p.m. night bite.

The lake has an excellent concession but no camping. Private boat launching depends on whether the ramps are accessible. The lake level fluctuates from draw-downs of its irrigation water. A large fleet of rental boats is available.

The bass fishing at Irvine can also be remarkably good for those willing to put up with crowds. The lake record is over 14 pounds, and many of the fish that are weighed in are typically nice 2 to 3 pounders.

Areas to Fish: When the water level is up there are some fence lines in the south fork, Santiago Flats area. In the Spring and Midsummer, these can be excellent bass-holding spots. There are also numerous old car tires and brushy structure scattered throughout these flats. The cliffs and the stickups in the

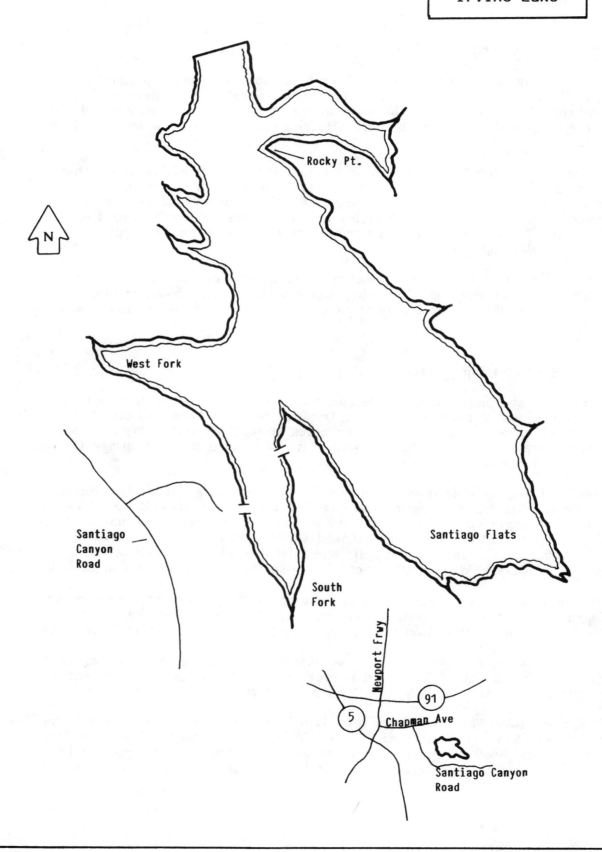

back of Sierra Cove to the north, the rocky points by the dam, and the coves in Wiley's mud flat on the western shore are also good bassin' areas. The rocky clay banks on the northeast shore are another worthwhile spot to try.

Best Times: Spring through Fall are the optimal times to fish Irvine for bass. The Summer night schedule is also productive, especially in a full-moon phase. Winter bassin' at this metropolitan lake is also effective with certain deepwater tactics -- but again, be prepared for the throng of trout fishermen. If possible, try to fish Irvine in the middle of the week for the lightest angling pressure.

Tips and Tricks: A variety of standard bassin' approaches will work at Irvine. Texas-rigged worms, crawled, shake'n baked, and doodled off the rocky ledges will get bit all year long. Purples and browns are the lake favorites including the brown/black Superfloat worm. Other colors to try are made by the hand-poured process and include, smoke/black bloodline, cinnamon/blue, and brown/smoke black in 4 inch curl-tail styles.

Subtle baits also work here. Fat Gitzits in smoke/sparkle and solid smoke, and small 3 inch curl-tail worms in smoke/blue flake fished on 1/8 ounce P-heads are good bets. There are a lot of shad in Irvine and that is why these dominant shad colors produce. Also, use a Garland Spider or Haddock Kreepy Krawler in similar shades cast off the deeper rocky points all year long.

Irvine does not really muster much of a surface bite, probably because it closes down so early in the Summer, unless you take advantage of that second fishing period starting at 5:00 p.m.

However, crankbaits consistently take nice fish worked along the rocky points and near shoreline cover. The Rapala Fat Rap in either foil or chartreuse is popular. Also, a chartreuse blade during the Summer months is worth tossing, especially in the shallow flats in the morning or when the wind comes up.

Live bait fishermen can only use nightcrawlers at this lake. Bass can be caught quietly walking the south west and east banks, carefully fly-lining a 'crawler in light 6 or 8 pound test line.

Lake Isabella (Map - p.168)

Travelling about 45 miles northeast of Bakersfield, the serious bassin' man will arrive at Lake Isabella -- without question, the premier trophy bass lake in Central California. Isabella is a good size impoundment, containing over 11,000 surface acres to fish. Many experts speculate that if the next world record largemouth doesn't come from one of the San Diego lakes or Casitas, then surely it will be landed at Isabella. The lake cranks out many fish over 10 pounds annually and a specimen pushing 19 pounds is already in the lake record books.

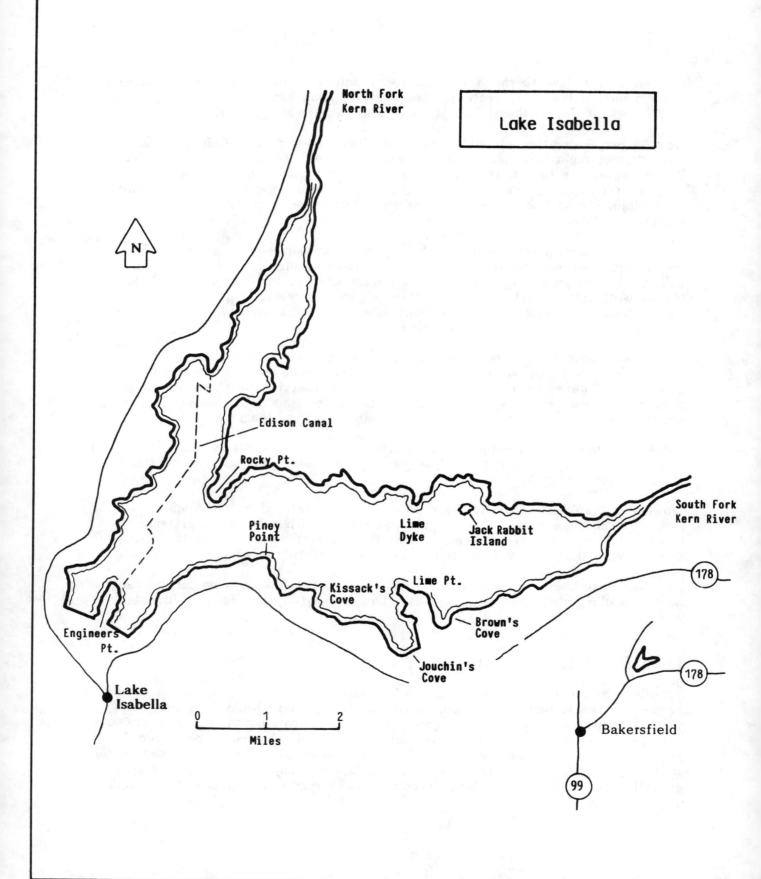

North Fork
Kern River

Lake Isabella

N

Edison Canal

Rocky Pt.

Piney
Point

Lime
Dyke

Jack Rabbit
Island

South Fork
Kern River

Kissack's
Cove

Lime Pt.

Brown's
Cove

Engineers
Pt.

Jouchin's
Cove

178

178

Lake
Isabella

0   1   2
Miles

Bakersfield

99

Campgrounds are plentiful around the lake, but don't look for too many resorts on the water. The launching conditions are excellent, along with a full service marina. Isabella's winds have a notorious reputation for spoiling a weekend outing. Be prepared to get off the water when conditions become too rough.

Areas to Fish: The flats up in the eastern fork of the lake by the airport are dotted with numerous submerged bushes and some visible trees that stand in the water. This is an excellent area in the Spring and is popular with tube fishermen. A submerged concrete canal runs midway up from the landing into the north fork. You can locate this with your electronics and fish all along it in 15 to 30 feet of water. The Lime Dyke area, Kissack Bay, and Brown's Cove in the south fork are equally productive year round. At the far end of the south fork is the fence line and additional trees. This is probably one of the few potentially good flippin' spots on the lake.

Best Times: Isabella is a tough lake through much of the Summer. It has an excellent population of northern and hybrid fish, but they seem to develop "lock-jaw" during the hot months. Concentrate on Spring and Fall. When the bass decide to "turn on" at this lake, the results can be memorable!

Tips and Tricks: In recent years, split-shottin' has become the most prevalent tactic to consistently put fish in the well at Isabella. Small 4 inch worms like the spaghetti-thin Fluttercraft baits are recommended. Good split shottin' colors include smoke/red flake, cinnamon/blue, mocassin brown, and motor oil/red flake. Another local favorite are the thicker 4 inch brown/black and "mean green" Superfloat worms (tails split of course), drifted behind a split-shot rig when the wind comes up.

The wall-hangers at Isabella will usually be caught on one of three baits: live crawdads, pig'n jig, or Bomber Long A's. The crawdads produce when they are still fished in the Spring. The same holds true for their closest imitation -- pork. Throw brown and black combinations with either #11 or #1 Jumbo Frogs. The Bomber Model A is a fairly well-kept secret trick among veterans familiar with this lake. You have to throw the BIG version of this lure (the one really made for saltwater) and jerk it with long sweeping strokes in the flats. Fish this bait with heavy tackle, and in the smoke/orange or orange/chartreuse finishes. This magnum-sized bait accounts for a lot of quality bass at Isabella, particularly in the Spring.

Other top-water success will be found with Zara Spooks, Rapalas #11 and #13-S and white buzzbaits. Sometimes the bass here will rise to the surface and feed on dragon flies in the coves and on the flats. A Storm Chug Bug, with its big eyes, in a phantom smoke/black pattern can be deadly.

A fairly standard array of crankbaits can be thrown as well in both crawdad and shad foil styles. You can fish somewhat larger cranks here including the Rapala #7 Fat Rap, Rapala #9 Shad Rap, Bagley's DBII and DBIII and Bill Norman's Deep Little N.

Lopez Lake (Map – p.171)

Fishermen living in nearby San Luis Obispo, Santa Barbara, and Ventura Counties have been fairly quiet about this lake and its budding bass community. Lopez is only 950 acres but it has over 22 miles of shoreline, and full facilities. These include a marina, a bait and tackle store, camping, grocery store, boat rentals, and even horseback riding. It is a short 10 mile drive from San Luis Obispo, but typically has minimal bass angling pressure for either largemouths or smallmouths.

Lopez is basically a canyon filled with water. It has steep banks, mostly very rocky shorelines, little visual structure, and few flats. There are good drop-offs, lots of rocky points and some good submerged structure.

In recent times, pro bassers felt that Lopez lacked any substantial number of largemouth bass, but those that were caught tended to be quality fish. In past years, a thriving smallmouth fishery has blossomed, with more and more bronzebacks showing up in the live wells.

Best Times: Lopez is a good Spring lake. You can do fairly well however, all the way through late Fall. The Summer is predictably tough, but not impossible. Lake regulars have mastered the Summer with a variety of plastic offerings. There is a Winter spoon bite, with hardly any bassers outside of a few locals ever taking advantage of it.

Best Areas: All around the immediate dam area is a popular bassin' spot. Look to the Wittenburg Arm for good action in the Spring. Vasques Canyon on the west shore is also a favorite pick among lake regulars.

Tips and Tricks: Ask any pro who fishes Lopez frequently what is the hot lure and there is a good chance they will recommend spinnerbaits. Both kinds of bass will jump on blades in either white or chartreuse skirts. It is estimated that over 50 percent of the largemouths taken during the Spring fall victim to a well-cast spinnerbait.

Lopez is also a good lake for plastic baits, particularly if you are looking for smallmouths. Popular choices here are C-O 4 1/2 inch curl-tail worms in hand-poured cimmanom/blue, motor oil, and purple/flake. Interestingly, sometimes a solid chartreuse worm is also effective in the Spring. You can use either Texas rigs or an open-hook 1/8 ounce darter head with these smaller worms. A three inch grub also fished with a 1/8 ounce darter works well at Lopez. Fish solid chartreuse or salt'n pepper. Lake experts recommend light, 6 pound monfilament for the best action with plastic baits.

Crawdads are a dominant forage food in the lake. Along these lines, crank the crawdad-colored Rebel Deep Wee R, Bagley DBII and DBIII, and the larger Rapala #7 Fat Rap off the deep, rocky banks. Occasionally, natural shad patterns will also produce. Pig'n jigs are also good crawdad imitations at Lopez. The basic

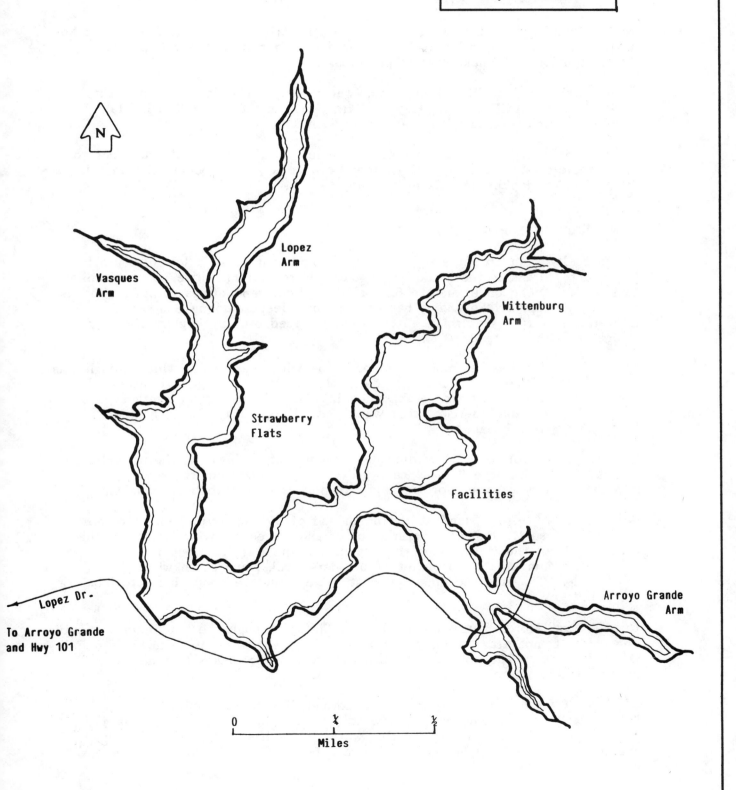

Lopez Lake

N

Lopez
Arm

Vasques
Arm

Wittenburg
Arm

Strawberry
Flats

Facilities

Lopez Dr.

To Arroyo Grande
and Hwy 101

Arroyo Grande
Arm

0   ¼   ½
        Miles

brown, black, and purple shades are best. Recently, the bass at Lopez have been introduced to Bobby Garland's Fat Gitzit and Spider Jigs. They like these lures, especially in smoke/sparkle patterns.

Sometimes there can be a limited top-water bite at this lake. White buzz baits, the Smithwick Devil's Horse, Heddon Zara Spook and floating Rapalas take a small number of surface-feeding fish at Lopez each season.

In the Winter try the deeper water to the left of the dam. Although not too many anglers take advantage of it, there can be a good spoonin' bite in this area on #075 Hopkins models in chrome.

Lake Morena (Map - p.173)

If you really want to get away from it all, and venture to a low pressure bass lake, then Morena is the place to go. To get to Morena, drive about 50 miles east of San Diego on Interstate 8. Take the Buckman Springs turnoff. This is basically an alpine lake and it has been a real sleeper among Southern California's bassin' fraternity. It is usually passed over by anglers choosing Hodges or Otay instead.

Keep some cold weather gear with you. The winds can really whip through this high elevation lake and it may get quite chilly. But, with good weather, the bass fishing will sometimes be sensational. There is just about every type of structure imaginable to fish: large weed beds, flats, rocky banks, boulders, brush, and gentle breaks.

In years past, Morena had a tremendous amount of sublegal northerns under 12 inches. Many of these "dinks" have grown up. In addition, there are a smattering of hawg-size Floridas up to 16 pounds that have been caught.

Areas to Fish: Goat Island at the north end of Morena is probably the most popular bass spot. Expect to fish a lot of submerged aquarium weeds in this area. Fish all the way around the island, and the flats between it and the east bank. The dam area offers a lot of boulders, rocks, and brush when the lake level is up. This and the adjacent west shore would be good places to look for big fish.

Best Times: Morena turns on in the late Spring through the hot Summer months. The water temperature drops dramatically along with the bass bite by late Fall through Winter. The cold alpine air temperature also makes Morena an uncomfortable Winter choice.

Tips and Tricks: Many veteran bass fishermen like to use Morena as a "classroom" for teaching novices how to fish the plastic worm. This is without a doubt the best overall bait on this water. The bass will usually bushwack the worms aggressively, and the action can be continuous throughout the entire

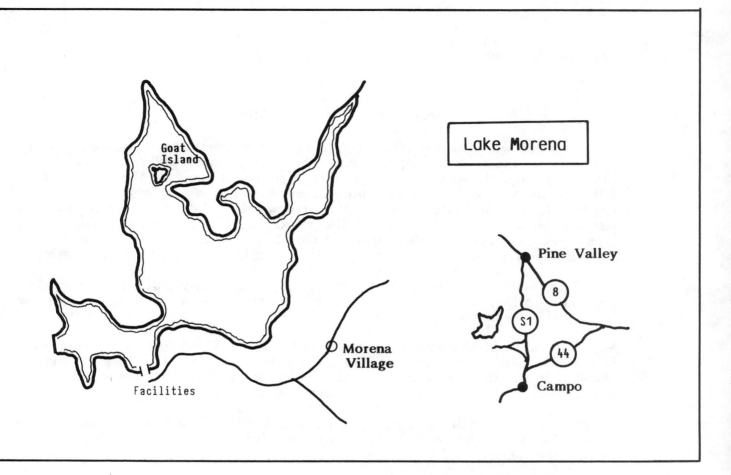

Lake Morena

Goat Island

Morena Village

Facilities

Pine Valley

8

S1

44

Campo

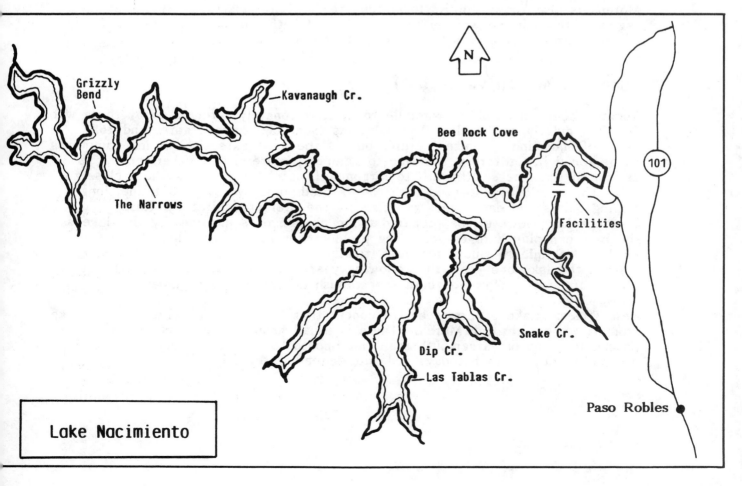

N

Grizzly Bend

Kavanaugh Cr.

Bee Rock Cove

The Narrows

101

Facilities

Dip Cr.

Snake Cr.

Las Tablas Cr.

Paso Robles

Lake Nacimiento

day. Rig the worm Texas-style for fishing areas without thick weed beds. When you fish the weeds, use a Carolina rig. The heavier sinker will penetrate through the aquatic vegetation better than a split-shot set up. The worm will fall seductively behind it settling into the weeds. Also try to drop a Texas-rigged bait vertically into the openings in the weeds and doodle or shake it just off the bottom. A P-head will also work. Six inch Superfloat worms in brown/black and purple are excellent. Solid black is good, along with the standard array of earth tone, "San Diego" colors, in both 4 and 6 inch lengths.

Top-water action at Morena can be pretty fair in the early morning. Assorted prop baits in shad or chrome, Zara Spooks, and the #11-S Rapala floating minnow have good track records at the lake.

Morena's bass will also chase crankbaits and blades. The favored bass plugs are in the foil finish: Rapala #5 Fat Rap and the Bagley DBII. Also toss a Bomber Model A in a foil/clear mirrored pattern. For blades, fish both white and chartreuse. Scale down to 1/4 to 3/8 ounce models.

In the dam area, pitch pig'n jigs. Brown or black live rubber skirts with either #11 or #1 frogs will catch some quality fish off the structure in this part of the lake.

Morena is also known for its loyal tube fishing enthusiasts who visit the lake regularly through the warmer months. Tubin' with standard bass tackle or fly fishing gear also accounts for some hefty stringers annually.

Lake Nacimiento (Map - p.173)

Located near Paso Robles, Nacimiento is affectionately referred to by those who fish it regularly as "Naci". This lake has over 5000 surface acres and 165 miles of shoreline. It also features one of the most extensive marina complexes to be found in California, catering to campers, boaters, and fishermen. It is estimated that the smallmouth to largemouth catch ratio is somwhere close to 3:1. This would be expected with Naci's prediminantly rocky shoreline, long sloping points and deep creek channels -- the prefect habitat for feisty bronzebacks. However, be prepared to be challenged sometimes by this lake as the bass can play hard-to-get. The problem lies in the fact that the water level at Nacimiento fluctuates dramatically. Just when you think you have learned the lake one year, the following year, the water could be drawn down almost 100 feet. Now you have to establish an entirely new gameplan.

Best Times: Lake experts seem to concur that Naci is an excellent Winter lake from November through March. There is usually some decent activity in the Spring, more so on largemouth than smallmouth bass. The Summer months become especially tough with hot days and wide-spread water skiing.

Areas to Fish: The backs and down the center of the larger creek arms are usually good places to look for Nacimiento's bass species. Snake Creek to the left of the launch, Las Tablas Creek, and Dip Creek are preferred by locals. The Narrows, where the river flows in, with its steep walls, is also a "must" spot to try for bronzeback action.

Tips and Tricks: Nacimiento is very suitable for some serious crankbait chuckin'. Without question, a dominant crawdad pattern should be given first preference. Try the Bomber Model A, Rapala #5 to #7 Fat Raps, and the Bagley DBI or II plugs. Another crankbait that has returned to the market and is a favorite Naci lure is the Rabble Rouser. Also, try to use crankbaits with a little more predominance of the color red at this lake.

Texas-rigged worms will generate some hot action at Nacimiento. Black, black/chartreuse tail, brown, and purple are especially effective. Any of the crawdad earthtone patterns also should be tossed, particularly at likely smallmouth hangouts. If the water level is fairly high, look for deadfall and trees in the water. If you are lucky, you may encounter some good flippin' in this type of area. Try plastic lizards in the Spring along with pig'n jigs.

Continue throwing pork and Superfloat/vinyl jig combinations with the onset of Winter. (Remember that the Superfloat is a great cold water lure.) Black and purple have been traditionally good at Naci for Winter jiggin' in #11 Pork Frogs.

There can definitely be some spinnerbait fish to be caught in the Spring and Summer on basic white or chartreuse blades. Stay with the smaller 1/4 to 3/8 ounce models. Grubs in black, brown, and purple are also a good bet, again particularly in Winter.

There are a lot of shad in this lake and subtle baits such as Fat Gitzits, P-heads, and darters fished along the rocky banks will work on hungry smallmouths. Similarly, smaller scaled-down spoons such as the Hopkins No-Equal, Kastmaster and Haddock Structure Spoon, should be fished on deeper outside structure at Naci when the bass school on tight meatballs of shad.

New Melones Lake (Map - p.177)

An excellent all-around bass lake, New Melones is a quick 60 miles from Stockton and 80 miles from Sacramento. This is a fairly large, 12,000 acre, lake spanning up to 8 miles across at its widest. New Melones has a very large contingency of northern largemouths and has become a popular spot for serious Northern California bassers.

The major forage bait of this lake is threadfin shad. The baitfish schools can be very large and you can often see the bass pushing the shad to the surface in a feeding frenzy (a similar phenomenon has been observed on San Diego lakes).

New Melones is open 24 hours a day and does experience a good night bite on bass during the warm Summer months. As for structure, you name it, the lake has got it: rocky shorelines, trees, ledges, brushy areas, plenty of coves and points. A complete range of facilities are found at various locations on the lake.

Areas to Fish: The Coyote and Angel Arms are regular bass hangouts. The Long Gulch Cove and the Glory Hole Coves are particularly good in the Spring. The small coves on the east side above the Highway 49 bridge are favored by lake regulars. Bass are found in the submerged trees in this hot spot.

Best Times: New Melones excels as a late Spring bass lake. But Summer fishing is consistently good all the way through the early Fall. Those who know the lake will also take a share of Winter bass with deepwater techniques.

Tips and Tricks: In the Spring, there can be a good flip bite. Pig'n jigs are the preferred baits, either with #11 or the larger #1 frogs. Black and purple are the standard choices.

From Spring through Fall, plastic worms are going to work, fished primarily on a Texas rig. In the Summer, be prepared to fish outside on deeper structure, drop-offs and ledges. The bass will often retreat down to 40 feet in the heat of the day. But, this will also be where a lot of the "kicker" quality fish will be caught.

Hand-poured P.R.O. worms in assorted styles are popular. Use blue, purple, motor oil, and black with and without some sparkle flake added. Shake'n bake or doodle these baits over the deep structure.

When the bass come up on the schools of shad, quietly start tossing some grubs, Scroungers, or Little Bit worms rigged on a 1/8 ounce P-head. White, green, chartreuse, and smoke will work in this situation. Fat Gitzits in smoke/sparkle also produce results.

Another top-water technique to use at New Melones is to jerk or rip a large #18 floating Rapala. Some of the locals custom paint these in salmon or rainbow trout finishes and then go hawg-huntin' with these big baits. The smaller #11 and #13 Rapalas also are effective in silver/black and blue anchovy colors.

More conventional top-water tactics will take fish in the late Spring through Fall. A large white buzzbait is good for big bass at New Melones. Heddon Zara Spooks and the Ozark Mountain Wood Chopper in shad finishes are also excellent surface lures for this lake.

Spinnerbaits in white and chartreuse are effective through late October along with an aggregate of crankbaits. The Bagley DBII in baby bass, and the Rebel Deep Wee-R plugs in shad pattern will take their share of fish.

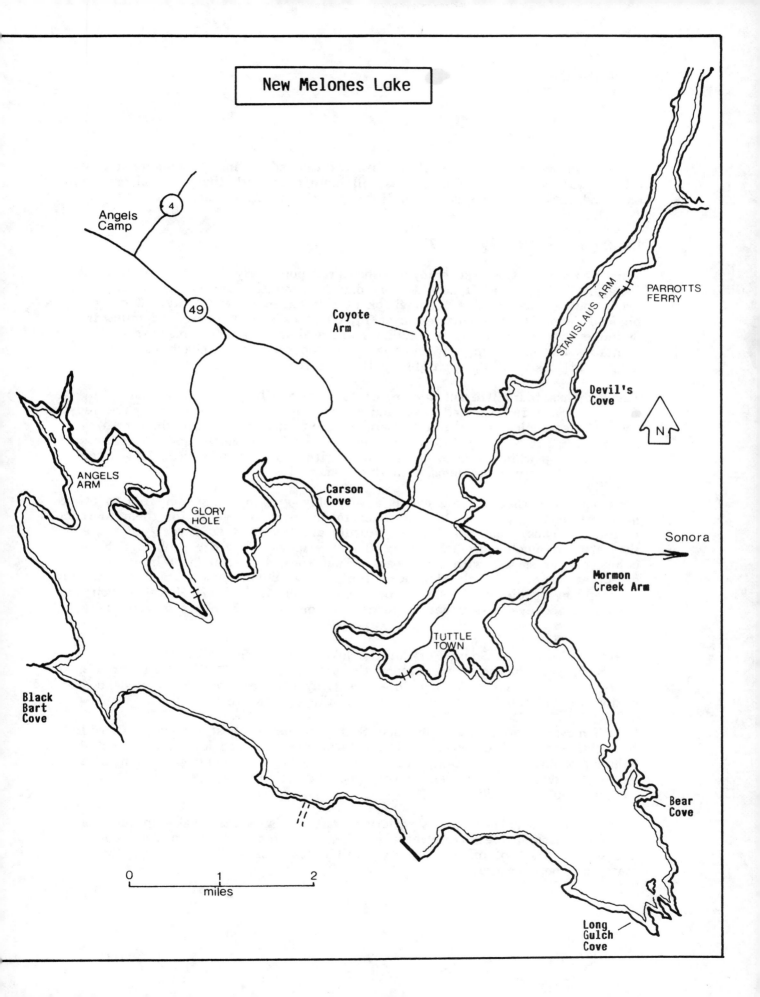

New Melones Lake

In the Winter, graph schools of baitfish off the ledges and in submerged trees all the way down to 60 feet. Bass will move deep with the bait and can be taken on standard spoonin' methods. A Hopkins #075 in chrome should do the job.

Lake Oroville (Map - p.179)

Many years ago, this lake enjoyed wide-spred popularity as a year around bass fishery. Fishing fell off considerably due to dramatic fluctuations in water levels, but is now making a comeback at this expansive waterway. Oroville is big and deep. It encompasses over 15,000 acres and is located 65 miles from Sacramento. A full array of facilities are available including marinas, numerous motels, campsites, and the unique opportunity to beach your bass boat at certain "boat-in" camps right on the water.

The lake has four different species of bass: primarily largemouths and smallmouths, a few spotted bass, and a junior member of the family, the red eye bass. This species is not too common in California and is very similar to the smallmouth. It has a distinctive red eye with slightly more reddish-bronze tones in its markings. Oroville is loaded with red eyes -- but don't get too excited. There are problems with this fish.

Biologists note that the red eye is a very slow-growing bass compared to other members of the species. It sometimes takes up to ten years for them to reach maturity. Thus, what you find at Oroville are lots of 4 to 5 year old red eyes that are not much more than 8 to 10 inches long. They are prolific fish and compete aggressively with other bass. Therefore, a special "slot limit" is in effect at Oroville to help thin down the red eye community. You are not allowed to keep any species of bass here between 12 and 15 inches. However, you may keep four red eye bass under 12 inches and one over 15 inches in your daily limit.

Areas to Fish: The South Fork of the lake is a favorite with locals. It is especially good in the Spring around the spawning period. The North Fork near Berry Creek and Spring Valley Cove, the Canyon Creek area in the mid-lake to the northeast, and the Middle Fork arms are all good bass haunts.

Best Times: There is no doubt that Spring offers the best fishing at Oroville for northerns and bronzebacks. The lake is open all year long, 24 hours a day. Summer fishing is predictably tough, but more anglers should give night time bassin' a try here. Fall can be very good, and there are still fish to be caught deep in the Winter.

Tips and Tricks: There are a variety of natural baits that make up the menu for Oroville's bass species: freshwater sculpin, pond smelt, threadfin shad, and crawdads. A lot of different tactics will catch bass at Oroville, with lures matching these natural offerings.

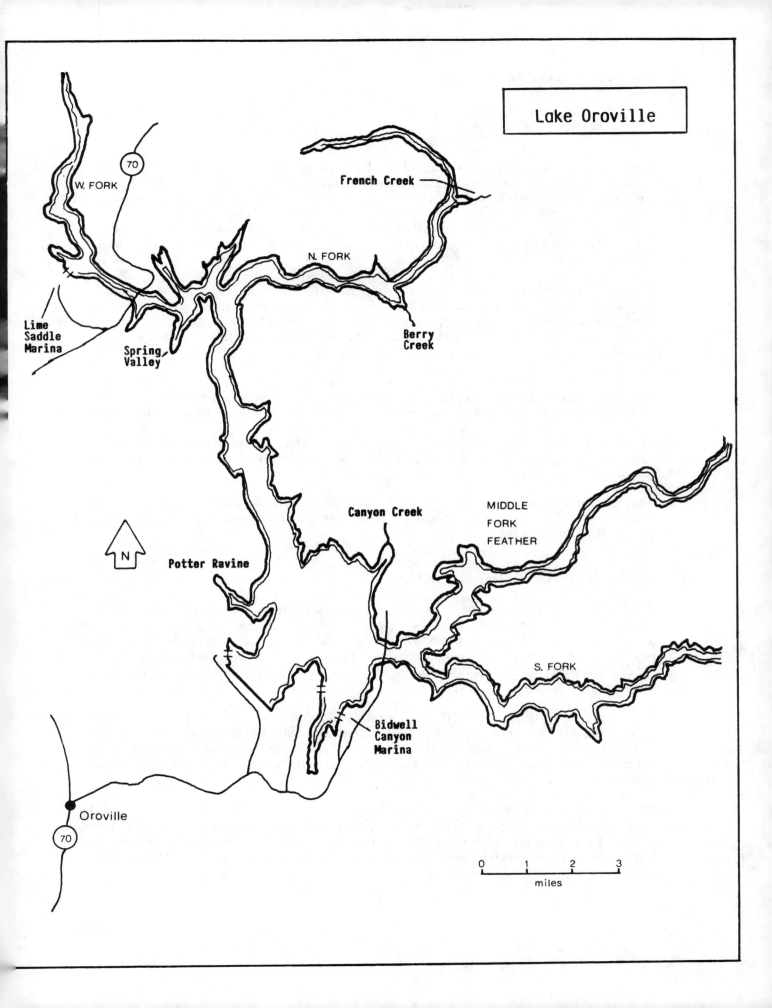

Plastic worms will take their share of fish. The Lil' Bit fished on a darter head is popular in smoke/sparkle, electric/grape, black/sparkle, and brown. The custom hand-poured Teazer worms in black/shad, smoke/orange, and cinnamon/blue have also caught on at Oroville. Again, fish these on light line with a 1/8 ounce jig head. Split-shottin' will definitely work here though it isn't used that often. When the fish are deep to 35 feet in the summer, wormin' will be your best approach.

In the Spring, throw white spinnerbaits. Blades will take a lot of nice fish this time of the year. Crankbaits also catch all the species of bass all season long. The Rapala #5 Fat Rap, Rebel Deep Wee-R, Storm Wiggle Wart, and Bomber Model A in crawdad finish are good. Stay with these small to medium sized cranks.

Standard pig'n jig combos with live rubber skirts and Fat Gitzits can be fished shallow to deep along Oroville's rocky banks. Later in the year, don't hesitate to do some vertical spoonin' down to 60 feet. The Hopkins #075 is productive.

There are also occasional good top-water bites that materialize. If the bass come up, try white buzz baits, Zara Spooks, and definitely twitch #9-S and #11-S Rapala floating minnows.

The live bait action can also be very good all year long. Crawdads, 'crawlers, and crickets are the standard faire. The crickets however, will account for a lot of smaller bronzebacks and red eyes.

Lower Otay Lake (Map - p.181)

Otay may very well be the best lake in the San Diego City system for early season bassin'. Located 20 miles to the southeast of San Diego, Otay kicks out an annual bumper crop of 8 pound plus Florida hybrids each year and is rivaled perhaps only by Lake Hodges. The lake is only 1100 acres, but is considered one of the premier big bass lakes in the world. The current lake record is pushing 19 pounds.

Like most San Diego lakes, Otay is open only certain times of the year, and then only three times per week. The lake opens in mid-February and shuts down in October. The crowds will be lining up sometimes for days in advance of the annual Otay season opener. It is during this early season that the largest number of bass fishermen frequent the lake.

There is no water skiing allowed at Otay, but still, the lake receives minimal summer angling pressure. The lake is fairly accessible from shore and has always been popular with bank fishermen. Campsites, boat rentals, and a small bait and tackle concession are available facilities.

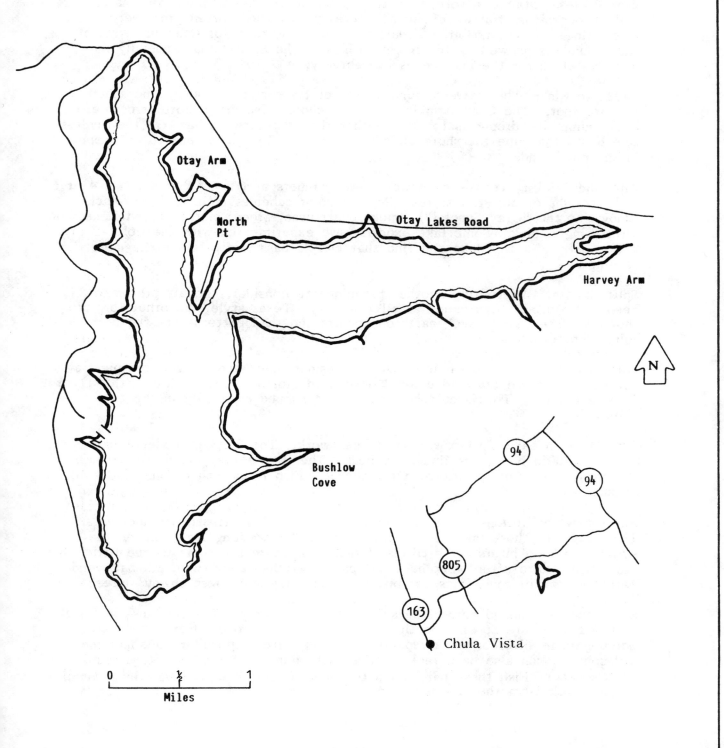

Lower Otay Lake

Otay Arm

North Pt

Otay Lakes Road

Harvey Arm

N

Bushlow Cove

94

94

805

163

Chula Vista

0   ½   1
Miles

Best Times: Otay is a very, very tough lake in the hot Summer months. There will be occasional flurries of surface activity, but these often prove very frustrating "see-but-no-bite" situations. The best time for Otay in terms of sheer numbers as well as for trophy fish is in the Spring and especially immediately after the lake opens in February.

Areas to Fish: The Harvey Arm has lots of trees and has been a perennial favorite spot. The Otay Arm is the other choice, featuring more structure and little hump-like drop-offs to fish. Other than these two areas, try the endless tule banks that line the shore all over the lake. The tules tend to be deeper in the north end.

Tips and Tricks: Texas-rigged worms are winners at Otay. You can use 4 or 6 inch straight or curl-tail styles. Popular color schemes include brown/black (known as the "Otay Special"), smoke/chartruese, green, motor oil/red flake, and interestingly, pink. Some lake experts have experimented with the Color-C-Lector meter at this lake and find that Otay's bass really follow the meter readings.

Split-shottin' is definitely another technique to consider. Locals prefer to keep two wormin' rigs handy at all times: one Texas style, the other for split-shottin'. The "San Diego" earthtone colors and shad patterns are the best split-shot options.

Pork-rind is a "big fish" bait at Otay. Besides black and brown jig'n pigs, a favorite is spotted crawdad-colored pork dyed mottled green. Stay with #11 or #1 size trailers. Pork should be pitched and flipped especially in the tule banks.

Crankbaits in early Spring will sometimes work. The Bomber Model A and Bagley DBII and III in baby bass finish are best. The Rattle Trap, a not so popular slab-style crankbait, is also an Otay secret. Fish it in both chrome and shad finishes.

For top-water action, be prepared for some potentially frustrating moments. This is one of those lakes where the bass can be crashing for hours on the surface with no biters for artificial lures. But there are some unique little tricks that quite often work here. Rapalas twitched along with buzzbaits and Zara Spooks will sometimes get bit. However, try some less obvious lures.

Small spoons cranked across the surface can be deadly. The Hopkins No-Equal, Haddock Structure Spoon, and the Schurmy Shad are good. Next try small Scroungers in silver or smoke/sparkle. The Spinrite, a peculiar-looking little tail-spinner, can also be a real surprise bait, along with a white Roostertail trout spinner. Fish these baits on 6 to 8 pound test line and make long casts. staying back from the frenzied schools.

One final tip: fish the little pot holes formed in the thick summer moss at Otay. A local secret has been the old fashion Johnson Silver Minnow, a weedless spoon, dropped into these little openings!

Pardee Lake (Map – p.185)

Nestled in between Sacramento and Stockton is one of the real secrets of Northern California, Pardee lake. This lake receives extensive publicity for its trophy rainbow trout and Kokanee salmon. What few fishermen realize is that Pardee is an outstanding warm water fishery for northern largemouth and smallmouth bass. Northern fish to over 13 pounds have been recorded with smallmouths topping 7 pounds. Numerous 6 to 8 pound largemouths are caught each year, with little word ever getting out about how really good the fishing is here.

The lake is fair-sized, covering over 2000 surface acres and with 43 miles of shoreline. It has a full-service marina, campsites, bait and tackle shops, and boat rentals. Pardee is an old lake by California standards, having been formed back in 1927. It is a drinking water reservoir, with absolutely no body contact with the water allowed. The lake closes in mid-November and then reopens in mid-February.

Be prepared to fish rocky banks if you plan to hunt bass at Pardee. There is not a lot of obvious shoreline structure here, and both the largemouths and bronzebacks will school together near rocky areas. Often a cast to the side of a rocky point produces a largemouth and on the next cast to the other side you might stick a bronzeback.

Areas to Fish: The best holding areas for both species of bass are clearly in the South Arm of the lake, where the Narrows are formed, following the rocky points and coves to where the river runs into the lake. The Channel Arm with the rocky shoreline around Shad Gulch and Cave Gulch can also be productive.

Best Times: Pardee is a remarkably good year 'round bass lake! Although the water gets cold, the angling pressure is very, very light for bass. May and June would have to be the best months overall. But the Summer months all the way to closing time in November are also good. A hot tip would be to fish Pardee when it reopens each year in mid-February. Lake regulars eagerly await the opener, for the bass haven't been tapped since the previous November. The bass bite during these first few weeks in February can be outstanding!

Tips and Tricks: Pardee does not have a threadfin shad population. The main forage baits here are crawdad and, surprisingly, the small Kokanee fingerlings planted each season. This lake has a remarkable reputation among knowledgeable insiders for being dynamite on top-water plugs -- all season long! Locals use surface baits in the cold of Winter, and all through the day in Summer on up to closing in November.

So, if you want to test Pardee, chose your top-water weapons. Both Rapala and Rebel floating minnows are effective but also tend to catch a lot of "short" smallmouths. The regulars will use the larger Bagley Bang-O, Heddon Zara Spook in silver glitter shad, the Tiny Torpedo, frog-colored Hula Poppers and buzzbaits. To emphasize, these lures can be thrown all day long with many strikes occuring during midday.

Crankbaits are also effective along the rocky ledges. Fish the Rapala Fat Raps in crawdad or chartreuse, along with the Rebel Suspend-R or Deep-R series. Pig'n jigs with brown, black, or black/orange live rubber skirts are productive on both species. Use black or brown #11 Pork Frogs.

Spinnerbaits are responsible for a lot of the 6 to 8 pound largemouths taken at Pardee. The standard white and chartreuse blades are popular. But also fish a tandem blade in brown or chartreuse/white skirts.

Pardee's better quality fish do not appear overly anxious to massacre a plastic worm or a Fat Gitzit. Top-water, pork and spinnerbaits take the heavyweights. But you will find some action on plastic, particularly with 4 inch brown worms and dark-colored Gitzits. Since there is minimal brushy structure to worry about, rig these 4 inch baits directly on a 1/8 ounce P-head or darter. Fish most of these plastic lures along the rocky points and shoreline with the open hook jig head.

Crawdads, shiner minnows, and nightcrawlers are viable live baits to use at Pardee. Crickets will catch a lot of smallmouths, but lose popularity because so many small bronzebacks quickly gobble them up.

Lake Perris (Map - p.185)

Located 70 miles east of Los Angeles and 80 miles to the north of San Diego, Perris is home to world record Alabama spotted bass. Any other species of bass found in this lake are "stragglers", for Perris was planned strictly as a trophy fishery for the "spots".

Don't expect great things from the lake in the way of extensive action. The spotted bass have been on the decline here and a recent moratorium has been enacted with a two fish, 15 inch size limit. However, the fish you catch here -- if you are lucky enough to hit them on the right day -- are healthy "footballs": fat, chunky, 2 to 5 pound class fish.

There are not that many places to fish on the lake. If the spots decide to eat, they will usually move on to one of these locations. Be prepared to slow down a little here, also. Typical run'n gun tactics are best for other lakes. Work Perris with diligence and patience. Spotted bass like to hug the bottom, but will often school together. If you latch onto one, another should be nearby.

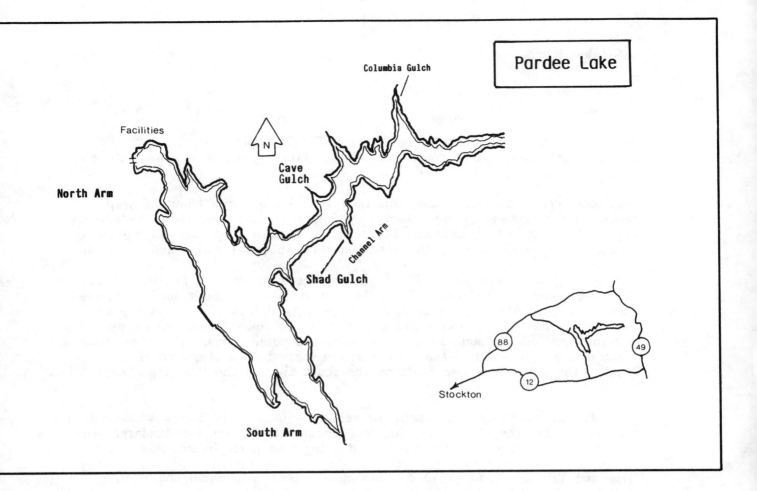

Pardee Lake

Columbia Gulch

Facilities

N

North Arm

Cave Gulch

Channel Arm

Shad Gulch

South Arm

88   49   12   Stockton

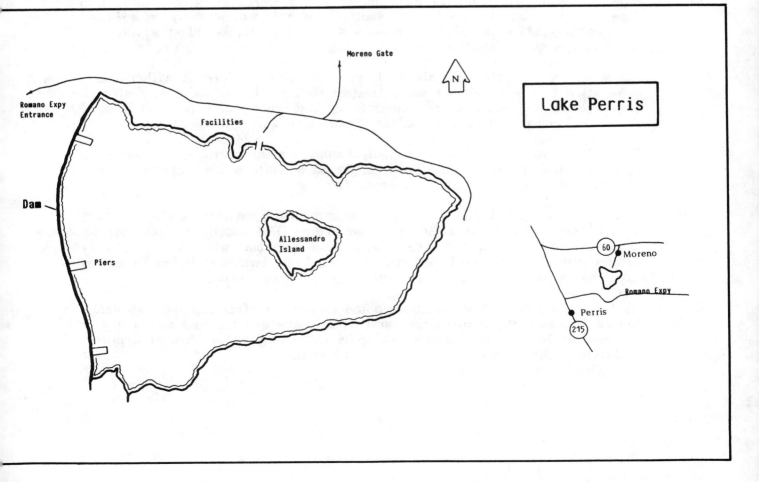

Lake Perris

Moreno Gate

N

Romano Expy Entrance

Facilities

Dam

Piers

Allessandro Island

60   Moreno

Romano Expy

Perris

215

The current world record spot comes from Perris tipping the scales at 9:06 pounds. Lake authorities are convinced that larger specimens remain to be caught.

So, most serious bassers fishing this lake are looking for a beautiful wall mount or perhaps even a line class or ultimate world record fish. Expect tough fishin', but if you tire, consider Perris' other extensive options ranging from campgrounds, picnic areas, full service marinas to water skiing and swimming.

Areas to Fish: There are basically six key areas to work at Perris. Fish them hard and return to each throughout the day in case the spots decide to move on them to feed. Along the dam in the large, jagged rocks is always a potential hot spot. The cove by the water outlet near the tower in the southwest corner and the rock piles around Allesandro Island are possibilities. The other rock piles at the east end and the jetties in the marina area also hold fish. Finally, the submerged tire reefs on the south side of the lake are always worth a shot.

Best Times: Spots can be caught all year long here. The locals who really know the lake prefer the Winter months, mid-December through mid-January. This time period will probably be your best bet at tying into a trophy size fish.

Tips and Tricks: Spots thrive on crawdads so bottom-bouncing baits are especially effective. Small 4 inch plastic worms, particularly the "mean green" Superfloat models, are the favorite baits. Fish this worm slowly on a Texas rig. Lake regulars also like to throw a 4 to 5 inch thick-bodied worm in a purple grape shade, split-shotted.

For some reason, green has always been a dominant preference with Perris' spots. In addition to the Superfloat worm, watermelon green grubs are very effective. The Haddock Split-Tail or the Manns Sting Ray grubs will catch fish here. Use them with either a P-head or darter, Texas-rigged or split-shotted.

These "footballs" will also occasionally chomp a spinnerbait. As a matter of fact, the current world record was caught on a white blade. Chartreuse (a variation of green) has also been productive.

Crankbaits, especially during the Summer, have also been responsible for some nice catches. The Bomber Model A and Bagley DBII and III in Tennessee Shad are local favorites. An inside tip here: also try a crankbait with some red in it, or one with a chartreuse base. This last color in particular is known as "baby bass chartreuse" and can be very "hot" sometimes at Perris.

As a general rule, the spots rarely come up for a surface bait so top-water fishing is practically non-existent at Perris. Lake experts also note that because of the Summer thermocline, spots will rarely be graphed at depths shallower than 15 feet during this time of year.

Lake Piru (Map - p.188)

You will find that Lake Piru is often overlooked by Southern California bass fishermen. It is a small, 1000 acre lake about 50 miles north of Los Angeles. But, usually the weekend angler opts for Castaic which is slightly closer to L.A. and features the possibility of a trophy fish. Or, they drive past Piru and seek their fame and fortune at Casitas, which is about another hour away.

The locals don't mind this at all, for they have sampled Piru's northern bass bite which can be fantastic at times. This is not an elaborately designed lake, but it does have good launching, a decent marina, a restaurant and camping nearby. There are rental boats available. Also, because of its small size, both car toppers and bass rigs will be able to cover the entire lake easily in a day's fishing. Most angling pressure on the lake is for planted trout.

Areas to Fish: Piru is not overly complicated to master, which is another reason the serious basser should give it a try. The northern fish are not as finicky as their cousins in Castaic and Casitas and are usually easier to catch. One key area to fish is the ski cove which is clearly marked with restricted buoys. Fishing is allowed in this arm, but fishing boat speed is restricted and skiers get first shot at the water. Felicia Cove is another hot spot, along with Bob Cat Cove on the opposite, southwest bank. The flats in front of the landing can be productive, along with the steeper cliffs on the east bank. When the water level is high, the west shore to the left of the launching area all the way up to the north fork can hold fish.

Best Times: A lot of bassers who fish Piru keep it as their "trump card" for the cold Winter months. Piru's northern strain fish will usually eat well -- if you can fish deep structure -- from December through February. The more obvious choice is March, April, and May when the bass spawn and move up shallow. Piru is characteristically a tough Summer lake.

Tips and Tricks: Piru can be a good worm lake at times. Even during the Winter the fish will often move up shallow for a few hours during the day, and a Texas rigged worm is your best chance. A hand-poured crawdad pattern is recommended. You can use the 4,5,6, and 7 inch models in both straight and curl-tail actions made by Teazer and A.A. Try a smoke/brown and black, straight brown/black, brown/crawdad belly, brown/watermelon or purple/red flake. Try doodlin' these same patterns in 4 inch straight or paddle-tail styles along Piru's deeper ledges and breaks from 20 to 50 feet. Small 2 to 4 inch worms split-shotted in typical shad tones can also be good.

Salt'n pepper grubs and Fat Gitzits in smoke/red flake and smoke/sparkle can generate strikes from the lazy Winter fish. Haddock Kreepy Krawlers in smoke, clear/sparkle and smoke/sparkle are also worth a try when Piru's bass are on shad.

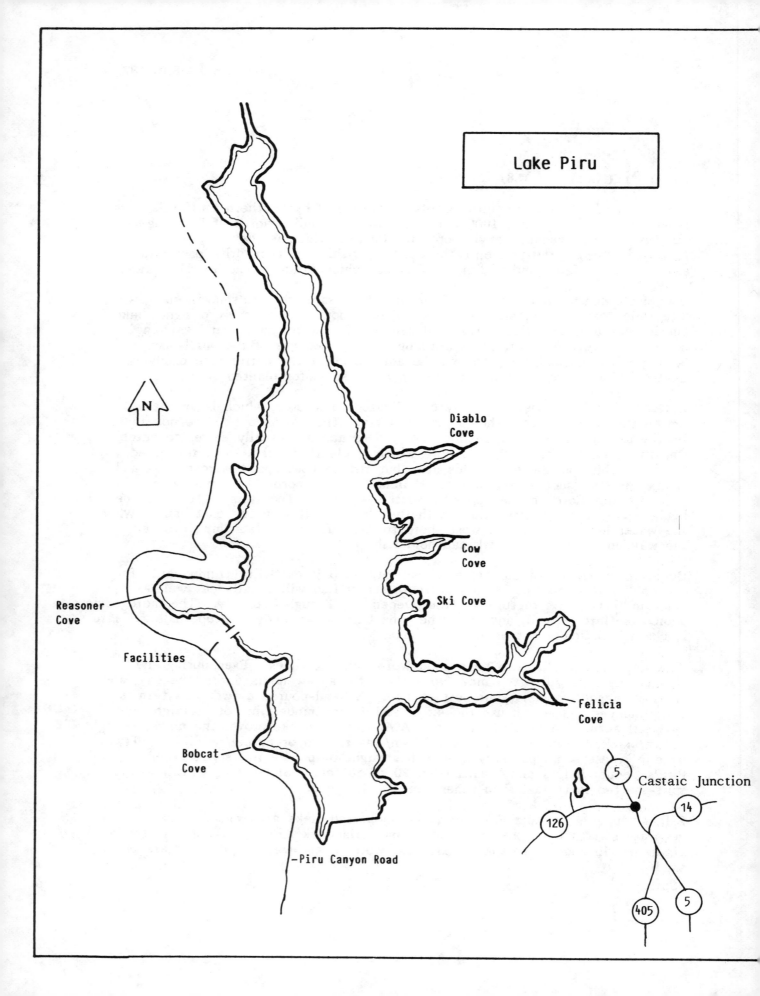

Lake Piru

N

Diablo
Cove

Cow
Cove

Ski Cove

Reasoner
Cove

Facilities

Felicia
Cove

Bobcat
Cove

Piru Canyon Road

Castaic Junction

5

14

126

405

5

Pork will also take some fish in the late Winter and Spring. Black, brown, and purple blends are best, but also think "big". These fish will occasionally jump on a big #1 Jumbo Frog or Spring Lizard crawled along the bottom. Spoonin' is also effective. The Hopkins #075 in chrome and the Haddock Structure Spoon in baby bass and smoke shad finishes are excellent picks.

Winter crankin' and blade fishing should also be given a fair shot at Piru. The larger crawdad-colored plugs such as the Rebel Maxi-R, and Rapala #7 Fat Rap have produced in the past. Similarly, the bass will also move up in the Winter to follow shad schools. The Bomber Model A in a silver-mirrored pattern matches well here.

If the lake is really filled to capacity, you can occasionally find some flip fish up in the north fork. During the Winter, there are small coves with heavy deadfall and riprap on the surface. A brown or black pig'n jig flipped into this cover will often take bass lying underneath it seeking radiant heat.

Baitfishermen will be wise to stick to nightcrawlers, fished with light 6 to 8 pound line, fly-lined along the brush and along the rocky banks.

Lake San Antonio (Map - p.190)

"San Anton'", as the locals refer to it, is a 16 mile long, 5500 acre lake on the edge of California's Central Valley just a short drive from Paso Robles. This is a full-service lake with marinas, bait'n tackle shops, camping, grocery stores, and house boats for rent. It is a very popular area also for pleasure boaters and water skiers, especially once school is out in late Spring.

There is a thriving northern and smallmouth bass fishery at San Anton'. When the lake level is up, there is a wealth of shoreline and outside structure to fish, compatible to a wide range of approaches. Many people who fish bass at San Anton' note that the lake seems to be divided into two distinct parts. To the west, there are the shallows and flats, with numerous coves and minor points. To the east, there is deeper cover, steep rocky walls, and long, extending points. Lake regulars say to be prepared for the bass to be predominantly biting in either one half of the lake or the other, but usually, not both.

Areas to Fish: In the east arm of the lake, Bee Rock Cove to the right of the dam has a lot of trees and broken rock banks worth trying. There can sometimes be a flip bite in these trees. To the left of the dam, the pipeline bank can be a good smallmouth spot, along with the white chalk cliffs and the south east shore. Harris Creek Campground and the half mile of shoreline to the right of the south launching area round out the picks for this side of the lake. To the west, try the trees in Dumb Dumb cove, the submerged "humps" in front of the floating outhouse on the north bank, or way back into the shallow flats in the Spring.

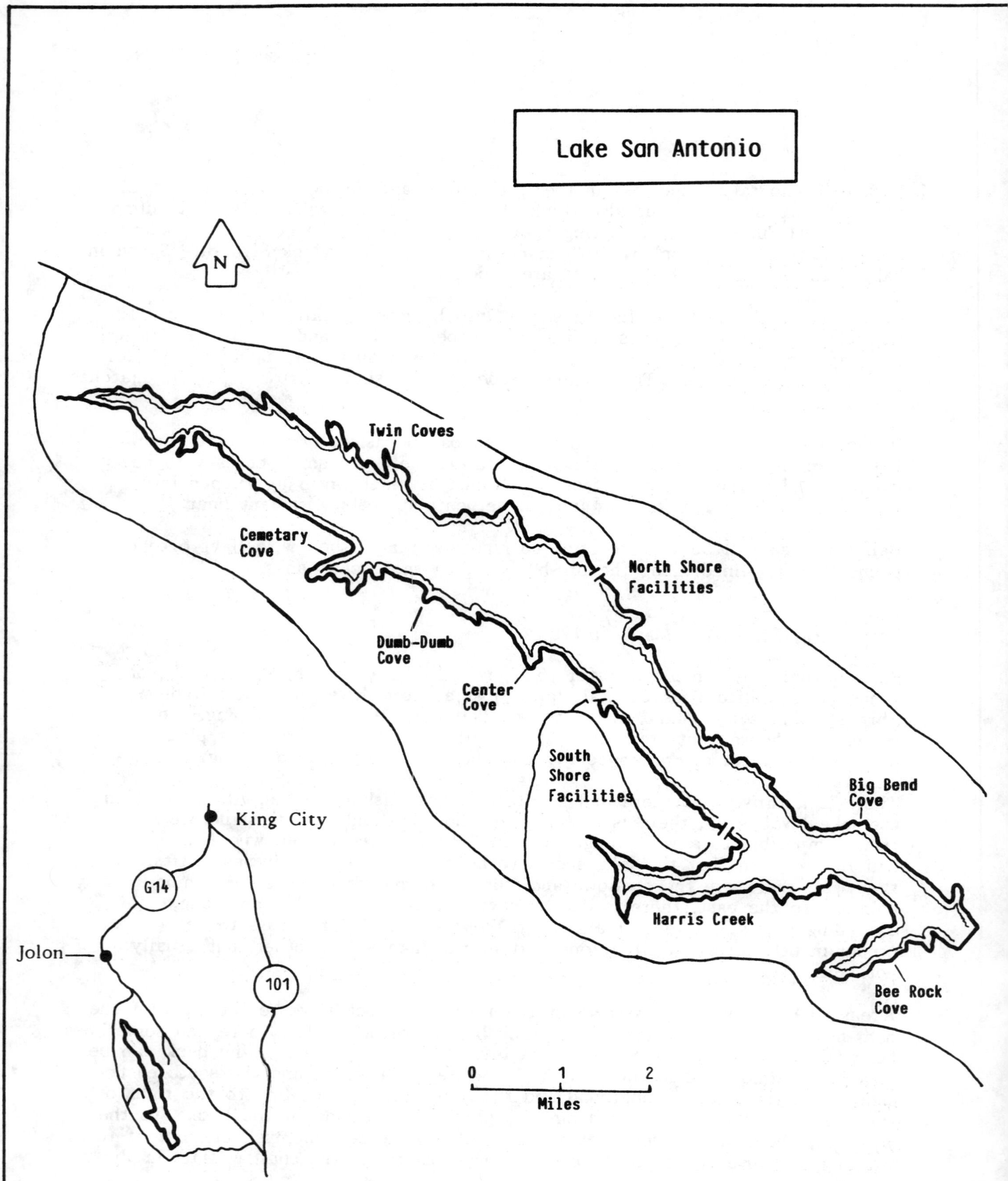

Lake San Antonio

N

Twin Coves

Cemetary
Cove

Dumb-Dumb
Cove

Center
Cove

North Shore
Facilities

South
Shore
Facilities

Big Bend
Cove

Harris Creek

Bee Rock
Cove

King City

G14

Jolon

101

0   1   2
Miles

Best Times: Spring and Fall can be very good periods to fish San Anton' for both smallmouth and largemouth action.   Bass can certainly be taken in the Summer, but here again, the water ski, jet ski, houseboat, and day cruiser traffic is very heavy.   In the Summer, fish early in the day, rest in the afternoon and then return for the evening action.

Tips and Tricks: There can be some large expansive weed and moss beds at San Anton' that shelter both species of bass.   White or chartruese buzzbaits fished over the heaviest concentrations of this vegetation can be sensational at times. If this doesn't produce, try casting some Fat Gitzits in and through these beds. Solid smoke, smoke/red flake and pumpkin green are the colors to use with these tube baits.

San Anton' is an excellent plastic worm lake.   The Texas rig crawled along the bottom is the preferred technique, but don't eliminate either doodlin' or split-shottin'.   Earth tone browns are a good choice, along with black/chartreuse tail, red/black, and smoke/red flake.   Also fish plastic jigs in the same areas. The Haddock Kreepy Krawler in smoke/sparkle, smoke/red flake, and smoke/blue flake is especially effective when the winds come up and muddy the water near the bank.   Shad move up into this off-colored water, and the Kreepy Krawler excels as a natural shad imitation here.

Crankbaits also produce results for both northerns and smallmouths.   Try Rapala Fat and Shad Raps, Bomber Model A's and Storm Wigglewarts in crawdad and shad finishes.   A real "sleeper" here can be a crankbait made by Rebel shaped to look like a natural crawdad.

In the Summer and Winter, San Anton's bass will often retreat deep to outside structure in 40 feet of water.   A lot of the lake locals opt for live bait under these tougher conditions.   Waterdogs are the preferred live offering, but don't hesitate to use deep-water wormin' techniques, too.

San Vicente Lake (Map – p.192)

"Vicente", as this lake is known in local circles, is one of the famous impoundments in the San Diego City Lakes system.   With Florida hybrids pushing 19 pounds, this lake is also a prime candidate for a potential world record fish.

Facilities, as with most lakes in this system, are limited: launch ramp, rental boats, a small concession for bait and tackle.   San Vicente, like the other City Lakes, is also open for a portion of the year on a three day per week basis.   Currently, the lake is scheduled to be open from October to July.

With only 1000 surface acres, the fishing in this canyon lake can be tough. There are lots of threadfin shad, but not a lot of visible shoreline cover.   You

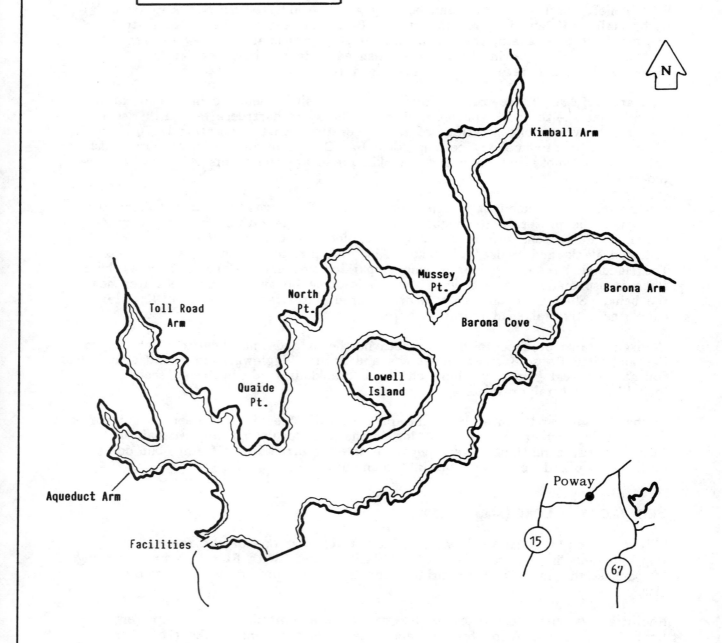

San Vicente Lake

N

Kimball Arm

Toll Road
Arm

North
Pt.

Mussey
Pt.

Barona Arm

Barona Cove

Quaide
Pt.

Lowell
Island

Aqueduct Arm

Facilities

Poway

15

67

will be fishing rocky banks and points, drop-offs, submerged "humps", underwater ledges, and the main island in the lake.

Water clarity varies here, ranging from very clear to stained. Lake regulars who have steady success at San Van scale down to 6 to 8 pound test line and learn to fish a variety of subtle baits.

Areas to Fish: The island is always a good place to start. Fish it downhill, casting to the bank. But also, pull your boat in tight to the shore and work your bait (usually plastics) uphill. The Barona Arm and the Aqueduct Arm are good big fish spots. The drop offs at Quaide Point and Mussey point are popular with local bassers. The chimney area (termed so due to an aging chimney-like structure on the bank) is east of the main island between the Barona and Kimball arms. This is also an excellent spot to try.

Best Times: This lake is basically tough all the time. However, if you can time your trip, mid-April to mid-May will be the best period for some sustained action. This is just prior to the spawn when these Florida hybrids start to move up shallower.

Tips and Tricks: It takes an accomplished worm fisherman to consistently put Vicente bass in the live well. Split-shottin' has really caught on here. Thin, 4 inch patterns in typical shad imitations, e.g. smoke/red, smoke/sparkle, and smoke/blue are good. So are the standard array of hand-poured, 4 inch worms in the "San Diego" colors: brown/smoke, cinnamon/blue, crawdad/green, brown/watermelon. The smaller 2 inch Cato Lil' Bit worm retrieved straight back from the bank slowly with a darter or P-head in light smoke color has been a "hot" secret. But also, rig up some longer, 8 inch, hand-poured worms, Texas-style, in the "San Diego" colors. The bigger fish at San Vicente will definitely eat these snake-like baits. This is the home of the "line feelin'" technique, so pick your spot and slowly "feel" that worm bait back to the boat.

Pork will occasionally take some nice fish from Vicente. In past seasons, a local favorite was a black bucktail hair jig with a black, 4 inch, Superfloat worm split to the sex collar as the trailer. Not too many fishermen know about this lure so it is still a good bet during the colder Winter months. Standard pig'n jig combinations are effective with live rubber skirts and #11 Pork Frogs. Work jigs primarily in the rockiest areas.

The top-water action at this lake can also be surprisingly outstanding at times. The #11-S floating Rapala worked twitchin' will stick the most surface-feeding fish. The Zara Spook and Smithwick Devils' Horse are good backups.

One other somewhat peculiar technique has maintained a limited popularity at San Vicente, but it does generate some trophy-sized fish. During the Winter months, bruiser-class bass often suspend at Vicente in 20 to 45 feet of water, picking off wayward planted rainbow trout as they pass by. A few innovative local fishermen theorized that they could get some of these large Winter bass to eat a rainbow trout pattern lure. The problem was getting it down to the bass. Lead core line trolled with a count down Rapala in rainbow trout finish did the trick. This little tip is definitely worth considering during the Winter months at Vicente for a trophy fish.

Bank fishermen should also like this lake. It is a good lake for this type of fishing particularly with bait such as 'crawlers or 'dads. Often the bank walkers at San Van will do as well, if not better than the guy in the bass boat.

Lake Shasta (Map - p.195)

With over 30,000 surface acres and numerous coves, arms, and inlets, Shasta comprises one of the largest and most varied inland waterways in the West. The facilities for camping, waterskiing, pleasure boating resorts, and houseboats are expansive all over this lake. The lake sports a year around bass fishery offering one of the finest opportunities to catch smallmouths you will ever encounter. There is also a thriving largemouth community with some of these Shasta bass having topped the scales at over 10 pounds. But overall, if you have a limited time to spend on this lake, direct your attention to the bronzebacks where action can be very hot and heavy.

As was mentioned in the previous chapter on smallmouths and spots, you have to scale down to be successful at catching these fish. Bring baitcasters loaded with 6 to 10 pound line and spinning outfits spooled with 6 and 8 pound test. This is very important to improve your catch here.

Best Times: Shasta's bassin' regulars prefer Spring as the best time overall to fish both smallmouth and largemouth bass. By April, look for the largemouths to move to the backs of coves for the annual spawn. The bronzebacks should then also be ready to nest in the gentle gravel areas in and around points and dropoffs. Smallmouths in particular can also be caught in the middle of Winter, which can prove to be a good trip, especially with diminished crowds.

Areas to Fish: Locals choose the Pit River Arm as their favorite spot for bassin' all year long with its submerged brush and trees. Other areas worth trying include the O'Brien inlet, the Sacramento Arm, the Salt Creek inlet, and Elmore Bay. The smallmouths are going to be found primarily on the rockier banks which are scattered throughout the lake.

Tips and Tricks: Small, 2 to 4 inch plastic worms and grubs will be good choices to start with. Fish them on darters, Texas-rigs, or split-shot setups. Shasta's bass orient to the dominant crawdads and threadfin shad found in the lake. Thus, keep your plastic baits fairly well aligned with these natural colorations. Clear/sparkle, smoke/sparkle, earth tone browns, and purple shades will all work with both the worms and the grubs.

Shasta's bronzebacks will inhale a Fat Gitzit fished on a 1/8 ounce P-head and 6

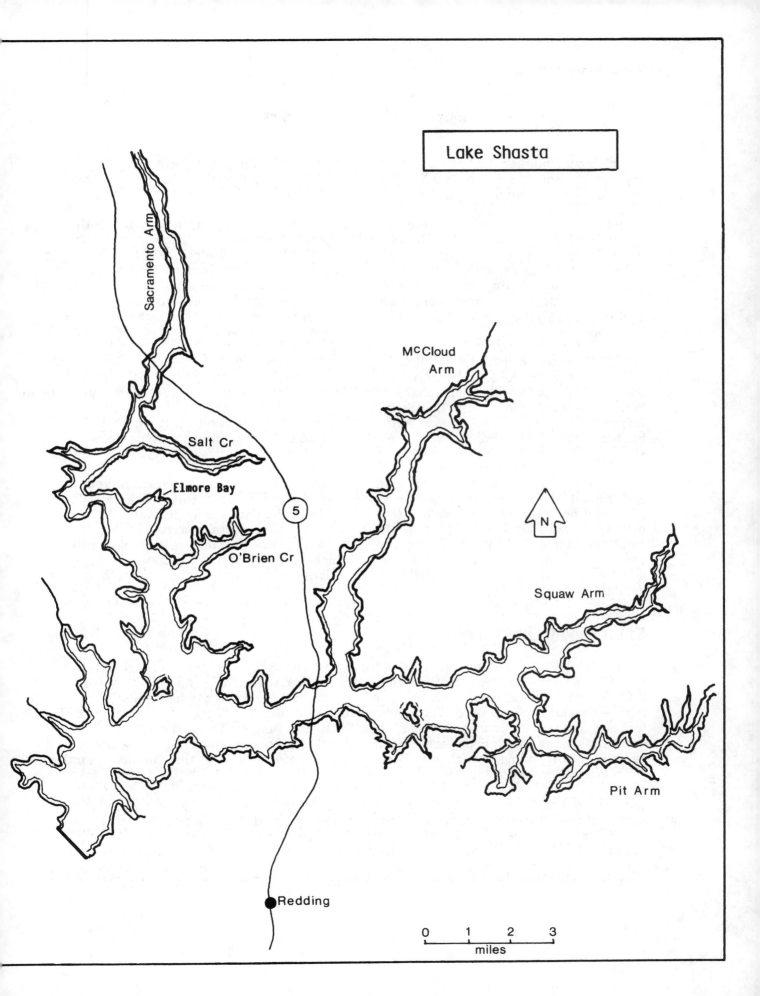

Lake Shasta

Sacramento Arm

McCloud
Arm

Salt Cr

Elmore Bay

5

O'Brien Cr

N

Squaw Arm

Pit Arm

●Redding

0   1   2   3
     miles

pound monofilament. There are three colors of this lure that have been responsible for some good smallmouth tallies: smoke/red flake, chartreuse, and a clear/chartreuse mix.

Keeping with the crawdad theme, you can't go wrong with pig'n jigs for both types of Shasta bass. The smallmouths predictably prefer a smaller presentation. A 1/4 ounce brown fine live rubber jig teamed with the diminutive #101 pork Spin Frog, also in brown, is a solid choice. But, don't be surprised to find these scrappers also inhaling larger offerings all the way up to the #1 Jumbo Frog in the Winter months. Experiment here with different pork combinations. Plastic jigs such as Garland Spiders and Kreepy Krawlers also catch both species. Use clear/sparkle and smoke/sparkle patterns tossed on 1/4 to 3/8 ounce lead heads.

If you concentrate on the smallmouth bass, then scale your crankbaits down a bit also, Smaller size cranks in crawdad, foil, and shad patterns are good. Try the Rebel Suspend-R, Rebel Humpback, Rapala #5 Fat Rap, Storm Wee Wart, and Wiggle Wart and the Bagley Balsa B. Switch to a Bagley DBIII in red/black for largemouth action. For spinnerbaits, a 1/4 to 3/8 ounce white with nickel blades is the preferred model. Use either a solid white, or white/chartreuse skirt.

The smaller, #9 Rapalas in both gold and silver can also be twitched, jerked, and ripped for Shastas's bronzebacks. If bait fishing is your forte, Shasta produces outstanding catches for the recreational basser. Live crickets, usually fished below a float from the bank or in a boat, take a toll on the smallmouth population. This is a hot bait -- the only problem is that you will catch a lot of short, sub-legal (under 12 inch) fish with them. Look for bigger smallmouths and largemouth with live crawdads or waterdogs when these baits are available.

Silverwood Lake (Map - p.198)

A small lake of a little over 1000 acres, Silverwood is a major recreational playground for week-enders throughout Southern California. This is an alpine lake located in the mountains north of San Bernardino. Don't be fooled by its high elevation. Silverwood has a year around fishery for largemouth bass, with lunkers topping 17 pounds. It has good facilities ranging from developed campsites, a marina, excellent launch ramps, and boat rentals. The lake also permits water skiing, which can become fairly intense during the Summer months, then diminishes until late Spring.

Silverwood can be miserably cold in this mountain setting. Always keep some cold weather gear stowed in your boat, even during the Summer. A chilling wind can rip through the canyon that forms this reservoir, generating some really rough wave action. Although the fishing can still be good in the winds, you would be wise to carry a strong anchor with you. There are times that even the best electric trolling motors will not cut through Silverwood's gales and there are very few places to take cover here.

Best Times: Most of the serious bass fishermen that visit Silverwood prefer the late Spring. The bass spawn later here than at lower elevation lakes. Thus, the last weeks in April all the way through June can be very exciting. The other times for Silverwood include mid-Fall and late Winter, around February. It is a good lake for deepwater tactics.

Areas to Fish: The best spots that recurrently produce at Silverwood are the various points on both sides of the main channel, and sometimes, within the channel itself, off deep structure. Other good areas include Outhouse Cove, the slide area across from the dam to the east, and the brushy shoreline next to the dam toward the west.

Tips and Tricks: One of the best ways to tackle Silverwood's bass population is to arm yourself with a good collection of spoons during the late Fall, Winter, and early Spring. This is one of the finest spoonin' spots in all of California. The main channel is the best location along the points there, the outside breaks, and just about on any submerged brush or schools of shad you happen to meter. The standard models will work including the Hopkins 3/4 ounce #075 in chrome, Kastmaster 1/2 ounce in silver, and Haddock Structure Spoon in anchovy blue or chartreuse. But, interestingly, also carry some spoons in gold finish (the Hopkins and the Kastmaster series) along with some smaller models. Sometimes Silverwood's largemouths turn on to these smaller spoons in 1/8 to 1/4 ounce in both gold and silver. The Hopkins slim No-Equal and the Bass Pro Shops Strata Spoons will be effective.

Next, bring along a good stock of salt'n pepper and green/flake single-tail grubs. Use them with P-heads or darters, but also rig them split-shot style. These can be dynamite here. Fat Gitzits fished slow in smoke/sparkle, smoke/red or pumpkin/green can also be effective all year long at this lake. Plastic worms fished both Texas-rigged and split-shotted are consistently good. Stay with mostly 4 inch straight and curl-tail models in purple/red flake, motor oil/red flake, chocolate/blue neon, and smoke/blue flake.

The flip bite here can also be spectacular when the bass move tight into the brush. Flip 1/4 to 3/8 ounce live rubber jigs in brown or brown/orange with #1 or #11 brown frogs. A #11 pork frog in "spotted craw" color, dyed mottled green, has also been a well kept secret trailed behind a brown jig. You can pitch pork all year at Silverwood, but when it comes to trophy fish, two other Spring lures stand out. Use the purple or brown vinyl jig/Superfloat worm combo off the points and along the brush. Then try the magnum Bomber Long A (saltwater size) jerked with heavy tackle. Smoke/orange is a good color. Be prepared to tie into one of Silverwood's chunky stripers while stroking this large lure.

Other top-water action can be found with Rapalas and Rebels twitched, jerked, and ripped. Stay with the medium-to-large versions of these floating minnows --

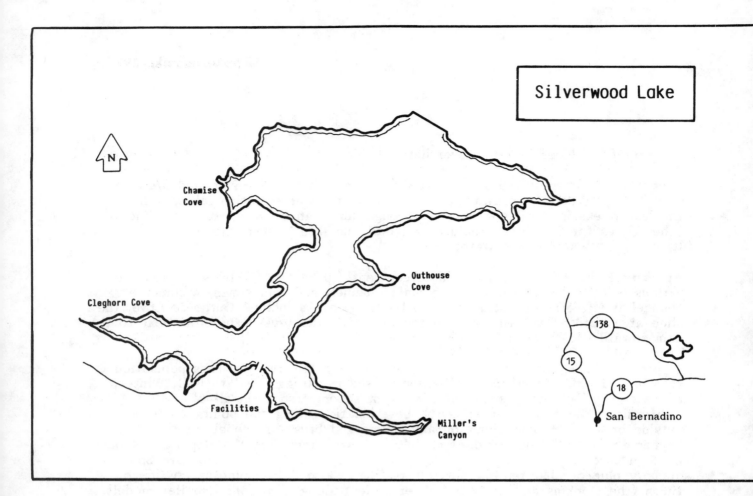

Silverwood Lake

N

Chamise
Cove

Outhouse
Cove

Cleghorn Cove

Facilities

Miller's
Canyon

138

15

18

San Bernadino

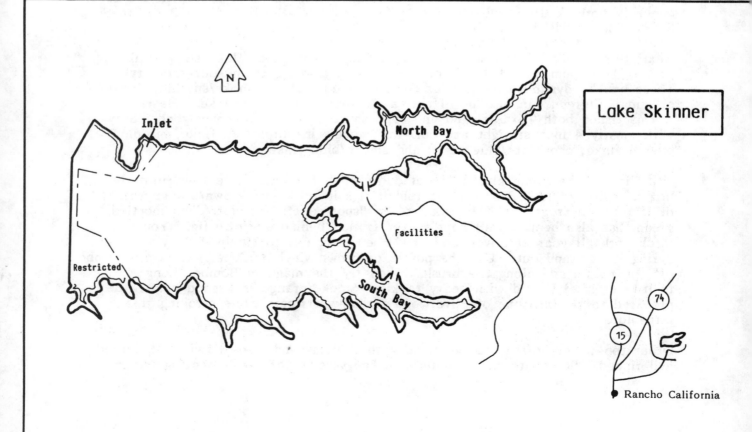

N

Lake Skinner

Inlet

North Bay

Facilities

Restricted

South Bay

74

15

Rancho California

Silverwood's largemouths will tear into a bigger bait. When that wind comes up in the warmer months, use a white buzzbait, thrown into heavy shoreline brush, and drag it back through the choppy water. This lure can also nail a few lunkers at this alpine lake.

Lake Skinner (Map - p.198)

This has to be one of the truly underrated bass lakes in California. Skinner is only 1200 acres when the water level is at its highest. It is located between San Diego and Riverside, 9 miles from Rancho California. It is a total non-contact lake, serving as a drinking water reservoir for Southern California. There are good facilities at Skinner, including an excellent boat ramp, large store, bait'n tackle, great campgrounds, and a boat rental fleet.

Skinner is a very uneventful lake in terms of its terrain. There are some gentle sloping banks, a few rocky points, some mud flats, a couple of underwater reefs, and when the lake is up, a fair amount of tule growth. All the bass are northern strain fish. The lake is open all year long and receives it greatest angling pressure when rainbow trout plants start in the late Fall.

Areas to Fish: The long bank to the right of the marina will hold bass throughout the year. The small coves on the east bank as you continue around hold fish on submerged boulders. The spillway at the northwest end is popular in the Summer when it is flowing. A lot of shad will school up here along with surface-feeding largemouths. A variety of coves, long points, and buoyed reefs on the south bank, along with an underwater rock jetty in the northwest corner are frequently productive.

Best Times: Skinner is an excellent Summer lake. Many bass fishermen prefer to fish it from June through September when the fish are actively feeding on threadfin shad. The Spring action is fair, but if the water is up, look for some nice fish in the tules. Late Fall and Winter are also good for slow-down presentations and deepwater spoonin'.

Tips and Tricks: To be successful at Skinner, you will have to master the subtle baits. Small 2 to 4 inch worms split-shotted, shake'n baked, doodled, crawled, and fished with darters and P-heads are dynamite baits for this lake. Light 6 pound test line is the key. The bass will strike these offerings shallow or deep, all year long here. The best colors to use include: motor oil/blue flake, amber/flake, salt'n pepper, smoke/gold flake, and all of the typical earth tone "San Diego" colors. Larger, six inch worms rigged Texas-style also catch their share of Skinner's northern bass. Here's a tip -- use a red/black blood line in the heat of Summer.

The salt'n pepper grub and the A.A. Reaper are also deadly at Skinner. Take your choice -- split-shot or P-heads with these small plastic baits. Lake experts also rig the grub on a pegged sinker, Texas-style and take outstanding larger fish flipped deep into Skinner's tule banks. Other subtle baits that are worth trying are the Fat Gitzit and the Haddock Twin-Tail fished on 1/8 ounce P-heads in smoke, smoke/sparkle, or clear/sparkle finishes.

As for jigs, Skinner's bass will eat a pig'n jig combo flipped into the tules. Browns and blacks are best, with #11 or #1 frogs, and 1/2 ounce live rubber jigs. For fishing the more open water, you cannot beat a plastic shad imitation. The Haddock Kreepy Krawler, and Garland spider jigs in smoke/sparkle, smoke/blue flake and clear/sparkle are the hot ticket. Definitely cast these into the bank when the winds come up and muddy the water. These plastic jigs, like the salt'n pepper grub, will also catch fish flipped into the tules when the water level is up.

Spinnerbaits and crankplugs will sometimes work at Skinner. A 1/4 to 3/8 ounce blade in white, chartreuse, or chartreuse and white combination pulled parallel to the tules can be very effective. Similarly, dominant shad-colored cranks will take fish here. The Rapala #5 Fat Rap, Bagley DBII, Rebel Deep Wee R, Storm Wiggle Wart, and Bomber Model A in Tennessee shad, foil, chrome, or mirrored surfaces are solid picks.

The surface action at Skinner is limited. There is an occasional warm weather bite on glitter shad Zara Spooks in the early morning. For evening action, try a smaller #9-S floating Rapala or chrome/blue Rebel. White/blue or solid brown buzzbaits in 1/4 to 3/8 ounce sizes are also effective top-water baits at this lake.

Lake Sutherland (Map - p.201)

One of the smallest lakes in the San Diego chain is Sutherland, with only 500 surface acres. This lake is also the most difficult to reach, stashed away in the hills outside of the little hamlet of Ramona about 45 miles northeast of San Diego.

There are minimal facilities, including boat ramp, rental fleet, and a small concession for bait and tackle. Waterskiing and swimming are not permitted. Sutherland opens approximately from March through October, and operates only three days a week.

In late Spring through Summer, you may witness one of the most spectacular sights you can ever imagine on a freshwater body of water. Sutherland is famous for its surface-busting hybrid bass that can literally keep acres of water churned up for hours. The volume of keeper to trophy-size fish you may see on a given day can be immense. Sutherland is similar to other lakes down South like Otay and Hodges that evidence what seems to be the same large-scale feeding frenzies. However, when a frenzy happens at Sutherland, any other alternate pattern usually gets completely shut off. Put simply, when the bass start boiling here, you either learn to catch them on top or phone it in!

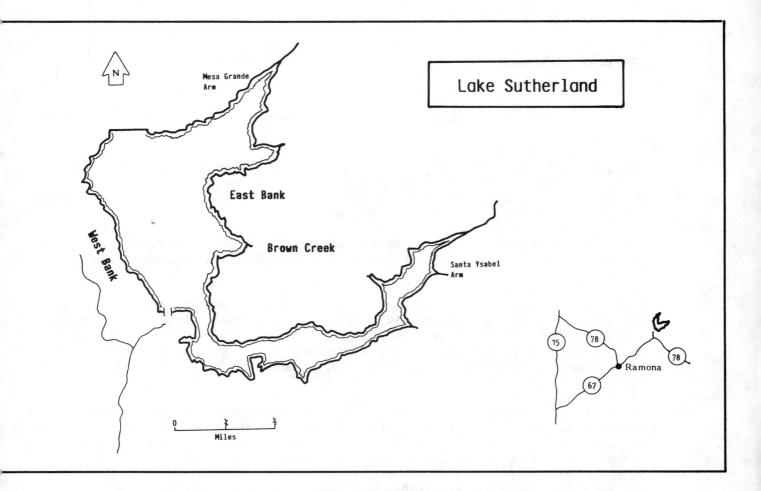

Lake Sutherland

Mesa Grande Arm

East Bank

Brown Creek

West Bank

Santa Ysabel Arm

0   ⅓   ⅔
Miles

15   78   78
67   Ramona

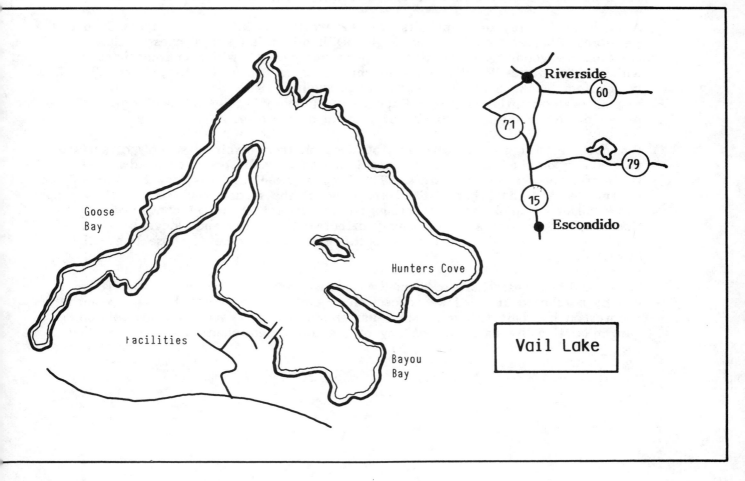

Goose Bay

Hunters Cove

Facilities

Bayou Bay

Riverside   60
71
79
15
Escondido

Vail Lake

Areas to Fish: The Santa Ysabel Arm has a lot of broken rock and submerged trees. This part of the lake usually holds fish throughout the season. Up in the northern portion of the lake, the Mesa Grande Arm and the dam area are good spots with lots of larger rocks and huge boulders.

Best Times: If you can master the bite on this lake, both Spring and Summer can afford good fishing. The surface fireworks are usually a late Spring to Summer event.

Tips and Tricks: Plastic worms account for many fish over 5 pounds here annually. Split-shottin' has quickly become the preferred method. Be ready to switch off from one worm color to another which is very typical for this lake. The Fluttercraft super thin, 4 inch, curl-tail worms are a regional favorite in shad tones. Go with smoke, smoke/sparkle, smoke/red flake, smoke/blue flake and salt'n pepper for starters.

A Texas-rigged worm will also catch fish, especially working along the tree trunks in the Santa Ysabel Arm and the big boulders in the Mesa Grande Arm. A larger, 6 inch, solid black, Superfloat worm is pretty standard. Smaller hand-poured baits in the popular earth tone "San Diego" colors also fish well on light line and a 1/8 ounce bullet weight. Try cinnamon/blue, chocolate/blue neon, smoke/brown, brown/watermelon, brown/black, and copper/neon green.

A fairly good array of crankbaits are also worth chuckin'. The Rapala Shad and Fat Raps, Bomber Model A, and Bagley DBII all in foil and Tennessee shad patterns are good. A conventional top-water approach will also sometimes work with the Smithwick Devil's Horse in chrome, Zara Spooks in shad, Storm Chug Bugs in phantom black, and white buzz baits producing. Sutherland's bass also respond well to either a #11-S Rapala or a Bomber Long-A in smoke/green finish jerked or ripped along the bank and even in open water.

But now let's figure out what can be done on those exciting schools of surface fish boiling on the shad. Locals have found that small spoons cranked across the surface will sometimes work. The Hopkins No-Equal, Haddock Structure Spoon, Kastmaster and the Schurmy Shad are some of the models they like. Salt'n pepper grubs, silver or smoke/sparkle Scroungers and even 1/16 to 1/4 ounce white Rooster Tail spinners are surprisingly effective (see Otay and Hodges). Gear down to 6 pound mono and stay with it. Eventually, some of those fish will bite!

Sutherland's largest bass are annually taken on golden shiner minnows. These can be purchased at the lake concession or caught right from the lake (see the chapter on live bait fishing). More lunker-size "toads" over 8 pounds will be caught on this live bait than on any of the lures mentioned.

Trinity Lake (Map - p.204)

With over 17,000 acres, 145 miles of shoreline, and some of the prettiest scenery in California, what more could you ask for from the premier smallmouth factory in the state? Trinity is located 45 miles north of Redding and 260 miles from Sacramento. This is an immense full-service waterway, with facilities including marinas, bait and tackle shops, resorts, campgrounds and houseboat rentals. Although it is situated in the northernmost part of the great state, the drive to Trinity is well worth the effort.

The lake is considered to be the best smallmouth fishery in the West. Numerous 5 to 6 pound bronzebacks are caught here annually. The lake record -- also the state record -- is a whopping 9:1 pound smallmouth. Trinity also has a thriving northern largemouth community that sometimes gets overlooked with all the attention given to the bronzebacks.

As with other smallmouth waters, gear down with 6 to 8 pound monofilament and small to medium size lures for the bronzebacks. Largemouths are also not that adverse to hitting the smaller offerings. Work the rockier areas for the bronzebacks, and the brushier, thicker shoreline cover for the bucketmouths. Occasionally, they will be mixed together, but normally, count on fishing each in different spots.

Areas to Fish: Look to find better smallmouth concentrations at the north end across from the Cedar Stock Resort on the Stuart Fork Arm. Mule Creek and the Estrelita Marina on that same fork are also good bronzeback territories. Also, try around the Fairview Marina north of the dam and the dredger piles in the North Fork by Trinity Center. Both largemouths and smallmouths congregate in cover around the East Fork of the Stuart Arm.

Best Times: April through mid-May is the best time for big bass of both species as they move up shallow preparing to spawn. The bass fishing at Trinity is good all the way through October. Smallmouths will be in 8 to 20 feet in the Spring moving down to 40 feet or deeper during the heat of August through September. The largemouths will be shallower in the Spring, but move off to deeper structure in 30 to 35 feet midday in the Summer months.

Tips and Tricks: Crankbaits are a good pick for both species of Trinity bass. Crawdad and chrome-colored patterns get bit best. Try the Storm Wee and Wiggle Warts, Rebel Suspend-R and Deep Wee-R, Bagley Balsa B, Bomber Model A, and the #5 Rapala Fat Rap.

Plastic worms fished on both darters and light bullet weight Texas rigs are always a staple. Stay with 2 to 4 inch patterns such as the Lil' Bit in blacks and purples. Also, throw some earth tone browns in hand-poured worms.

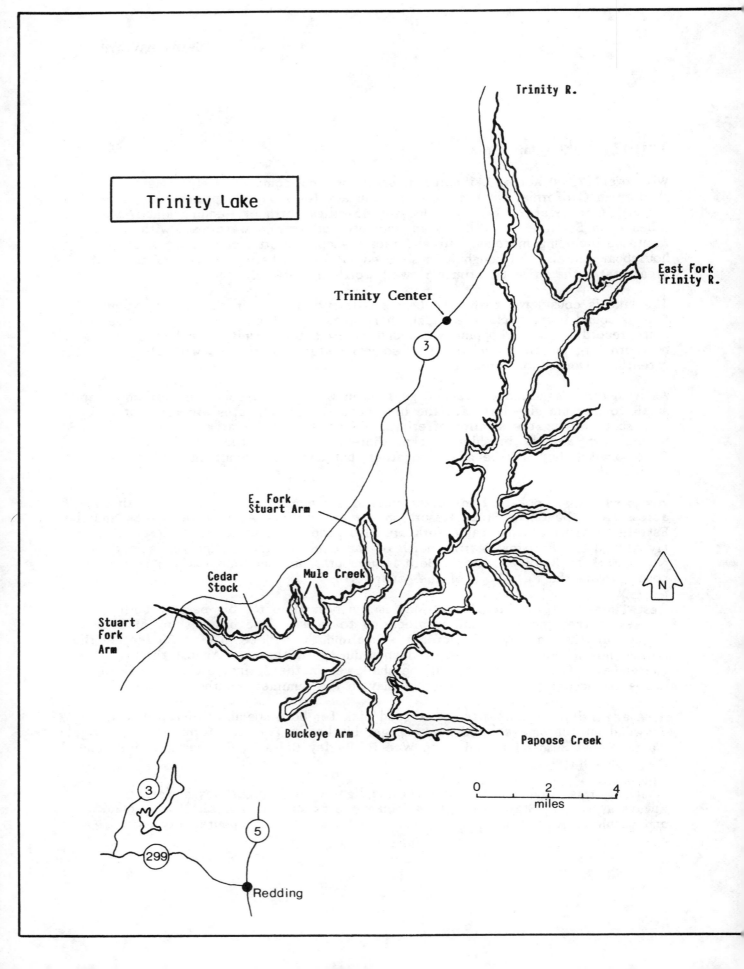

Trinity Lake

Trinity R.

East Fork
Trinity R.

Trinity Center

③

E. Fork
Stuart Arm

Cedar
Stock

Mule Creek

N

Stuart
Fork
Arm

Buckeye Arm

Papoose Creek

0   2   4
        miles

③

⑤

299

Redding

Grubs in similar colors, in additon to smoke/sparkle, clear/sparkle and salt'n pepper will take both species fished on 1/16 to 1/8 ounce P-heads. The Fat Gitzit in typical shad imitations, especially smoke/sparkle is an additional subtle bait that Trinity bass will eat.

Small pig'n jig in 1/4 ounce super fine live rubber skirts and #101 Spin Frogs, brown-on-brown, are good for pitchin' to rocky banks where bronzebacks hang out. Try the larger #11 Pork Frogs in brown and 3/8 ounce jigs for both large and smallmouths.

A Rapala or Bill Norman Rip-N floating minnow, ripped off rocks or brush can also be a dynamite presentation for Trinity's smallmouths. Largemouths strike these too. A white spinnerbait with nickel blades in 1/4 to 3/8 ounce is yet another good lure here.

Live bait will put a dent in the smallmouth numbers at Trinity. Crickets account for a lot of small bass, but some real lunkers, too. Split-shot these with a #6 to #8 baitholder hook. 'Crawlers and 'dads will also be effective for both types of bass.

Vail Lake (Map - P.201)

Vail is slowly becoming recognized as a trophy lake for lunker-size bass. The lake is located between Riverside and San Diego about 12 miles east of the town of Temecula. Facilities here are minimal. There is a small store and bait and tackle concession, rental boats, and one boat ramp. When the word gets out that the fish have turned on here, be prepared to sometimes sit up to an hour and a half in line waiting to launch your rig. However, when the bite is hot, the wait can be worth the trouble. Many hefty limits come out of Vail up to a 17 pound record bass. There is speculation that larger specimens loom to be caught, especially since the lake started planting trout in past Winters.

If you could ever imagine a near-perfect lake designed for bass fishing, Vail would have to come to mind. Although it is just 1000 surface acres when full, you will find every conceivable type of structure. There are groves of trees, tule banks, deadfall, scattered brush, rocky points, steep walls, submerged humps and islands, river channels and assorted ledges and breaks. Your necessary tackle can range from 6 pound test for split-shottin' all the way to 30 pound test for some very serious flippin'!

Areas to Fish: Bayou Bay to the right of the dock with its stumps and brush holds some shallow fish all twelve months. When the winds come up, it is a good place to hide. This bay and Hunter's Cove to the northeast are good Springtime spots. There is a good drop-off in front of the boat docks that is popular split-shot territory. The submerged island, the north coves to the right of the dam, and the far end of Goose Bay have historically been very good.

Best Times: Spring is the best period to look for a wall-hanger at Vail. Numerous fish are caught during March through June that top the 8 pound mark. Summer is the toughest time, but limits are still possible. In Fall, the action starts to pick up again. Deep water tricks will take bass at Vail in the middle of Winter. It is an excellent lake to fish when most others have shut off by November.

Tips and Tricks: Plastic worms are always a good pick at Vail. Texas-rigs shake'n baked, doodled, flipped, and crawled produce. Split-shottin' especially in the Spring, can be deadly in terms of sheer numbers. Worm preferences range from the thin profile split-shot worms made by Fluttercraft to earthtone hand-poured versions marketed by Teazer and AA. Lengths vary from 4 inch all the way up to a magnum size 12 inch snake flipped in the Spring. Popular colors include smoke/sparkle chartreuse tail, purple/chartreuse tail, watermelon/brown, smoke/blue flake, cinnamon/blue and salt'n pepper. The Mr. Twister 6 inch red/black bloodline and the 4 and 6 inch Superfloats in black, brown/black and "mean green", are good injection-molded worms.

Subtle presentations such as P-heads, darters, and Gitzits all catch fish here. A hot local trick, is to split-shot or P-head the salt'n pepper grub. This lure will take fish in the moss during the Summer when nothing else seems to work. Small 2 inch plastic worms and A.A. Reapers are also definitely worth a try.

The top-water activity at Vail can also be sensational. A number of trophy bass are caught each year on the Heddon Zara Spook. Toss shad glitter, blue shore minnow, and solid chrome. The Smithwick Devil's Horse and the Ozark Mountain Boy Howdie are good prop baits. A white buzzbait in the wind is also a bonafide hawg hunter. A #11-S Rapala or a Bagley Bang-O lure are preferred baits for Vail's twitch or jerk bite.

Spinnerbaits and cranks are also solid choices. Don't hesitate to throw the #6 to #8 giant Willowleaf blades in white or chartreuse. Crankbait selections include the #5 and #7 Rapala Fat Raps, the Shad Rap, Bill Norman Deep Little N, or Bagley DBII. Tennessee shad, smokey joe, and foil finishes are consistently best.

For jigs, flip and pitch pig'n jigs all year long at Vail. Brown on brown is the local's choice. Use #11 or #1 frogs. Black. black/chartreuse, and purple mixes also work. Brown/black vinyl skirts are a good tip for Winter. Along this line, spoon the breaks and ledges for cold weather bass. Use #075 Hopkins and the Haddock Structure Spoon in chartruese or blue.

The Delta

The California Delta(or the Sacramento-San Joaquin Delta) is a vast array of rivers, sloughs and backwaters located in a triangular area between Sacramento, Stockton and Rio Vista. In total, it encompasses over 1000 miles of navigable waters. The Delta is most famous for species other than black bass, including striped bass, sturgeon, salmon, steelhead and shad. All these species move through the Delta during spawning migrations. With all the other angling at-tractions, the good population of northern-strain largemouth bass are often over-looked. But bass anglers, who know better catch a lot of fish in the 5-10 pound class.

Areas to Fish: One key to success in this vast area is identifying promising habitat. Try these likely spots: a)tule beds along shore or islands, b)along rock jetties and breakwaters, c)around and under piers and pilings, d)around logs and fallen trees, e)in and around protected harbors, f)at points of land especially if it has overhanging growth, g)where irrigation pipes are dumping water into the main waterway.

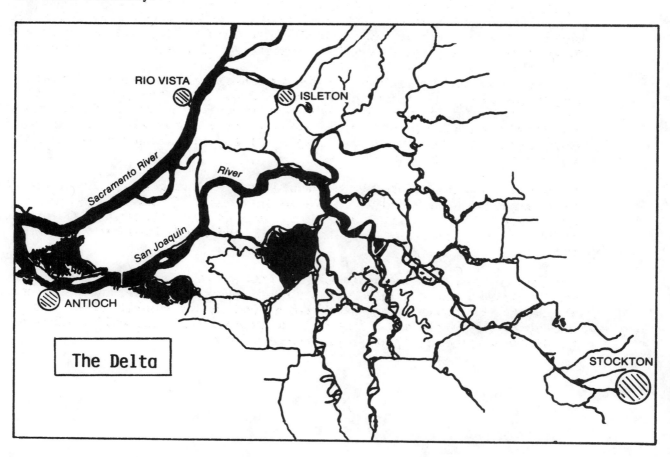

Best Times: Early mornings are usually the most productive although fish can be caught at any time. Evenings are also good after the boat traffic has subsided and the light is off the water. April and May are the best months. Summer is slower with the Fall improving into early Winter, but bass can be caught most months of the year.

Tips and Tricks: There are tons of crawdads in the Delta, enough to support a commercial fishery. So live crawdads, along with offerings like the Pig'n Jig and crawdad colored crankbaits are winners. Flippin' in the tules can be very productive with plastic worms(6 inch Jellywaggler or Super Float in black), or black or brown rubber-skirted jigs with attached frog-shaped pork rinds(use 17 pound test). White, green or black skirted, single-blade spinnerbaits(3/8 to 1/2 ounce) are winners. Try adding a pork rind trailer for scent and better visibility. Spinnerbaits are especially good at irrigation inflows. Remember the Delta is tidal water and tide movements are delayed from reported changes along the coast. The best bass fishing is during large tidal swings as water movement sweeps natural baits through the Delta waters. Fish the incoming tide.

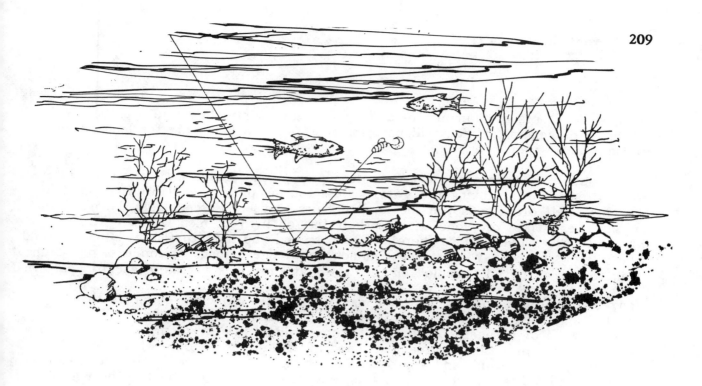

Bassin' Strategies

Bass fishermen are often amazed at the way top-level professionals are able to tame a lake and nail a limit of fish. The pros do this by deciphering what kind of "pattern" the bass are on. Most accomplished Bassmasters cite the ability to pattern their quarry as the foundation of the sport.

Learning to pattern the fish, however, is not as simple as it sounds. But, if the angler takes into account some basic factors beforehand, the primary feeding pattern may be easier to isolate. There are certain pre-pattern conditions that the pros review, sometimes for days prior to the tournament. They will examine the lakes general history, emergent weather patterns, water conditions and differences in specie behavior **before** they even make that first cast.

Assessing these pre-pattern variables serves to give professional bass fishermen an initial idea of how to select and prepare their tackle prior to a tournament. This knowledge also allows the anglers to more precisely draw up an opening game plan for the contest. They can begin to formulate in advance the probable baits and techniques to use as well as the best potential spots to try. A lot of valuable time can be saved and unproductive water eliminated when the Bassmaster reviews variables before working the lake.

Lake History

Most impoundments demonstrate certain seasonal characteristics year after year. Some are recognized, for instance as stellar worm lakes in the spring while others are early season spinnerbait havens. Some reservoirs are known for summer moss

Portions of this chapter originally appeared in
B.A.S.S. Times, published by Bass Anglers Sportsman Society, Inc.

beds, while others are famous for a deep structure wintertime bite. These are examples of generalized seasonal patterns that seem to hold true for long periods of time on a given lake.

Taking such history into account can often provide the angler with some reliable starting points in attacking the water. Bass touring pro, Jake Bedwell, feels that the lake itself often tells you the kind of baits to use. For example, he notes that on San Diego lakes everyone catches their fish on 9 to 11 inch worms. Then you go to Clear Lake where there's huge bass and you have to fish a 4 inch worm. Bedwell goes on to say that such common knowledge among veteran bass pros helps them to get an initial "handle" on the water as they look for more specific patterns.

Many Bassmasters also keep detailed logs. All of the principle elements that affected a particular outing are entered into a journal. Over a period of time, some features of a specific lake may become evident. Western pro, Larry Hopper, goes to a lake and fishes tournaments, and afterwards he records what the conditions were, what he did, and any other key things that happened. He puts these variables into a file on the lake, so the next time he goes to the lake he begins by looking over his notes.

With such historical and seasonal information, top level bassers like Bedwell and Hopper can begin to narrow down their tackle repertoire for an upcoming contest. Specific lures, types of viable retrieves and traditional fish-holding spots are contemplated as they design their strategies. They then lay out the appropriate rods, reels and lines, assembling the diverse outfits they feel they will need to start attacking the water.

Emergent Weather Patterns

Some Bassmasters frequently listen to weather reports days before setting out to the lake. Bass are an extremely tempermental specie. There is considerable evidence to indicate that these fish are affected by climatic changes.

Another California pro, Chuck English, actually utilizes a weather radio to monitor both prevailing and emergent conditions on the lake he is planning to fish. He will try to always watch for low pressure storms coming into the region. If possible, he likes to fish before it starts to rain. This can spark bass movement. English will then pre-rig his rods with items that will catch big, active fish like larger plastic worms and jig-and-pigs.

Larry Hopper also tries to gather as much information about weather conditions as he can before he arrives at the tournament. For example, in the Spring if Hopper was going to fish one of the desert lakes and it had been cold and windy all week and the water is in the low fifties, he wouldn't be going into the backs of coves even though it is springtime. He would start outside and work his way in, outside and inside points. Because it's been cold and windy, the fish should be holding outside.

Checking the weather reports for an uncoming tournament can also influence **how** you decide to present your baits. For instance English feels that with reports of bad weather, he knows he will have to focus on the most productive areas of the lake that he remembers from past knowledge. He'll plan on being more deliberate from the start with his presentations as he looks for bass holding tight to structure.

Thus by parlaying such information about the weather into their overall line of attack, pros like English and Hopper waste little time exploring "dead" stretches of water or trying out useless methods.

Water Conditions

If possible, try to also acquire some knowledge about the water conditions of the lake you are traveling to. Ask questions about clarity, rising and flowing levels, movement of current, pH and surface temperatures. There is a wealth of information to be gleaned from reviewing these variables prior to your trip.

Hopper and Bedwell often call the lake marina operator or dam manager to check beforehand if there is a lot of water being put in or drained out of the lake. This can be an integral component in establishing a fishing pattern. For example, Hopper routinely calls ahead when he fishes Lake Mojave to ascertain information on water flow. If he discovers that a lot of water is being run through the lake he will expect the bass to move out of the main river channel where the current is ripping. He will then concentrate on the coves where there is less turbulence. This eliminates considerable unproductive water as Hopper attempts to establish a complete pattern.

Bedwell, on the other hand, will key in on water levels. Depending upon whether or not a lake is high or low, he will set out a different line up of baits for the situation. Bedwell claims that the most critical thing he has learned in ten years of bass fishing is that if the lake is real high and flooded, use a bigger lure that covers a lot of water fast - like a spinnerbait. When a lake is low, a lot of times a little subtle lure works better. But, when the water is up, stay with a big, fast-moving bait.

In either case, both pros rely upon information about the specific impoundment's water conditions to decide what tackle to bring and what sort of initial strategy to devise once they arrive on the lake. By assessing this pre-pattern variable, the angler is once again able to limit his approach and focus on the potentially best areas using the best baits.

Specie Differentiation

Smart bassers will also review the different aspects of bass feeding habits in lakes with multiple species present. Some reservoirs can have Florida largemouths and spotted bass, for example. Others may have smallmouths and spots living together. A bass is not a "bass". Each separate specie has distinct behavioral traits.

Accounting for these differences in feeding habits before you reach the lake can also help to isolate a certain pattern. English points out that he often finds himself in a position to fish for multiple species in a tournament situation. He will review his logs and compare the previous methods he has successfully employed for largemouths and smallmouths. He will then rig up the right baits for both species the night before. English notes that if one specie is not active, he always has rigs ready for the other. He likes to start out with larger baits to catch large-mouths, because they represent bigger weights for tournament bassin'. But then he'll switch to little baits for smallmouths if the largemouths don't cooperate.

In this situation, expert bassers like English "cover all bases", by carefully analyzing the bass species they are stalking. By carrying an arsenal of lures and rigs to accommodate each specie, the pro is then able to respond to a full range of possible patterns. Successfully patterning bass on a given impoundment takes a lot of forethought with a measure of skill, experience and luck thrown in. Still considerable guesswork can be eliminated if these pre-pattern variables are assessed prior to leaving for the lake.

Attacking Small lakes

Tournament style bassin' in the West is often a tough proposition. This is particularly true for popular club level and team events. Many of these contests are held on small 1000 acre impoundments that serve as multi-use reservoirs. In San Diego, for instance, local promoters routinely stage major two-man team tournaments on tiny lakes such as Hodges, El Capitan and San Vicente. Weekend anglers are lured to these smaller impoundments because they are close to home. Many of these lakes also kick out some extraordinary double-digit class bass on a regular basis. Hence, many area Bassmasters reckon it may take only one big fish to win .

Still, the pressure on such small waters is immense. There can be over one hundred teams in the tournament. An additional fleet of sixty or so rental skiffs will be taken by recreational fisherman. There are typically another hundred shore anglers, a few dozen float tubers and at least fifty pleasure boats all sharing the water the day of the tournament. Put simply, this scene has all the earmarks of a virtual "zoo" as far as serious bassin' is concerned. Bassmasters in the West learn to accept this crowding as a feature of their environment. The successful competitors carefully devise strategies to work around this congestion.

Learn the Spots

Most of these small lakes are characterized by stark shoreline cover. There are a few minor targets to throw at such as boat docks, scattered boulders or the rip rap along a dam. Count on seeing boats blanket these visual targets immediately at the start of the tournament.

The other primary spots are found mostly on outside structure, often some distance from the bank. Your electronics will help you find ledges, drop-offs, submerged islands and gentle "humps". Most likely, you will not need topographical maps to locate the spots you failed to find with your electronics. There will already be boats on them. There are few secrets left to be discovered on such small lakes.

The Strategies

To begin with, if you think you can attack a 1000 acre lake on tournament day by quickly running down a shoreline, you will probably not do well. There are too many other boats you will have to maneuver around. Plus, the bass will be extremely wary after the first hour of competition. The boat traffic will definitely inhibit these fish from readily striking a reaction bait used in a rapid-fire presentation.

Mike Folkestad is a frequent competitor and high finisher in these small local contests. In these tournament conditions he will fish the more subtle baits such as a reaper, a small grub, or worm, with four or six pound test line, a 1/8 ounce sliding sinker or split-shot. It takes these kinds of baits, because the fish have so much pressure with the boats running around. That's the primary way you are going to get them.

Folkestad goes on to say that if you persist in using the larger reaction lures associated with a run-and-gun approach, you may not even get a single strike on these highly pressured waters. However, he does recommend firing off a few casts in the morning or late evening with a spinnerbait or crankplug as you approach a spot during that time. Folkestad feels that there is always a remote possibility at this time of day of finding one bass that is aggressive enough to attack a larger lure.

One alternative to the run-and-gun strategy then, is to locate a good spot and practically "camp" on it. The theory is that the bass in the lake will invariably use that particular location as a major feeding area **sometime during the day.** Anglers who camp on such a spot believe that it will only be a matter of time before a movement of bass occurs in that area. Sometimes this strategy really pays off. Both large bass and a volume of fish can often be taken from a single spot. Florida bass and San Diego lakes expert Chuck English has been known to patiently wait for that movement of fish on one of his prime locations. There are generally two movements, according to English, one in the morning and one in the evening. The Floridas will typically move up in the late afternoon. There are spots that he finds from trial and error that the fish use as a feeding shelf or ambush point. Pretty soon if he waits long enough, he will invariably stick some fish.

The trick is to place your boat in position to take advantage of the best presentation possible. For instance, it might be better to work a spot uphill instead of the more commonly used downhill retrieve. In this situation, it would be wise to keep the boat close to the shore and work uphill. Similarly, it might be important to anchor on an outside flat and fan cast the adjacent area. The anchor keeps the boat fairly stationary. The anglers won't have to fight the elements while they concentrate on every inch of the immediate terrain in casting distance from the boat. This is another method that sometimes accounts for limit catches on these little reservoirs.

Another option is to plan out a "rotation sequence", which will allow you to cover a greater amount of productive water. Design a game plan before the tourney. Pick out a half dozen prime spots that you figure should hold fish. Try to get to those locations during the time of day that they historically have held fish. The object is to rotate from spot to spot hoping to intercept the bass at the time they move on that particular area. This tactic is risky since quite often most of the productive areas have boats on them when you want to fish that spot.

Forget the Obvious

Most anglers will thus relegate themselves to fishing the most recognizable "hot" spots by either "camping" on the area or rotating between a small number or normally productive locations. Mike Folkestad instead takes a dramatically different approach. His secret ploy is to look for some of the least obvious water he can find. If you happen to get a good number in the tournament, Folkestad recommends going to a prime spot. These are spots all the good bass fishermen know. You can run to that spot and sit on it all day. If you get a low draw number so you go out late, then you aren't going to get on any of the good spots. What you do when you prefish is to look for little subtle structure between the good spots where the boats don't fish because it looks poor. If you examine these areas hard, you will find a little rockpile, maybe a little rough spot, or something that holds one or two fish.

Hence, Folkestad intentially focuses on otherwise bland, nondescript stretches of bank that might be overlooked by locals working the primary spots. Above all, Folkestad and English recommend a slow, meticulous presentation. These bass will more often than not be highly selective with regard to the baits they strike. They will have seen literally hundreds of offerings all day. Pick the lure you have confidence in then fish it slowly. Take some time to work these less obvious stretches. But continue to move from one to another, picking off a bass here and there. Five separate stretches can hold five solitary fish. This can translate into a limit catch!

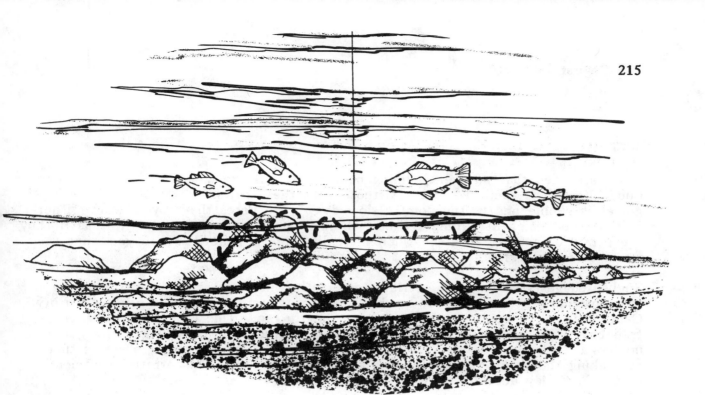

Beginner's Mistakes

If you haven't noticed lately, more and more anglers are getting hooked on serious bass fishing. The proliferation of organized clubs, dramatic increases in bass boat sales, and the formation of various tournament circuits are indications of the booming popularity of this sport.

Sometimes, however, it is very difficult for the novice angler to acquire the core information that will help him develop the diverse techniques necessary to fish bass competitively. As with any professional sport, there are always certain "basics" that serve as the cornerstone for successfully performing in the game. Pro athletes are constantly being told by coaches that they "have to get back to fundamentals" before they can refine their play. It's really no different with competitive bassin'. There are certain rudimentary things that the angler has to learn to do, day in and day out, if he is to bring fish to the scales on a consistent basis.

I surveyed top pros who fish the various bass circuits. Each of these fishermen is recognized as an expert of sorts in a particular facet of the bassin' game. I asked each one to discuss what they saw as the primary mistakes beginners make while utilizing a specific technique.

I might add that for this writer, working on this part of the book served as an excellent refresher course. Sometimes as athletes become more sophisticated in their approach to their sport, they lose sight of such fundamentals. The insights that these pros are willing to share may serve as a reminder that we have to master the basics before we try to "fine tune" our presentations. Here's what they had to say:

Wormin'

It is estimated that an overwhelming number of bass are caught on plastic worms. Chuck English is recognized as a virtuoso with these baits. His advice to the beginner is simple and to the point: **slow down!** He notes that novice worm fishermen are too quick at pulling the bait through submerged structure. It is as if they are afraid of getting hung up, when in reality this is exactly where you want the worm to really perform.

English suggests slowing the retrieve, especially when you feel the bait bumping into obstructions like rocks or brush. Ease the worm through this prime territory. Gently lift it, shake it, or "pop" it over the rip rap. This is an amazingly snag-free lure. By dancing it over and through the structure, you will actually get hung up less than by just dragging it along the bottom. English further observes that by making the worm "jump" through the rocks and brush, this erratic movement of the bait may actually trigger otherwise lethargic bass into striking.

Crankin'

The crankbait is a marvelous lure to use when you are looking for fish, particularly on unknown waters. However, as veteran pro Chuck Boydstun relates, too often the beginning basser simply fails to **put the plug where the fish live.**

Boydstun has watched many novices fish these baits in an overly cautious manner. The high cost of the plug, combined with two sets of deadly treble hooks, perhaps compels the recreational angler to be a little hesitant with regard to where he tosses these lures. Boydstun is emphatic that you have to be somewhat adventuresome when it comes to chuckin' and windin'. For instance, if the crankplug hits some brush, don't stop - keep winding! The diving bill on these lures will actually help to deflect it away from the structure.

Picture the crankbait working like a bumper car at the carnival. You must be willing to kind of "plow" it through the structure as it deflects from one stick-up to another. As was just said about wormin', the deflection of the plug off of the brush is precisely the action that stimulates the strike mechanism of the bass.

Spinnerbaits

As a former U.S. Bass "Angler of the Year" and prominent lure manufacturer, Fred Borders can make a spinnerbait sing. Beginners, he notes, often fail to make these blades work for them. Rookie bassers commonly cast the spinnerbait to a given target and then just grind it back in on a straight retrieve.

Borders claims that the secret to being successful with these lures is to learn to **fish the fall.** By this he means, as the lure approaches the structure(e.g. a boulder, stick-up, bridge piling, etc.) slow the retrieve and actually stop if necessary to allow the blades to flutter down into the strike zone in imitation of an errant baitfish. Once again, a little trick like this can aggravate the bass holding tight to cover into bushwhacking this rather uncomplicated lure.

Jiggin'

When it comes to fishing jigs, you would be hard pressed to find a pro to rival Utah's Bobby Garland. Using innovative designs and color schemes, this perennial high finisher set the tournament trail ablaze a few years ago with his famous Bassin' Man Spider and Creature jigs. He is very clear as to what is the single most important thing neophytes must do when pitching jigs: **maintain control and feel of the lure.**

Bobby Garland relates that quite often bassers just starting out fish jigs with either the line too tight or with too much slack. They are then unaware of whether the bait is making contact with the bottom or is just free-swimming through the water. His remedy is not that simple.

The angler has to spend some time working these baits. Usually jigs are most effective when they are bounced along the bottom. After repeated outings, you can develop a feel for when the line has to be tight as the lure swims unencumbered along a flat terrain. At other times, it is necessary to loosen up on the tension, creating a little slack. This is important to do as the jig hits some structure so it can tumble down deeper into the fish-holding cover. Hence, there is no substitute for practice in becoming proficient with a jig. You just have to stay with it to develop that uncanny feel for when the lure hits structure or when a bass inhales it.

Flippin'

Don Payne is a long-time touring pro who also spends much time guiding on the expansive Sacramento River Delta. He is a magician with a flippin' stick. He notes that if you are confronting water that is lined extensively with shallow brush, tules, or deadfall, flippin' has to be the name of the game.

On his guiding trips, Payne works with many "green" bassers who want to learn how to flip. Over the years, he has found that fishermen have to learn to **hit the target accurately and quietly** when they first try to flip a bait. Accomplished flippers know that the lure's entry is critical with this technique if you don't want to spook the fish.

Rather than flippin' with the more conventional pig'n jig combo, Payne states that novices should start with a plastic worm. Interestingly, he feels that the plastic bait allows for a more splashless entry, especially for the beginner. The worm is softer than pork rind bait and can be flipped slightly past the target, then gently slid into the little pockets that comprise the flipper's strike zone.

Top-Water

Perhaps the most spectacular type of bass fishing you can experience is to see a lunker bass literally explode on a surface lure. Veteran guide and teaching pro, Dave Mitchell, has this style of bassin' down to an art and encourages beginners to definitely give top-water a try. Surface action produces a lot of larger "kicker" fish under tournament conditions.

Over the years, Mitchell has taught many of his students to **set the hook when they feel the resistance of the bass rather than on the commotion.** What happens is that the fish literally bursts through the surface when attacking the top-water plug or buzzbait, creating a lot of noise and excitement. In reaction to this spectacular strike, many anglers instantly go to set the hook. The problem is that far too often, the bass has either just swirled near the bait, rolled over it, or simply missed the hook. Thus, as the quick hook-set is made, the lure is suddenly pulled away from the fish.

The way Mitchell corrects this with his clients is simple: he has them relax, be a little less "trigger happy", and set the hook only when they feel the weight of the bass pulling the line taut after all the splash and noise. This is a very important ploy that should improve your top-water success significantly.

Subtle Baits

Arizona bass pro Gary Garland manufactures Canyon lures. He specializes in fishing diminutive plastic baits on super light lines. Lures like the exotic-looking Mini-Squid with its long tubular body and multiple tentacles, grubs, and teeny Mini Jigs are staples in Gary Garland's repertoire. He states that most recreational anglers must remember to fish these unique lures **slowly in the major strike zone.**

Miniature baits like these are designed to kind of sensually dart back and forth under water. They generate strikes under some of the toughest conditions the pros encounter. The trick Gary Garland says is to get these lures down into the bass' immediate feeding area. It is easiest to start around 15 feet and work downward. Although some traditional bassers turn their noses up at this gear, he strongly recommends using spinning tackle with subtle baits. These outfits match well with 6 to 8 pound monofilament. They also provide a lot of sensitivity to detect even the slightest amount of **pressure** as the fish mouths the bait.

Gary Garland further recommends that the beginner should stay with about 1/8 ounce jig heads, fished with an open hook. In contrast to weedless baits, the exposed jig hook makes it easier to stick fish with just the slightest strike. He wants his customers to initially throw these lures to visible structure, into areas in which they have confidence. This pro adds that if you are not getting hung up once in a while, you are not fishing where the bass live. Thus, you should definitely expect to loose some of these little baits if they are being worked in the proper zones.

Big Baits

There has been a strong trend toward using smaller plastic baits on a routine basis for fishing many deep, clear impoundments. So-called "sissy baits" like 4 inch worms, grubs, Reapers, and Gitzits have won the hearts of many Western anglers. Without a doubt, these small lures take a lion's share of keeper fish out West.

Bob Bringhurst is a Western pro who has also held the world record for brown trout. He knows the merits of using **big baits for big fish.** Bringhurst feels that too many new bas fishermen are getting into a rut by restricting themselves to throwing small baits. Too often, when pre-fishing a particular tournament, anglers using little plastic lures fall into what he terms a **false pattern.** They catch what appear to be keeper bass in the pre-fish, but they usually do not accurately measure the fish. When tournament day arrives, they continue to catch bass on the same baits. But, when the fish are put on the Wil-E-Go Board, they invariably come up short. Hence a false pattern was established that worked only for sub-legal fish.

Borrowing a page from his Dixie counterparts, Bringhurst encourages the beginning basser to diversify and fish larger baits for better quality bass. He feels that under stained water conditions it is not that necessary to scale down to that super fine mono with minuscule baits. Instead, Bringhurst will toss 6 to 9 inch worms, larger crankbaits, top-water, and magnum willowleaf blades, looking for a limit of kicker fish. He concedes that he may catch fewer bass than "light liners", but invariably he also weighs in heaviers limits. I might also add that Bringhurst has caught over 30 bass topping the 8 pound mark - all of these on bigger baits!

Electronics

Don Seifert is considered to be one of the foremost authorities on electronic bassin'. Seifert emphasizes that beginners should **use their graph recorders at increased speed.** He notes that in perhaps an effort to conserve graph paper, the novice cheats himself, since he is unable to see what Siefert terms "the whole parade of action".

This is a simple concept to understand. By increasing paper speed, the graph recorder will give you a much finer, more accurate picture of what is going on in the unerwater environment. Bass movements are also more precisely charted with the faster speed of the recording, So, just as a photographer should not scrimp on film with his expensive hi-tech camera, the recreational basser would be wise to use more graph paper. In this way he will receive a better view of the bass' world.

Fishing Structure

Over many years Larry Hopper has refined fishing deep outside water into a science. Inexperienced bass fishermen - and even seasoned pros - are simply overly bank-oriented and must focus on **fishing offshore structure.** Too often they fish primarily casting to shallow, visual targets. Hopper notes that this is a major shortcoming. Working submerged brush, points, ledges, humps, and similar deep structure, this Western pro fished his way to a $50,000 paycheck as the 1987 U.S. Open victor at Lake Mead.

Hopper feels that the most frequent mistake novices make are running their electronics too much, taking only a cursory picture of the underwater topography, making a few casts, and then moving on. It is as if they are giving "lip-service" to fishing structure and really feel more comfortable working the shoreline.

There is an approach, however, that might give the novice more confidence in fishing structure. As simple as it sounds, Hopper recommends they concentrate on long, sugmerged points. This type of terrain, when you think about it, is actually a transition from the bank to the deep water. The beginner may feel more comfortable out at the ends of these points, running their electronics, monitoring the ledges, breaks and bottom. Hopper also adds that points can hold bass all year long - another feature that may enhance proficiency in fishing out into deeper water.

Well, there you have it: ten concise, basic tips from ten veteran pros. Novice anglers should review these key pointers. Work hard, refine them each time out, and don't forget these fundamentals as you progress in the bassin' game. Even the best bass fishermen realize that this can be a very humbling sport. Fred Borders said it best when he noted, "Too many beginners are looking for some miracle lure rather than fishing a small number of baits and concentrating on presentation". As with any athletic endeavor, there is simply so substitute for practice!

Big Baits, Big Bass

Since the days of Isaac Walton, anglers of all ages have anxiously awaited the arrival of Spring each year to signal the start of another bass season. Spring is when the less-than-diehard fishermen bring their tackle out of mothballs in anticipation of that first weekend since last Fall. But Spring is also the time of year when "hard Core" bassin' men throughout the country begin to think of one thing - a big fish and a potential trophy catch.

Throughout this book, I have presented the thesis that the key to catching fish in the Golden State is to master certain techniques suitable to lakes out West that experience extensive recreational and angler pressure. These methods revolve around the presentation of such subtle offerings as diminutive split-shot worms, darter jigs, grubs and tube baits. Make no doubt about it these lures will not only catch substantial numbers of bass all year long, but also that occasional nice "kicker" fish when more traditional baits fail. However, during the Spring, it might be best to go back to basics, so to speak, working with the simple theory that "big baits catch big fish". During this pre-spawn period, larger fish are more active, they have greater appetites, and are typically aggressive towards lures intruding into their territory.

If you are looking for a wall-hanger fish this Spring, put away the little baits and light line for a few weeks and concentrate on tossing a lure with a larger profile. Your best choices will be made from crankbaits, blades, jigs and top-water lures.

Crankbaits

In the early Spring, the bass will often be in a transition state as they begin to move up from deep water to shallow coves. Many pros look to the outside points of quiet coves as the best place to intercept a big bruiser-class bass on its migration from deeper water. Smaller crankbaits such as the Bomber Model A, Storm Wiggle Wart, or Rapala #5 Fat Rap are good for medium-to-shallow water. But for reaching depths over 10 feet along these outside points, start with a larger plug. The Bagley DBIII has been a longtime favorite along with the bigger #7 Rapala Fat Rap. Both of these lures represent large natural offerings such as crawdads, shad, bass fry, or even rainbow trout to hungry pre-spawn bass. Quite often in lakes where Florida-strain bass and rainbow trout co-habitate, the bass will push the trout up, feeding on them, and creating surface boils similar to saltwater gamefish. This is the time to throw one of these larger crankbaits. All too often many Spring tournaments are won by some angler crankin' up a "toad" to round out his limit.

For extra deep crankin' along these points or down the center of the coves, try one of the even larger Poe's Super Cedar or Mann's 20+ Deep Hog plugs that dive to 18 to 20 foot depths. After an initial flurry of popularity in the pro ranks some years ago, the Poe lures disappeared from the market. They are now back in a whole new array of designs and colors. The #400 Series is especially good for reaching this deeper range. Bass rarely see an artificial lure swimming through this deep strike zone on a retrieve. Hence it is basically uncharted water that you will be fishing with these oversize plugs in search of that trophy fish.

Spinnerbaits

Spinnerbaits are also a versatile Spring lure that allows the basser to cover a lot of shoreline during a springtime outing. Here again, think **"BIG"**. Tie on one of those Magnum-size spinnerbaits with the large #6 to #8 willowleaf blade. When I first saw these gigantic spinnerbaits, I figured that there was no way that they would be effective. They simply looked too bulky and overwhelming. But, after watching the pros throw these lures and following their recommendations, I found that they really do work - and on quality fish!

You need to gear heavier for this 1/2 to 5/8 ounce lure. Fish 14 to 17 pound test with a longer 7 foot rod. These larger blades have considerable torque, displacing a lot of water and generating a significant amount of vibration. They will indeed aggravate big fish into striking, but they will also thrash the angler after a few hours of casting with lighter baitcasting rigs. Use the longer rod with a strong reel to make easier two-handed casts with this big bait. Work the blades on the shallow flats around brush and similar cover. Retrieve them all the way from just under the surface to plowing them right along the bottom. This lure creates a lot of commotion and really "calls in" the larger bass during the Spring months.

Jigs

However, if I had to pick just one type of lure to use for nailing that trophy in the Spring, my choice would be a jig. I would either flip or pitch this bait consistently in lakes where large Florida-strain bass are found. During this time of the year, crawdads also move up into the shallows and comprise a major portion of the diet for these big Floridas. Of all the lures a pro can choose from, a pork rind-tipped jig in either vinyl, live rubber, or natural bucktail skirt perhaps comes closest to resembling a crawdad. The pig'n jig casts a nice bulky silhouette in the water comparable to that of a crayfish. In addition, the soft tender pork has the texture of a live creature to a bass with a man-size appetite.

Veteran West Coast pro, Mike Folkestad, is a pig'n jig specialist extraordinaire, having finished high in many tournaments throwing primarily this simple bait. Although he fishes the popular #11 Uncle Josh Pork Frog almost exclusively, other pro bassers prefer to toss an even larger super bulky pork rind bait during the Spring. The Uncle Josh #1 Jumbo Frog and the Spring Lizard are favorites when they are looking for a lunker fish. Here's a further tip: big bass can't resist **black** pork in the Spring. For some reason, the larger fish during this time of the year are simply provoked by seeing one of these menacing-looking dark pork combinations drift into their shallow lair.

The other jig pattern I prefer has been a fairly well-kept secret within the pro ranks for some time. Expert Western jig fishermen like Jim Emmett, Larry Hopper, and Dave Nollar have been using a jig made from vinyl and a Superfloat worm. Cut it in half and split the tail portion up to about one inch from the tip. (You actually end up with two usable sections). Thread this trailer behind a lead head with a reversed nylon skirt. The vinyl flares out and the Superfloat tail portions rise off the bottom presenting the appearance of a crawdad raising its claws. This jig combination is thrown or pitched primarily along points or the shallow flats for springtime action. The best colors are purple and brown blends. Some truly large trophies have been taken in California on this customized jig in recent years.

Top-Water Baits

The final category of lures to consider using to catch that trophy bass are big top-water baits. The Heddon Zara Spook in silver glitter shad finish accounts for a lot of big fish this time of year. Spend some time with this bait and practice one little tip passed along to me that may require some patience. Gary Robson, a Southern California touring pro, notes that bass will occasionally "blow up" on this surface plug without truly eating the bait. When this happens, the first inclination is to quickly reel in and fire off another cast. Instead, immediately after the bass misses the plug, Robson just lets it sit still for a moment. Then he gives it a single twitch. This will often generate a second, more vicious and aggravated strike resulting in a hook-up.

Floating minnow-like baits such as the Rapala, Rebel, or Norman Rip-N-Minnow also produce some tallies on large, early season fish. These can be jerked or rhythmically twitched along the bank or even in seemingly open water. The little secret I mentioned in regard to letting the Spook rest after a missed strike, works equally well with these lightweight minnows. Interestingly, a really unique twist in top-water lure selection is to use one of the Bomber Long #16-A plugs. These six inch heavy duty lures were really designed for saltwater striper fishing. Some of the locals at big fish lakes such as Isabella, Silverwood, Vail, or San Vincente have been throwing these ocean lures for years stroking some trophy-size Floridas. The inside tip is to use a medium weight saltwater spinning outfit. An oversize spin reel will allow you to pick up greater amounts of line with minimal effort when you twitch or jerk this jumbo bait.

Shallow Water Tactics

Over the last few years, flippin' has become a widely practiced method for catching shallow water bass. As a specialized technique, flippin' can be productive all year long at a variety of Western lakes. Invariably, you will find high finishers at large scale tournaments attributing much of their success to getting on a good flip bite.

Flippin' not only keeps your lure in the strike zone ninety percent of the time, but also produces quality fish. For tournament level bassin', many of the larger "kicker" fish will be caught with this shallow water approach. There is no question that on smaller, heavily-pressured water, fine diameter line and small, subtle baits are the order of the day. But, on big expansive Western lakes such as Clear, Mead, Havasu, and Martinez, you would be wise to pack your flippin' rod and some heavier 20 to 30 pound monofilament along with your lighter gear. Many "toads" and hefty stringers are taken annually from big water like this by flippin'.

Most Western bass fishermen that have tried flippin' tend to stay with two basic presentations. The customary pattern has been to use the popular pig'n jig combination in the Spring and cold water months, then switch to a plastic worm when the water warms. Both of these lures traditionally have been shown to replicate a crawdad that has tumbled into the shoreline cover. Occasionally, some bassers will also flip a plastic lizard in the Spring as an alternative to the pork rind baits.

However, to become an accomplished shallow water fisherman, try to expand your range of possible flippin' lures to include some less obvious choices. Although much has been written highlighting how flippin' involves primarily aggressive reaction strikes, this is not always the case. Quite often, the bass rooted into shallow cover will completely "shut off" on a particular bait just as fish holding on other structure do. For example, on popular, small, 1000 acre trophy lakes such as Otay or Hodges in San Diego County, the available flippin' water can really take a pounding on the weekend. This is especially true if multiple club tournaments are scheduled there. The Florida bass in lakes like these are finicky eaters to begin with, and can really develop a major case of "lockjaw" after seeing endless casts of the same flippin' baits put in front of them.

Some dedicated flippers that regularly fish lakes like these have successfully developed approaches with a wide array of lures that dramatically expand upon the typical menu of pork rind or plastic worm selections. Keep in mind that most of these more "exotic" flippin' lures will be effective on a variety of lakes throughout the West irrespective of size or weekly angling pressure. Here is a brief sketch of what some of these less obvious flippin' baits are and how to fish them.

Plastic Worms

With plastic worms, be more experimental and move away from standard six inch models, scaling up or down in size. Sometimes, a smaller four inch worm fished on lighter 12 to 14 pound line can be the "hot ticket" if you are fishing a popular bank behind other flip fishermen. On the other hand, you might want to consider using a "little larger" than normal plastic worm. By a "little larger", how about a 12 inch snake! These are available in custom hand-poured models or from commercial manufacturers such as Manns and Mr. Twister.

Many West Coast fishermen make the mistake of thinking that this type of jumbo plastic worm is more appropriate for Southern style bassin'. This is a real oversight because these magnum baits really produce some lunker fish on our lakes when teamed with a flippin' outfit. Rig this worm with a large #5/0 hook and a small bullet weight pegged or crimped at the head. Fish it the same way you would with either a pig'n jig or a smaller plastic worm. However, when you feel the initial strike, let the fish run with the bait just a little longer than you normally would before setting up. Most of the time, the larger bass will go right for the head of the bait when they bushwack this big worm.

Another variation to try if you prefer to flip plastic worms is the customized Super Floater. This worm in either four or six inch lengths has been around for a long time. It is a very unspectacular lure, especially in today's market of specialized hand-poured worms in the latest shapes and colors. Still, this simple, straight-tail bait can be transformed into a sensational flippin' lure with a little do-it-yourself modification. For flippin', use the six inch version in either purple, black/chartreuse tail, or brown/black stripe. Take a razor knife and slice the worm down the center starting from behind the sex collar. Next, with surgeon-like skill, run the blade down through the two tail sections. This leaves the worm with four, undulating tentacles. Combined with a #3/0 to #4/0 worm hook and a pegged sinker, this customized worm can be a terrific year long flippin' bait. This worm is especially deadly when the flip bite gets very tough on sluggish fish. As the worm's head rests on the bottom, the four tail sections float and sensually wave back and forth with no effort. The bait has the appearance of a crawdad putting up its claws in its last line of defense.

Other Possibilities

Conventional plastic jigs such as Bobby Garland's Spider and Haddock's Kreepy Krawdad can also be potent weapons in the hands of a good flip fisherman. Lately on the big Colorado River lakes, the locals have been flippin' these baits in the brushy areas. You can flip them with either polypropeline or fiber brush guards, or rig them Texas-style with a #2/0 to #4/0 worm hook and pegged bullet weight. Popular color patterns include smoke/sparkle, smoke/red flake, solid brown, and solid silver.

A variation on this theme would be to flip two other plastic baits that have received most of their notoriety as subtle offerings on light line. These are Canyon Lures Fatzee and the Kalin Lunker Salty Grub. The Fatzee makes for an outstanding flippin' bait when a super delicate entry is needed. The best way to flip this little tube lure is to rig it with either a 1/8 to 3/16 ounce jig head shoved inside the hollow body. Use a mono guard for shoreline with heavy brush. These small jig heads have fine wire hooks that might bend with too much pressure. Thus, it is recommended to gear down to 12 to 14 pound test when they are used for flippin'.

The Salty Grub with its distinctive flagellating tail can be flipped with heavier line. You can use all the way up to 30 pound test for the most dense cover. Rig the grub Texas-style. Peg a 1/8 to 1/4 ounce bullet weight matched with a #2/0 to #3/0 worm hook. This lure is particularly soft and the bass will really crunch it hard, especially when they are ambushing shad in shallow water. Popular choices for flippin' colors in the Fatzee include smoke/sparkle and purple/red flake. For the Salty Grub, try salt'n pepper, green/flake, or silver/gold flake. Add a plastic jig skirt for additional bulk and contrast.

There are also a few other plastic baits that are characterized by prominent whip-tails which also fish well as a flippin' bait. The Rebel Red Neck, designed to look like a plastic salamander with flared red gills, has been very effective on those large Colorado River lakes, particularly in the back waters and sloughs off the main river. Similarly, the Boogie Tail was marketed primarily as a jig trailer for saltwater species. Rigged Texas-style in shad finish, this big whip-tail bait will often generate some solid strikes when gently lowered into the thickest brush, deadfall, or tules. Like the other plastic jigs, grubs, and tube baits, the Boogie Tail excels when the bass are up shallow feeding on shad.

Finally, two more options are worth mentioning: Kalin's Lunker Shad and Canyon's Mr. In-Between. The Lunker Shad is a fairly large knob-tail lure used extensively at the Salton Sea and on offshore marine species. It works quite well on large-mouths flipped in shallow reeds, mimicking a fluttering shad minnow. Rig the Lunker Shad Texas-style. The Mr. In-Between is used primarily on a jig-head. It is a bizarre cross between a plastic worm and a lizard. This lure nails many quality bass in the hands of a skilled flip fisherman.

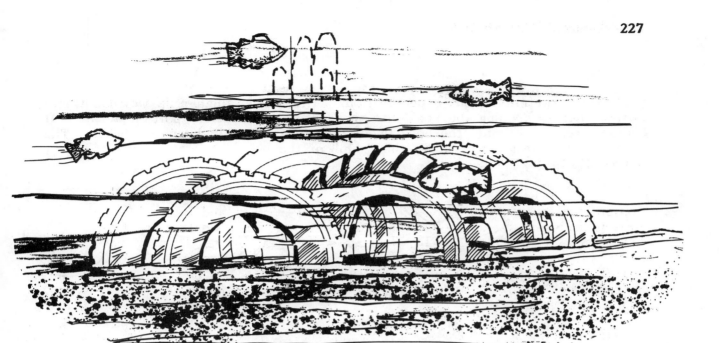

Advanced Tips and Tricks

Sometimes, on tough fishing days, a subtle change in presentation or technique can make the difference between success and failure. But at other times it takes more radical departure to produce fish. This chapter is packed-full of advanced fish-hooking methods that range from adjustments and refinements to outright reversals of conventional wisdom. The one thing that all these methods have in common is that they come highly recommended by top Western pros and bass guides.

The "Doodle Stitch"

Long-time Western pro Chuck English is recognized as a magician when it comes to working a plastic worm. English fishes for large, world-class Florida bass. Using a combination of the line feelin' technique(also known as "stitchin'") and the doodlin' strategy, English will do the "doodle stitch" to coax the big Floridas. This presentation is relatively easy to master. While pulling the mono through the guides as is done with line feelin', add a short rhythmic shaking action with the rod tip. The slow line feelin' combined with the worm erratically dancing from side-to-side, is sometimes the secret trick for inducing jumbo Florida bass to strike!

Skin-Hooking

Quite frequently many strikes will be missed by embedding the worm hook directly into the center of the plastic bait. Sometimes the worms, lizards, or snakes will too thick to permit adequate penetration.   Here is a valuable tip worth noting. Rather than embedding the hook into the center or "meatier" portion of the soft-bodied lure, gently slide the hook under the outermost thin layer of plastic.   The hook now will rest barely under the "skin" of the bait.

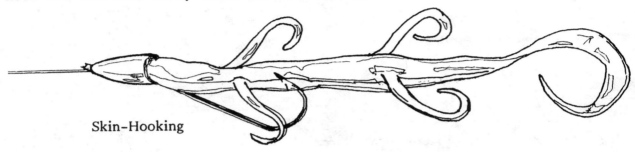

Skin-Hooking

Although the lure is now not as weedless as it would be with a center hooking, better penetration is possible with the skin-hook technique. The worm hook will pull free with the slightest swing of the rod. This is a key ploy to use when the bass do not seem to want to hold onto the plastic bait for long. It is also excellent when combined with fine diameter 4 to 8 pound test line which typically exhibits a lot of stretch. The skin-hooking makes quick, efficient hook-sets possible with the light mono associated with doodlin', split-shottin', or line feelin'. Lizards should definitely be skin-hooked for optimal hook penetration.

Plastic Crawdads

Plastic crawdads are designed along two basic patterns. One shape is made to replicate a natural 2 to 4 inch crayfish in terms of texture and silhouette. The Haddock Kreepy Krawdad and Executive Tackle's Billy's C-Dad are excellent examples of these life-like imitations. Bill Craig, the originator of the Billy's C-Dad notes that plastic 'dads in this genre are terrific for split shottin'. Craig uses his C-Dad on numerous deep Western lakes teamed with 6 to 8 pound test line. A Mr. Twister Keeper Hook can be used to rig the C-Dad Texas-style. The skin-hooking technique is also applicable in using these thick-bodied crawdad replicas.

Both the Billy's C-Dad and the Kreepy Krawdad also excel crawled along the bottom, simple Texas-style. Don't overlook either of these plastic 'dads when it comes to flippin'. Flip them either with a pegged or crimped slide sinker, or laced behind a live rubber jig. These can be super alternatives to pig'n jigs when flipped into brush, rocks, tules, and reeds. The other plastic crawdad design is actually a combination - half crayfish, half worm. Stanley's Craw Worm and the Mr. Twister Salty Pockit Dad exemplifying this kind of bait.

Craw-worms in this design are commonly used as flippin' offerings, particularly along stretches of the lower Colorado River. Occasionally anglers will also fish craw-worms behind a jig head or with a bullet weight for Texas-style wormin'. Crawdads seem to produce best in the Spring when bass are actively working the shallows in preparation for spawning.

The Tandem Hook Worm

Quite frequently bass will "short strike" a plastic worm, nipping at the tail portion. One method the pros use to combat this is to construct a tandem hook bait.

Take a 4 inch Super Floater worm and slide it onto a 1/8 to 3/8 ounce darter or p-head. Next, carefully thread a long-shank #4 to #6 Carlisle or Aberdeen hook into the tail section. Tie a small 2 to 3 inch piece of 12 pound mono to the bend in the front jig hook. Don't be concerned that the connecting leader is exposed with this worm rig. It doesn't seem to inhibit the action or the strike potential of the bait.

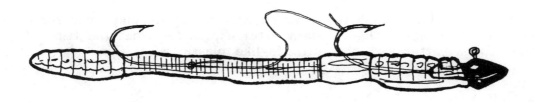

Tandem-hooked Worm

This tandem hook worm excels as a deepwater lure. Use it in the same way you would vertically doodle a 4 inch worm. Quickly set on any unusual pressure felt when working this bait. More often than not, the bass will be nailed in the rear "stinger" hook. It is important to maintain steady tension on the line when retrieving a fish caught on the tandem hook worm. Also, pre-sharpen the small rear hook to maximize this bait's hooking power.

Kalin's Topwater Secret

Al Kalin is the manufacturer of the popular Kalin Salty Lunker Grub. These 5 inch long, single, curl-tail grubs are used extensively on Texas rigs, split-shot set-ups, and with darter and p-head jigs.

One appraoch rarely thought of with this type of soft plastic lure is to employ it as a surface lure. Kalin will rig his grubs Texas-style with the worm hook embedded into the soft plastic body. But the trick is to rig it **without any slide sinker or other weight.** Cast this practically weedless grub out near the bank and especially around thick vegetation. Reel it in with a moderately fast retrieve. The whippy, elongated tail generates considerable vibration coming across the surface. The grub imitates a frantic baitfish struggling at the water line. The topwater strike with this technique can be explosive at times!

The "Soft Spoon"

A recent innovation has been the usage of so-called "soft spoons". These are simple to construct. Take a narrow-bodied spoon such as a Haddock Jig'n Spoon and slide a soft plastic tube bait over it. Both the Fatzee and Fat Gitzit tube lures will work. Push the line eyelet split-ring or snap up through the soft plastic in the head area of the tube bait. This unique lure combines both the features of a vertical spoon and a hollow tubular bait like the Gitzits or the Fatzee.

You can "dress up" old worn out spoons with the wide variety of plastic tube baits on the market. As the soft spoon is vertically jigged, the dangling tentacles that are part of the tube baits add terrific seductive action to an otherwise bland-looking metal spoon.

Also, the soft plastic "skin" that now encases the spoon may generate more pronounced strikes from the bass. Many veteran pros feel that the fish will hold onto the spoon better with the soft life-like plastic outer skin.

Pork Rind Trailers

Northern California pro, John Bedwell passes along another insider's trick for custom-coloring pork rind trailers. He feels that the pork rind used straight from the jar is too saturated with the color dye from the factory. Bedwell theorizes that crawdads in their natural state usually are found in a series of patchy dark color hues. Therefore, pork rind in similar shades should work best.

Bedwell removes the colored pork frogs from the factory bottle and places them in another jar of white-bellied frogs in clear water. He then lets this jar of frogs sit out in the sun. The sunlight penetrating the pork fades the darker color into the white frogs creating mottled tones of purple, brown, or black. This simple procedure results in a customized pork frog, whose coloration more closely resembles live crayfish.

Strike Rind - An Alternative to Pork

An interesting alternative to the pork rind trailer is Berkley's Strike Rind. The "frogs" made from this material have both the appearance and feel of trailers made from natural pork. In reality, the Strike Rind baits are manufactured from a leather-like substance similar to chamois material.

These jig trailers can be re-used numerous times even after they dry out. Simply dip them in the water again and they become soft and pliable. Like pork rind, they can be trimmed and customized. The added benefit of the Strike Rind jig trailers is that each one is soaked in a solution of Berkley Strike. This attractant impregnates the leather material, making this kind of "pork" highly tasty to hook-shy bass.

Fish Attractants

The Berkley Company also markets two other items that can be utilized as fish attractants. Berkley's Alive is sold in powder form. After you wet your artificial lure, sprinkle some of the Alive powder on the bait. Within seconds the powder reacts with the water and an incredible slimy film envelopes the lure. This gives a plastic worm, snake, or lizard - or even a hard plastic crankplug - the appearance of a live critter.

Berkley's other product is Moldable Strike. This is a solid form of their popular liquid strike attractant. Smart plastic worm fishermen will take a pinch of the solid Strike and carefully mold it into the hollow portion of a bullet weight. As the plastic worm is crawled along the bottom, the Moldable Srike slowly releases the scent locked into the slide sinker.

Folkestad's "Plowing" Tactic

Mike Folkestad is one of the premier bass pros in the United States. He has caught over 50 bass topping the 8 pound mark capped by a 16 pounder this author had the pleasure of netting. Folkestad nails many of these lunkers using pig'n jig combinations. Most bass anglers are taught to fish jigs by gently hopping then along the bottom. In contrast, Folkestad prefers to "plow" the pig'n jig slowly through every inch of underwater terrain.

His plowing technique is similar to crawling a plastic worm. Virtually no action is imparted to the lure. Folkestad wants his pork to make contact with the most subtle structure such as rocks and brush. He feels that live crawdads slowly plod along the bottom. Rarely do they "hop" as is portrayed with most jig retrieves. So Folkestad carefully plows his jigs through the structure minimizing any exaggerated motions in the lure.

California Bass Club Councils

There are a number of organizations that are involved in promoting club-level bassin' in California. The San Diego, Southern California, and Central California Bass Councils function as a "United Nations" for regional bass clubs. A similar group working more in Northern California is the Black Bass Advisory Council. All of these groups endorse the catch-and-release ethic. Anglers interested in contacting these organizations can usually acquire information from area tackle stores. The chairmen of the various groups will refer potential club-level bassers to specific clubs that might fit their individual needs.

Special Bass Lakes

In an earlier major section of this book(starting on page 124), 36 premier California bass lakes are profiled, in detail. **Special Bass Lakes** is a bonus section that details the great bass fishing opportunities of four lakes that are probably best known for trout or striper fishing. But don't let that fool you. Big Bear, Davis, Mojave, and Mead provide some excellent bucket-mouth action.

Big Bear Lake(Map - p.233)

This longtime favorite Southern California trout lake also has a budding "sleeper" population of bass. At 7,500 foot elevation and 3 hours from downtown Los Angeles, Big Bear has both largemouth and smallmouth species. The largemouths overwhelmingly comprise the bulk of the bass fishery.

Big Bear is 7½ miles and up to 1¼ miles wide. It has over 22 miles of shoreline. Numerous hotels, motels, restaurants, and fast-food operations are located in the nearby towns of Big Bear Lake and Fawnskin. There are public boat ramps and rental boats available at lake-side marinas.

Areas to Fish: The bass will commonly be found along the numerous weed lines scattered throughout the lake. The north side towards Juniper Creek is a popular spot as is the eastern region known as the Stanfield Cut Off. Bass are also found around the docks and boulders in Boulder and Metcalf Bays. The rocky structures near the dam in the western sector will also hold bass near the shoreline.

Best Times: Big Bear exels from late Spring through late Fall. This mountain lake will frequently freeze over in the dead of winter. Big Bear can become quite windy and chilly even during the mid-summer period. Anglers should always carry cold weather gear when bassin' at this lake.

Tips and Tricks: Spinnerbait enthusiasts will absolutely fall in love with Big Bear's weed beds. Tandem and single blade spinnerbaits are excellent here in smaller 1/4 to 1/2 ounce sizes. Try some of the more opulent skirt combinations such as blue/chartreuse, yellow/green, brown/yellow, orange/brown, and solid black. Gold blades seem to work particularly well.

Plastic worms in basic "earth tone" browns, blacks, and purples are perfect around the docks flipped, pitched, or crawled. Crawdad-colored crankplugs, along with purple, black, or brown jig'n pig combos mimic Big Bear's crawdads perfectly, especially near the rocky shorelines.

Top water specialists should try buzz baits, Zara Spooks, Chug Bugs, floating Rebels and Rapalas, and the Rebel Pop-R. Fishermen using chest waders or float tubes can take advantage of this surface activity in the summertime.

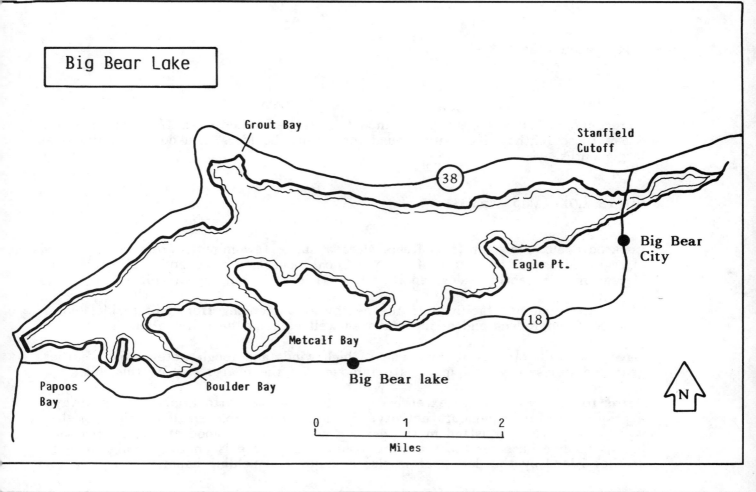

Big Bear Lake

Grout Bay
Stanfield Cutoff
38
Eagle Pt.
Big Bear City
18
Metcalf Bay
Big Bear lake
Papoos Bay
Boulder Bay

0   1   2
Miles

N

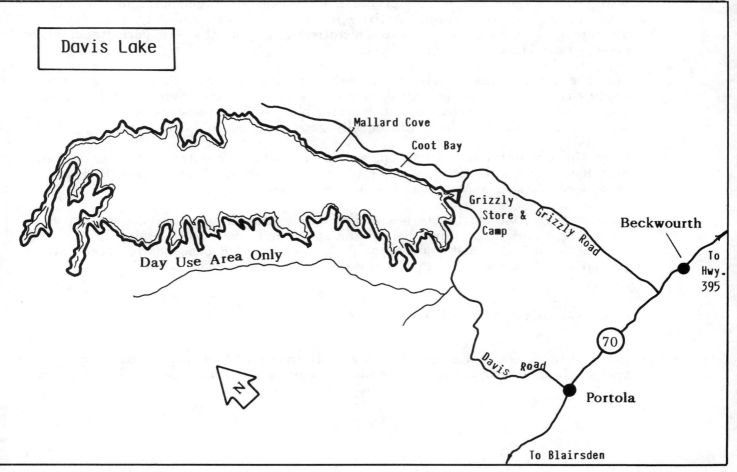

Davis Lake

Mallard Cove
Coot Bay
Grizzly Store & Camp
Grizzly Road
Beckwourth
To Hwy. 395
Day Use Area Only
70
Davis Road
Portola
N
To Blairsden

A recent "hot" lure has been a 3 inch long reaper fished on a 1/8 ounce p-head. Shake these feather-like baits around the weeds, boulders, and docks for Big Bear's largemouths.

Davis Lake(Map – p.233)

Located about one hour from Reno, Nevada and a few minutes from Portola, Davis is regarded as a stellar trout factory. Local fishermen from both California and Nevada have recently discovered Davis' sensational bassin' opportunities.

There are moderate facilities in the nearby areas ranging from bait, tackle and food to campgrounds and hiking trails as well as some beautiful alpine scenery.

Davis can be hazardous at times due to high winds and rough water. Cold weather gear and full safety equipment is paramount for the boater visiting this lake.

Areas to Fish: There are extensive grass beds in the north arm. This is always a prime spot for largemouth activity. Look for any viable small openings in the weed lines. The big island in the eastern sector can be good at times with subtle breaks holding bass for the structure fisherman. There is another semi-submerged, smaller island by the dam that is also a major fish-holding haunt.

Best Times: Davis begins to kick out a lot of keeper largemouths in late May with the start of the spawn. Activity intensifies through mid-July, then tapers off through late Fall. Water levels historically drop as the Fall period approaches, making boat launching more difficult.

Tips and Tricks: The massive weed beds here are the key. Bass will lie deep inside the beds, so weedless-type baits are a must in this cover. Locals prefer to flip jumbo Fatzee tube baits in electric blue or chartreuse patterns. Plastic worms and brown pork frogs are equally good choices.

When the top-water bite heats up, switch to white or chartreuse 1/2 ounce Cato Buzz Baits. An alternative is the Haddock Counterblade Buzzer. The Heddon Zara Spook is still another surface lure worth tossing.

Look through that old tackle box and tie on a Johnson silver weedless minnow. Pin a white pork rind trailer behind the spoon and continue to probe Davis' massive weed beds. Salt and pepper grubs laced on 1/8 ounce darter heads are also effective, casted toward the points where weed growth is minimal.

Lake Mojave (Map – p.235)

Although it is not in California, many Californians visit Mojave annually to experience casino life at nearby Laughlin, Nevada as well as to fish. Laughlin has extensive

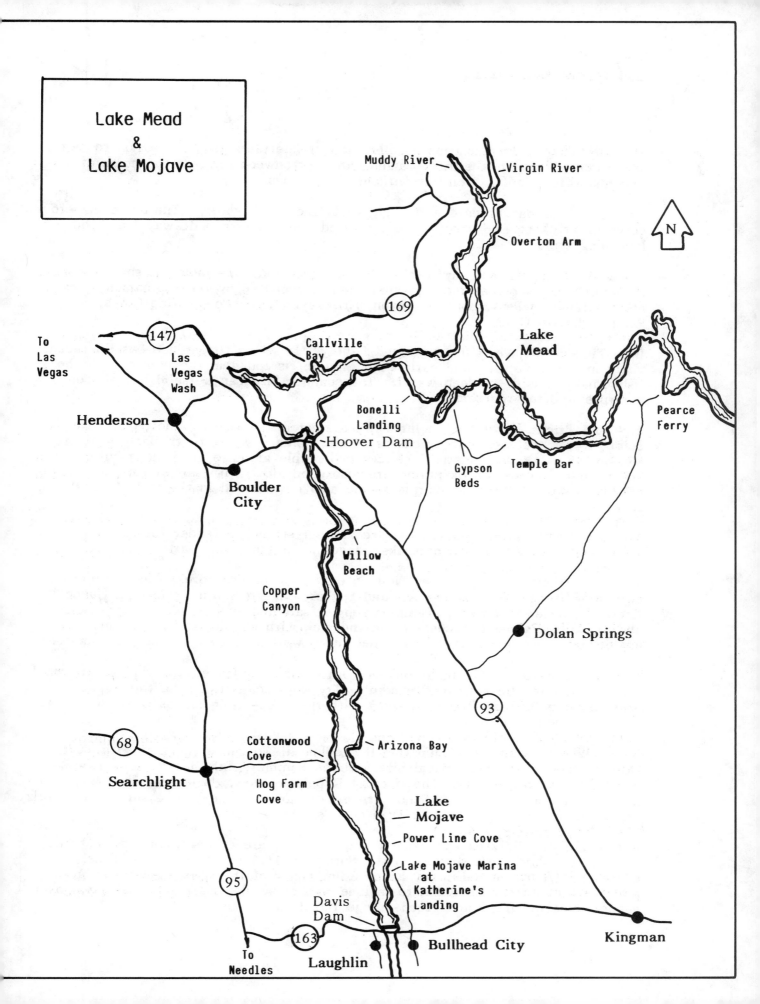

facilities ranging from marine supplies, lodging, restaurants, R.V. parks, to bait and tackle shops. Katherine's Landing and Cottonwood Cove to the north of Laughlin offer similar facilities without the casinos.

Mojave can be dangerous due to high winds and rough water. There are numerous coves in which to find sanctuary if you find yourself stranded away from your launching spot.

Areas to Fish: Almost any of the endless coves that line Mojave's shoreline can hold fish. Some of the more popular areas frequented by the tournament pros include the Hog Pens, Copper Canyon, Arizona Bay, the Power Line Coves, Owl's Point and Carp Cove.

Best Times: Mojave is a year round fishery. It seems to produce best in recent years in the late Spring and early Fall. Bassin' is tough in the Winter with the fish usually holding in deep water. The summer bite can be solid but air temperature is often scorching.

Tips and Tricks: Soft plastic lures are preferred at Mojave. The basic "river color" worm - purple with traces of red and blue - works particularly well at Mojave. Earth tone patterns in brown and purple are also good along with salt and pepper. Tandem hook purple are also good along with salt and pepper. Tandem hook worms in red or purple should also be included in the Mojave tackle repertoire.

Salt and pepper grubs and reapers are another strong contender for limit catches. These can be split-shotted or shaked, laced on a 1/8 ounce darter head.

Jigs have traditionally produced well on outside structure here. Plastic tail-swimming models such as the Garland Spyder, Canyon Cap'n Gown, and Haddock Kreepy Krawler will work. Pumpkin/pepper, salt and pepper, electric grape, smoke, and smoke/sparkle color schemes are the pick with plastic jigs. Although few anglers use pork on Mojave, it will definitely work in brown and purple combos.

Mojave can be a good crankin' lake. Both medium and deep-diving plugs are viable for some serious chuckin' and windin'. Try shad-colored Rebels, the Rapala Fat Rap, and the Bomber Model-A, along with the deep-diving Manns Deep 20 Hawg and Poes Super Cedar.

In the Winter, consider doodlin' small paddle-tail worms or spoonin' with #075 Hopkins spoons for the vertical bite. In the Summer, shift gears and use buzz-baits over the moss beds. The floating Rapala minnow, the Storm Chug Bug, Heddon Tiny Torpedo, and Zara Spook are great choices for explosive surface fireworks. Stay with light colored shad or even clear/smoke patterns.

Fat Gitzits and Fatzees in a wide range of colors are a year round staple bait at Mojave. Toss them shallow in the Spring on 1/16 to 1/8 ounce p-heads, and deeper on 1/8 to 1/4 ounce jig heads other times of the year. Some of the time proven colors for tube baits here include smoke/sparkle, smoke/red flake, pumpkin pepper, electric grape and green-orange flake("Christmas Tree").

Lake Mead (Map - p.235)

Although this expansive waterway is not in California, many California anglers feel that Mead is a "second home". The lake is located about one hour from downtown Las Vegas. Its shoreline is dotted with numerous hotels, casinos, marinas and restaurants. Mead can be a treacherous lake. Wave action can become life-threatening during wind storms. It is absolutely imperative to monitor weather conditions on a daily basis when boating on Mead.

Areas to Fish: There is literally endless secions of this waterway that are perfect for bass fishing. These include Callville Bay, Las Vegas Marina, Vegas Wash, the Gypson Beds, the Grand Wash, Temple Bar, Overton, and the Muddy and Virgin River areas.

Best Times: Mead is sometimes sensational in the Spring. The Summer heat often soars above 110° making bassin' uncomfortable. Nevertheless, the fish will co-operate in the Summer although deepwater tactics may be necessary. The Fall bite can also be productive. Mead is a tough, though not impossible lake to fish in the Winter. As in the Summer, anglers will switch to deepwater strategies in the colder periods.

Tips and Tricks: Soft plastic baits are clearly the best overall choices for Mead. Plastic worms in 3 to 6 inch lengths are recommended. A popular color combination is purple with red or blue flake. Salt and pepper, solid purple, red black and pumpkin/pepper, and "earth tone" patterns should also be included in the Mead war-chest. Texas rigs, p-heads, and darters match well with these worms.

Tandem hook Superfloat worms in bright red or solid purple are another favorite, worked at greater depths. Similarly, Kalin and Twin-T's curl-tail grubs split-shotted or on small jig heads can be used in place of the worm. Salt and pepper is the number one pick.

Jigs - both pork and plastic - will nail some of the better "kicker" bass. Pitch or flip these into shoreline cover. Garland Spyder, canyon Cap'n Gown, and Haddock Kreepy Krawler jigs can be plodded along the bottom to depths of fifty feet. Try pork in brown and purple combos, plastic jigs in pumpkin/pepper, salt and pepper, smoke/sparkle, and smoke/red flake.

Mead can also yeild some fantastic top-water action in the warmer months. The medium-size Rebel Pop-R in assorted finishes and the Heddon Zara Spook in silver flake shad are longtime favorites..

Crankplugs - particularly the deep diving Poes Super Cedar and Manns Deep 20 Hawg are excellent choices when the bass suspend down the center of coves or on outside structure. Stay with traditional shad-colored patterns. Spinnerbaits in lighter shades are similarly productive at times.

Finally, subtle offering such as reapers and tube baits have tremendous application on Mead, especially during hot weather. These should be teamed with fine diameter 6 to 8 pound test premium mono.

California Bass Information Directory

Major Bass Tournament Organizations

B.A.S.S.
One Bell Rd., Montgomery, AL 36117
(205) 272-9530

Operation Bass (Redman Tournaments)
Route 2, Box 74-B
Gilbertsville, KY 42044
(502) 362-4880

West Coast Bass
3239-B Monier Cir.,
Rancho Cordova, CA 95670
(9160 635-0111

Western Outdoor News (W.O.N. -- Bass)
3197-E Airport Loop Dr.
Costa Mesa, CA 92626
(714) 546-4370

California Bass Lakes

Alamanor
Chamber of Commerce
Box 198, Chester, CA 96020
(916) 258-2426

Amador
Lake Amador Resort
7500 Amador Dr., Ione, CA 95640
(209) 274-2625, 274-4739

Berryessa
Park Headquarters, Chamber of Commerce
Spanish Flat Station, Napa, CA 94558
(707) 966-2111

Big Bear
Chamber of Commerce
41647 Big Bear Blvd., Big Bear Lake, CA 92315
(714) 866-5652

Cachuma
Cachuma Lake Resort
Star Route, Santa Barbara, CA 93105
(805) 688-4658

Camanche
Camanche North Shore Resort
2000 Jackson Vly/Cam. Rd., Ione, CA 95840
(209) 763-5121
Camanche South Shore Resort
P.O. Box 92, Wallace, CA 95254
(209) 763-5178

Casitas
Casitas Recreation Area
11311 Santa Ana Rd., Venture, CA 93001
(805) 649-2233

Clear
Chamber of Commerce
875 Lakeport Blvd., Lakeport, CA 95453
(707) 263-6131

Colorado River (Blythe)
Blythe Chamber of Commerce
201 S. Broadway, Blythe, CA 92225
(619) 922-8166

Don Pedro
Don Pedro Recreation Area
Box 160, La Grange, CA 95329
(209) 852-2396

El Capitan
El Capitan Lake (619) 465-4500
Current Fishing Info (619) 465-3474

Elsinore
State Recreation Area
32040 Riverside Dr., Lake Elsinore, CA 92330
(714) 674-3177

Folsom
Folsom Lake Recreation
7806 Folsom-Auburn Rd., Folsom, CA 95630
(916) 988-0205

Havasu
Lake Havasu Area Chamber of Commerce
65 N. Lake Havasu Ave.
Lake Havasu City, AZ 86403
(602) 855-4114 or (602) 453-3444

Henshaw
Lake Henshaw Resort
26439 Hwy. 76, Santa Ysabel, CA 92070
(619) 782-3501

Hodges
Lake Hodges
Lake Drive, Escondido, CA 92025
(619) 465-4500
Current Fishing Info (619) 465-3374

Indian Valley
Indian Valley Store
P.O. Box 4939, Clear Lake, CA 95422
(916) 662-0607

Irvine
Irvine Lake
Star Route Box 38, Orange, CA 92667
(714) 649-2560

Isabella
Corps of Engineers
P.O. Box 997, Lake Isabella, CA 93240
(619) 379-2742

Lopez
Lopez Lake
6800 Lopez Dr., Arroyo Drande, CA 93420
(805) 489-2095

Mead
Lake Mead National Recreation Area
601 Nevada Hwy., Boulder City, NV 89005
(702) 293-4041

Mojave
Lake Mead National Recreation Area
601 Nevada Hwy., Boulder City, NV 89005
(702) 293-4041

Morena
San Diego County Parks
5201 Ruffin Rd., Suite P
San Diego, CA 92123
(619) 565-3600
Current Fishing Info (619) 565-3618

Nacimiento
Lake Nacimiento Resort
Star Route, Bradley, CA 93426
(805) 238-3256

New Melones
Resources Manager
Star Route, Box 155C, Jamestown, CA 95327
(209) 984-5248

Oroville
Oroville State Recreation Area
400 Glen Dr., Oroville, CA 95965
(916) 534-2409

Otay
Lower Otay Lake, Chula Vista, CA 92010
(619) 465-4500
Current Fishing Info (619) 465-3474

Pardee
Pardee Lake Resort
4900 Stony Creek Rd., Ione, CA 95640
(209) 772-1472

Perris
Lake Perris State Recreation Area
17801 Lake Perris Dr., Perris, CA 92370
(714) 657-0676

Piru
Park Manager
P.O. Box 202, Piru, CA 93040
(805) 521-1500

San Antonio
Lake San Antonio Resort, Bradley, CA 93426
(805) 472-2311 or 472-2313

San Vincente
San Vincente Lake, Lakeside, CA 92040
(619) 465-4500
Current Fishing Info (619) 465-3474

Shasta
Shasta-Cascade Wonderland Association
1250 Parkview Ave., Redding, CA 96001
(916) 243-2643

Silverwood
Silverwood State Recreation Area
Star Route, Box 7A, Hesperia, CA 92345
(619) 389-2281 or 389-2303

Skinner
Lake Skinner
37701 Warren Rd., Winchester, CA 92396
(714) 926-1541

Sutherland
Lake Sutherland
Box 429, Ramona, CA 92065
(619) 465-4500
Current Fishing Info (619) 465-3474

Trinity
U.S. Forest Ser., #T, Weaverville, CA 96093
(916) 623-2121
Chamber of Commerce
Box 517, Weaverville, CA 96093
(916) 623-6101

Vail
Vail Lake
44500 Vail Lake Rd. #201, Aguanga, CA 92302
(714) 676-5280

Glossary

Bangin' - Using a heavy jig head and vertically shaking it off the bottom, banging rocks and similar structure.

'Blades - Another commonly used name for spinnerbaits (also lead'n blades).

Break - A ledge with a drop-off leading into deeper water. A prime fish-holding structure.

Bullet Weight - A cone-shaped sliding sinker designed especially for plastic worm fishing.

Buzzin' - Retrieving either a spinnerbait or a buzzbait along or barely under the surface.

Carolina Rig - A rig characterized by a sliding sinker butted by either a swivel, snap or similar device. A lengthy 18 to 36 inch leader with a soft plastic lure attached. (See illustration page 46.)

Chugger - A specialized topwater lure, combining the cylindrical body of a stickbait and the cupped mouth of a surface popper. (See illustration page 60.)

Crankin' - The retrieve associated with winding in a crankplug or similar hard plastic lure.

Curl Tail - The tail design on many soft plastic lures which makes the bait appear to be fluttering in the water.

'Dads - Another name for crawdads or crayfish.

Darter - A 1/16 to 3/8 ounce jig head, arrowhead-like in design, used with a small plastic worm or grub trailer.

Dead Bait - When a soft plastic lure such as a worm or grub is allowed to rest motionless on the bottom.

Doodlin' - The art of rythmically shaking a small 3 to 4 inch long worm vertically over deep underwater structure.

Drop Bait - Lures typically casted following an explosive attack and miss with a surface plug. The angler then casts a soft plastic lure into the commotion, letting it "drop" into the sport where the commotion occurred.

Fall Bait - A lure allowed to momentary sink midway through the retrieve such as fishing a spinnerbait "on-the-fall."

Fan Casting - Making repeated casts in either a semi or full circular pattern to thoroughly explore a potential fish-holding area.

Flippin' - Making short, vertical presentations to shallow, shoreline targets.

Floater - A soft plastic bait that will float above the bottom even with a hook in it. Air bubbles are injected into the plastic during the manufacturing process to create this effect.

Flyline - Presenting natural live bait without any additional weight or sinkers added to the line.

Grub - A short compact 3 to 5 inch long soft plastic lure designed to resemble a crawdad or baitfish. Can often be used in place of a plastic worm. (See illustration page 103.)

Jerkin' - Making rhythmic sweeps of the rod to drive a floating minnow plug down under the surface.

Jig'n Pig - A pork rind trailer laced behind a lead head jig. (See illustration page 83.)

Kneel-and-Reel - Intentionally extending the rod tip underwater to make a crankplug dive deeper while retrieving.

Lift-and-Drop - Lifting the rod, then lowering it when presenting a metal spoon in a vertical fashion. The "lift" raises the lure through the water; the "drop" lets it flutter down.

Line Feelin' - (also known as "stitchin'") Retrieving the line by hand in order to slowly pull a soft plastic bait along the bottom. Commonly practiced on the San Diego Lakes.

Live Rubber - The strands of rubberband-like material used in jig and spinnerbait skirts.

Lizard - Soft plastic replica of the land-based reptile. Used primarily for flippin'.

Pegging - Breaking off the tip of a wooden toothpick into the head of a bullet weight. This makes the sinker immobile when using a Texas rig. (See illustration page 44.)

Paddle Tail - A flat paddle-shaped tail portion found on certain plastic worms used with doodlin' technique.

pH - The acid or alkaline quality of the water, which can affect the areas where bass will seek cover.

P-Head - A small round pea-shaped lead head jig in 1/32 to 1/4 ounce used with subtle soft plastic lures. (See illustration page 100.)

Pitch - A gentle underhand or side-arm presentation involving a short cast to nearby shoreline targets.

Plastics - Another term for soft plastic lures such as worms, grubs, tube baits, and lizards.

Glossary (continued)

Plowing - A slow methodical retrieve of a jig being inched along the bottom.

Popper - A surface lure with a prominent cupped mouth to create a "popping" sound when retrieved. (See illustration page 60.)

Pork - Another term for any pork rind trailer used behind a jig, spinnerbait, or other lure.

Pressure - Any dull resistance on the end of the line when bass mouth a soft plastic lure.

Reaper - A small 2 to 3 inch soft plastic lure shaped like a feather or leach. Commonly used with the split-shot method.

Rippin' - Using short rhythmic rod twitches to keep a floating-diving plastic or wood minnow under the surface.

Riprap - Any broken rock that lines the bank in continuous fashion.

Run'n gun - A rapid fire series of casts made quickly to cover expanses of shoreline.

Safety-pin Spinner - Common spinnerbait design with wire frame bent to resemble an open safety-pin. (See illustration page 94.)

Shakin' - Short repeated rod twitches that make the plastic worm "shake" as it is retrieved along the bottom.

The Sink - When a bass hits a lure while it is vertically dropping through a strike zone.

Skin-hooking - Barely embedding the plastic worm hook into the outer layer (or "skin") or plastic. This facilitates quick easy hook sets.

Slab Bait- Any hard plastic crankbait with a flat slab-like surface and without a diving lip. (See illustration page 53.)

Slide Sinker - Another term for a bullet weight. Can also apply to larger oval egg-shaped sinkers made to slide up the line when used with a Carolina set-up.

Snake - Any long 8 to 18 inch plastic worm resembling either an aquatic or terrestrial snake.

Split-shottin' - A variation of the Carolina rig A lead shot is crimped 12 to 36 inches above a soft plastic lure to suspend the bait slightly off the bottom.

Stitchin' - See "line feelin."

Spoonin' - Vertically presenting metal spoons in a lift-and-drop fashion.

Stickbait - Topwater lures without a diving lip, cupped mouth, or propeller (See illustration page 60.)

Stick-ups - Decayed brush that is exposed somewhat out of water.

Straight-tail - A plastic worm with a simple straight tail structure, resembling a live nightcrawler.

Structure - Any fish-holding area from docks and boulders to underwater ledges and grass beds.

Stop'n Go - A specific retrieve where the angler intentionally stops, pausing to allow the lure to rest motionless.

Subtle Baits - A variety of smaller soft plastic lures typically fished on lighter 4 to 8 pound test, including grubs, reapers and tube lures.

Suspend - When bass move off the bottom or from structure and position themselves at a mid-water level.

Texas-rig - Most common way to use a plastic worm. Comprised of a bullet weight, worm hook, and the plastic worm. The hook is embedded into the worm to make the lure virtually weedless. (See illustration page 40.)

Tail-Spinner - A jig with a revolving spinner blade attached to the rear. Also known as a "mattie." (See illustration page 97.)

Trailer - Anything used behind a jig, spinnerbait, or other lure.

Tube Bait - Any hollow soft plastic tubular lure usually with multiple "tentacles' in the tail portion. (See illustration page 105.)

Turnover - When the surface layer of water quickly chills and sinks to the bottom. The warmer bottom layer in turn rises to the surface. Typically this is a tough time to catch bass.

Twin-spinner - A spinnerbait with two distinct wire arms, with either one or two blades attached to each arm. (See illustration page 98.)

Walk-the-Dog - A specialized retrieve designed to make a stickbait or chugger sashay across the surface.

Worm Hook - A hook especially designed for fishing with plastic worms and similar soft plastic baits.

Yo-yoing - The lift'n-drop motion associated with vertically presented spoons, slab baits, spinnerbaits, and other lures.